MW01504366

Fiscal Policy in Early Modern Europe

This book examines the gradual assembly and consolidation of Portuguese fiscal policy in the second half of the fifteenth century, providing a comparative analysis of the Portuguese State's finances and fiscal dynamics with other Western European monarchies.

This volume scrutinizes relevant aspects of the Portuguese Royal finances, particularly the different instruments employed to provide income, both ordinary and extraordinary, and the rubrics involving all types of expenditure, permanent or temporary, between the reigns of Afonso V and Manuel I at the dawn of the Modern Ages. The analysis of Portugal's case will also serve as a main conducting wire to a broader fiscal examination of other Latin-rooted Mediterranean and North Atlantic kingdoms.

This book will be of interest to students and researchers of economic history, fiscal history, economic theory and history of economic thought, as well as students of medieval history, the history of the Western Europe and the Iberian Peninsula.

Rodrigo da Costa Dominguez is an economic history junior researcher in the Interdisciplinary Centre of Social Sciences at the University of Minho–Portugal.

Perspectives in Economic and Social History
Series Editors: Andrew August and Jari Eloranta

The Economic and Business History of Occupied Japan
New Perspectives
Edited by Thomas French

An Urban History of The Plague
Socio-Economic, Political and Medical Impacts
in a Scottish Community, 1500–1650
Karen Jillings

Mercantilism, Account Keeping and the Periphery-Core Relationship
Edited by Cheryl Susan McWatters

Small and Medium Powers in Global History
Trade, Conflicts, and Neutrality from the 18th to the 20th Centuries
*Edited by Jari Eloranta, Eric Golson, Peter Hedburg,
and Maria Cristina Moreira*

Labor Before the Industrial Revolution
Work, Technology and their Ecologies in an Age of Early Capitalism
Edited by Thomas Max Safley

Workers, Unions and Payment in Kind
The Fight for Real Wages in Britain, 1820–1986
Christopher Frank

A History of States and Economic Policies in Early Modern Europe
Silvia A. Conca Messina

Fiscal Policy in Early Modern Europe
Portugal in Comparative Context
Rodrigo da Costa Dominguez

For more information about this series, please visit www.routledge.com/series/PESH

Fiscal Policy in Early Modern Europe

Portugal in Comparative Context

Rodrigo da Costa Dominguez

LONDON AND NEW YORK

First published 2020
by Routledge
2 Park Square, Milton Park, Abingdon, Oxon OX14 4RN

and by Routledge
52 Vanderbilt Avenue, New York, NY 10017

Routledge is an imprint of the Taylor & Francis Group, an informa business

British Library Cataloguing-in-Publication Data
A catalogue record for this book is available from the British Library

Library of Congress Cataloging-in-Publication Data
A catalog record for this book has been requested

ISBN: 978-0-8153-6781-9 (hbk)
ISBN: 978-1-351-25648-3 (ebk)

Typeset in Times New Roman
by Apex CoVantage, LLC

Contents

List of figures   vi
List of tables   vii
List of maps   viii
Preface   ix
Abbreviations   xi
Acknowledgments   xii

1   Introduction   1

2   Toward a fiscal model: building a framework   13

3   European fiscal panorama during the later Middle Ages
    and early modern times: comparisons   41

4   A Portuguese "Fiscal X-Ray": one study, two moments   66

5   The geography of early modern Portuguese fiscal dynamics   106

6   Administrative and fiscal structures in Western European
    context   137

7   Conclusion: a contribution for further Portuguese
    early modern fiscal studies   170

Index   179

Figures

4.1   Guarda's fiscal revenue development (1436–1522)   75
4.2   Lamego's fiscal revenue development (1434–1520)   77
4.3   Setúbal's fiscal revenue development (1439–1523)   78
4.4   Beja's fiscal revenue development (1439–1519)   79
5.1   Guarda's revenues (in approximate percentages of total local)
      in 1436   119
5.2   Setúbal's revenues (in approximate percentages of total local)
      in 1439   121
5.3   Beja's revenues (in approximate percentages of total local)
      in 1440   122
5.4   Total leased versus total received regarding the sales taxes
      (*sisa*) on colored cloth in Lisbon (in reais brancos/white
      reais – Portuguese Medieval Currency)   126

Tables

4.1 Ordinary revenues versus extraordinary revenues in Portugal,
c.1436–1449 (in pounds and reais brancos) 84

4.2 Detailed expenditure at Guarda's fiscal branch (*almoxarifado*)
(in approximate percentages of local total expenditure) in 1436,
1437, 1438 and 1449 90

4.3 Detailed expenditure at Lamego's fiscal branch (*almoxarifado*)
(in approximate percentages of local total expenditure),
c.1434–1441 91

4.4 Detailed expenditure at Setúbal's fiscal branch (*almoxarifado*)
(in approximate percentages of local total expenditure) in 1449
and 1450 93

4.5 Detailed expenditure at Beja's fiscal branch (*almoxarifado*) (in
approximate percentages of local total expenditure), c.1439–1442 95

5.1 Kingdom's fiscal branches (*almoxarifados*) and its respective
revenues in 1473 (in reais brancos) 107

5.2 Lisbon's revenues versus rest of the kingdom (in reais brancos) 114

5.3 Revenues of *aver-do-peso* in Lisbon (in reais brancos) 124

5.4 Revenues of sales taxes (*sisa*) on colored cloth in Lisbon
(in reais brancos) 125

5.5 Revenues of royal dwellings' payments, c.1446–1449 (in reais
brancos) 126

Maps

4.1   Portuguese Crown's documented revenues in the later Middle
Ages, c.1448 (average value between 1447 and 1449)   74

5.1   Portuguese Crown's documented revenues in the later Middle
Ages, c.1473 (average value between 1472 and 1474)   109

5.2   Portuguese Crown's documented revenues in the later Middle
Ages, c.1494 (average value between 1493 and 1495)   116

5.3   Portuguese Crown's documented revenues in the later Middle
Ages, c.1504 (average value between 1503 and 1505)   120

5.4   Portuguese Crown's documented revenues in the later Middle
Ages, c.1512 (average value between 1511 and 1513)   128

5.5   Portuguese Crown's documented revenues in the later Middle
Ages, c.1520 (average value between 1519 and 1521)   130

7.1   Total volume of revenues by wider categories c.1434–1525   173

Preface

Returning to a place where you were happy is not a hard task at all, despite your feelings for your home country, for the place that saw you grow up. The connection that the human race creates with a new environment is amazing – a very dear ground where you have a set of experiences that shape you, which becomes part of your existence. Things that you will carry, no matter where you go. Bottom line, a place that you can call *home*.

This is what Portugal, Porto and the faculty of arts means to my life. The same places where I learned the skills to become a researcher and historian opened its arms to host me once again in 2009. On the other hand, this return also meant a great responsibility in the sense that I had previously set the performance bar during my graduate studies between 2004 and 2006. In a very pragmatic standpoint, my objective was to push it further.

Nevertheless, the context was different. The environment was tenser. The severe crisis that resulted from the Lehman Brothers bankruptcy process in the US reverberated also in Europe and hit Portugal even more severely in the following years. The imposition of a combined austerity regime on the need to cut spending formed a completely dark scenario regarding credit. Increasingly difficult access to money for the poorest, middle class families and also for the small and medium-sized business sector created a shortage of cash flow for the maintenance of their businesses and investments. Furthermore, an increase in the tax burden brought the Portuguese economy into a state of stagnation. The dilemma faced was – and somehow still is – how to generate economic growth? To invest first, even tortuously, to generate a surplus and pay off debt or pay the debt first to grow sustainably afterwards?

Based on these expectations, the principle of this whole process of reinventing and reassessing the Portuguese economy and its early fiscal constitution, or at least part of it, was the central motor of the subject of this investigation. Where would the first Portuguese "state budgets" be? Were they already unbalanced from their origin? Where did the revenues come from? What about expenditure? What was the balance? How was management done? Were there more or fewer revenues? A relevant set of questions readily came up.

One of the key aspects of this work, in a broader perspective, is to insert Portugal into the range of major case studies mentioned by Richard Bonney in order to complete that fiscal studies' scenario. Furthermore, it also seeks to establish a connection between the Portuguese contemporary fiscal and financial situation and its medieval roots: had Portugal, in the early modern times, sufficient revenues? Would it be possible to see an administrative and tax network ready at that time? There are several issues to be analyzed and compared. There are some prospects for discussion on this aspect. At least, with regard to tax transformations, it is believed that reflections and the current discussion derived from the historical origins is pertinent, given the importance of the moment that the country is currently experiencing.

Hard as it may be to realize, a leading country like Portugal, a central player during the European maritime expansion in the early modern times and holder of a vast colonial empire, had major issues regarding its fiscal structure and financial management. In many ways, Portugal built its taxation mechanisms according to the historical contexts and economic demands imposed by the respective commercial change in course from the fourteenth century onwards. Practically all Western European kingdoms were going through similar structural transition processes, from old seigneurial domains to modern states equipped with proper bureaucracy skilled to deal with financial issues and support national armies and navies. Many merchants and businessmen had the opportunity to reinvest their money and become partners with kings, assuming control of tax collection. However, the Portuguese pioneerism regarding the great voyages in the fifteenth and sixteenth centuries took its toll on the kingdom's economic and fiscal organization. The luxury and riches underpinned by the profitable trade monopoly with India pushed Portugal away from a more conscious and stable financial condition.

Based on this brief essay and on the surviving sources, I want to invite the reader to a journey behind the scenes of Portuguese fiscal policy, its gradual assembly and consolidation and how it links with the major political decisions that enable the kingdom to be the leader of oceanic expansion, beating strong competitors such as England, France, Spain and the Netherlands.

Abbreviations

ANTT	Arquivo Nacional da Torre do Tombo, Portuguese National Archives.
Chanc. D. Afonso V	King Afonso V's Chancery records.
Chanc. D. João II	King João II's Chancery records.
Chanc. D. Manuel I	King Manuel I's Chancery records.
Chanc. D. João III	King João III's Chancery records.
Gavetas	drawers: it corresponds to the arrangement of the diplomas in the old Royal Archive. In each drawer it was kept the documents relating to a certain state matter: organization charts, wills, treaties, sentences, among others. This nomenclature has fallen into disuse and, currently, the drawers are referenced by numbers.
Leitura Nova	new reading: copies of documents considered most important, which composed a new collection. Those copies were produced under Manuel I's rule, starting in 1504, and ordered by regions, masters and diverse topics, known as miscellaneous (Místicos). The copied documents were organized in books and separated by districts: Além-Douro (Northern Portugal, North of Douro River), Estremadura (Western Portugal, between the Douro and Tagus River), Odiana or Guadiana (Southern Portugal, South of Tagus River, which includes the Algarve) and Beira (Eastern Portugal, close to the Castilian Border, between the Douro and Tagus River). Moreover, there was an extra book (Livro dos Extras) which contains decrees of the officers who did work in or out of the kingdom, letters of the king's officers, donations, contracts and other financial information.

Acknowledgments

Before anything else, it is time for me to thank some institutions, and some people as well. Without their help, this book would not be possible. This journey started back in 2009. Thanks to my *alma mater*, the University of Porto, and to all professors within my Ph.D. program.

Thanks to the Fundação para a Ciência e Tecnologia (FCT), the Portuguese science funding agency, for supporting my Ph.D. research on which this book is based.

Thanks to the Municipal Archive of Cascais, as well as to the Torre do Tombo, regarding their staff, for all the attention, availability and help.

Thanks to the geography cabinet of the faculty of arts (Infografia), and its supervisor, Dr. Miguel Nogueira, for his help, advice, effort and outstanding work.

I want also to dedicate this to my dear friends/colleagues at the University of Porto. But also to my very dear historian friends who remain in Brazil. For your trust, scientific stimulus and friendship, I salute you all.

To my former advisors/supervisors, Dr. Luís Miguel Duarte and Dr. Hilario Casado Alonso, as well as other colleagues, Dr. Leonor Freire Costa, Dr. Amândio Barros, Dr. António Castro Henriques and Dr. Joaquim Romero Magalhães (in memory), who provided me great input on this book.

Nevertheless, this book became real after my internship at Appalachian State University in 2016. I want to thank Dr. Jari Eloranta, Dr. Bruce Stewart, Dr. Victoria Yeoman and Dr. Michael Behrent, who generously provided valuable comments and suggestions when it was still an idea and early project. Moreover, I want to thank Dr. Jeremy Land, Dr. Tony Moore and Dr. Evan Wallace for english review and scientific support.

And, finally, to my close friends and dear family. Thanks to your vital emotional support, this became possible. Thank you for your love, and for making me feel incredibly loved. Thanks, Nina, for all. For existing, for being this great human being, full of light and wisdom, and for giving me our major sources of inspiration: João and Luís. Thanks for your endless effort to make me every day a better man, always by your side.

RD

1 Introduction

1.1 In the name of the Portuguese economic and fiscal history

This work is the result of an initial desire to investigate the organizational structure of state finances in Portugal during the fifteenth and sixteenth centuries, which resulted in my Ph.D. dissertation – a wish awakened by reading a classic (Rau, 2009) of Portuguese economic historiography, recently reprinted, for one of the disciplines within the scope of the University of Porto's Ph.D. program in history back in 2009.

Observing the structuring and consolidation of the *Casa dos Contos* as the Portuguese central fiscal structure of the period, we were struck by some of the sources used for that study and in particular the politico-economic context of the mid-fifteenth century, which stimulated the research at that moment. There were some studies regarding the kingdom's revenue-centralizing mechanism. However, little is known about the organics of fiscal organization and the internal tax collection network effectively constituted. The reigns of Afonso V, João II and Manuel I are important in this sense, i.e., from the perspectives of finance, credit and economic dynamics, as Portugal seeks to recover from an extremely exhausting period for the treasury. The wars against Castile for the kingdom's maintenance at the end of the fourteenth century,[1] the various monetary devaluations that followed this period and the political developments related to these events, such as the financial reform implemented by Duarte I (1433–38) in 1435, the administration of intense military activities on three fronts from 1448 onwards – internal, external and overseas – allied to the large amount of costs with the royal entourage, all these events led us to a simple questioning: would there be enough income to carry out all these initiatives in a "relatively short" time period or, put another way, would it be possible to do all of this at the same time?

As time passed, more and more questions arose but the key issue was: with new challenges, new expenses (the extension of the Portuguese presence in Morocco and the Atlantic expansion) but also new and powerful income sources, would it still require some extra credit, internal or external? Where did these extraordinary revenues come from? In order to elucidate many of my doubts about fundamental Portuguese economic features and concepts, economic history and, more particularly, economic history studied and produced in Portugal, I chose to follow this path.

It is quite clear that much has already been done in this branch of history. However, it also seems that, mainly in Portugal, there is still room for contributions to the study of finances and taxation, in the relations between those who collected the taxes, those who paid and those who managed them, within a dynamic of resource circulation: how they get to the central office in Lisbon, how they were applied, where and how they were centralized in terms of spending, what was the logistics behind this administrative apparatus and what would be the consequences of these processes, both for those who channeled these financial resources and for the receivers of these reserves in some way. In general, studies of the process of public and private financing in the Portuguese medieval economy have been scarce, just as fiscal history (within the same chronology) as well as the concept of "public debt". A few years ago, in a historiographical balance, this same "lack of works" in this area was mentioned, besides the difficulty with the available sources (Gonçalves, 1999: 107).

It is also worth noting the development of these studies all over Europe, in Spanish institutes or in France, with cooperation between the various research units and departments within the Ministry of Economy of that country. In Italy, with a variety of research centers and universities, whether in the field of economics or history, supported either by the government or by relevant private foundations, or even in England, in centers like Cambridge, Oxford, York, Reading and the London School of Economics. Although from a peninsular perspective, the Spanish fiscal and economic history, closely linked to the Portuguese and of many common characteristics – albeit with all the problems faced by the central governments and autonomous communities –, and even with severe financial restrictions that scientific research has been submitted to recently in that country, it is still capable of progressing. On the other hand, in Portugal the integration between history and economics, particularly with regard to studies related to the Middle Ages and early modern periods, both in scientific terms and in institutional terms, is still lacking a major collective, connected and coordinated effort. A better effort between the faculties of economics and history all over the country is mandatory, together with the Center for Levies and Customs' Studies, linked to the Taxation and Customs' Authority, collaborating more with seminars, congresses, Ph.D. programs, grants and funding for fiscal studies, in this period and others, which holds as much value as modern or even contemporary discussions, whether on state budgets, expenditure cuts or revenues' maximization.

We do believe that more intense work and greater attention to Portuguese economic history and fiscal issues – within a broader comparative framework, particularly related to the process of developing a fiscal and administrative machinery capable of sustaining and benefiting from Portuguese overseas expansion – would lead to lucrative efforts to realize financial dynamics. In addition, it would also be possible to establish connections through the consequent process of colonization and management of the respective discovered regions, which would assume the "Lusitanian tax gene" in its economic and financial matrix. We can extend this relation to Brazil, a possible partner in this search for alternatives to the historiographical debate, and, at the same time, to resume contact with Brazilian historiographical production in this field, traditionally more focused on North and Central European schools (France and Germany) than on its own Iberian origins, thus undertaking a kind of "reconversion". Other future works may emerge following this contribution, to back, to a great extent, more studies related to this particular area, as well as medieval and early modern Peninsular History in a wider perspective.

1.2 Structuring process

In terms of methodologies and definitions for this book's organization, the initial idea was to revisit the *Contos'* studies and the kingdom's economic administrative organizational structures as a pragmatic strategy related to the purpose of competing for Ph.D. grants, in which we succeeded. Subsequently, as the first bibliographical readings were taken, the lack of balance was evident in all aspects of the available economic historiography and its general approach, from concepts and theories, to the technical terms. This in itself has taken a lot of effort and time to identify and eliminate this handicap as soon as possible. On the other hand, all this commitment elicited great rejoicing from studies in this area. On first sight, we had chosen to study the financing sources of the Portuguese Crown during the reigns of Afonso V and João II and to understand the internal structure of these finances and the prominence of each component – own assets, ordinary and extraordinary revenues, requests and loans, confiscations and other businesses related to the Crown – in order to try to determine some degree of revenue predictability.

However, through a previous sources' analysis, we realized that it would be useful for this volume to widen the observation spectrum a bit, to better comprehend the changes, and even for comparative purposes. To achieve that, we used, albeit more broadly, the sources of Manuel I's reign, although from some points of view, these sources have already surpassed the "limits of the Middle Ages", as well as it mixed some "overseas' income". Despite any chronological issue, it resulted in something positive, especially in terms of comparison of values and comparative scale benchmarks. The criteria for the sources' selection was simply to have clear and feasible revenue and expenditure numerical data that we could work with, which would allow the composition of a budgetary table framework – albeit rudimentary –with gaps to be filled.

Confronted with the limitations imposed during the Ph.D. research process and thesis writing itself, the most realistic and achievable option was made to reconstitute this taxation network through the numbers and values found. It is clear that this volume, at that point, would not be more complete and comprehensive due to those issues. Nevertheless, after a few years and lots of tension involved in that writing process, it turned out to be more constructive to properly observe, identify and compare the Portuguese taxation system with other Western European Monarchies' economic and fiscal dynamics, with more time available to do all the required reading and research with no regrets, whether personal or professional, regarding casual imperfections.

1.3 Sources utilized

To this end, we sought to use the Royal Chancery's records of the kings previously mentioned, as well as the documentation of the *Leitura Nova*,[2] regarding some acquittance letters, which were the primary element for the volume content. Although a large number of these letters were already published by Anselmo Braamcamp Freire (1903–1916), the retrieval of many others in the Torre do Tombo archives, as well as in the Cascais' Municipal Archives, was of a fundamental importance for the assembly of a better and broader comprehensive perspective, with the help of tables and graphs produced with the data compiled and processed in a databases, with several of those letters found, some of them already transcribed and published in previous works elaborated in the same scope.

It is also important to emphasize the importance of Portuguese medieval sources' transcription and edition for different periods, such as the royal chancelleries prior to 1531 concerning Morocco (Azevedo, 1915–1934), the Portuguese Oceanic expansion (Marques, 1988), as well as the period influenced by the *Infante* Henrique, o Navegador, known as Henry the Navigator[3] (*Monumenta Henricina*, 1960–1974), which have greatly reinforced the main set of documents used, altogether with collections of laws compiled, mostly related to officers' conduct and procedures of fiscal nature (Carneiro, 1818). All this production related to the history of law served to complement the financial activity with the necessary legal support for the exercise of tax collection, whether ordinary or extraordinary. In this sense, Maria José Ferro Tavares's studies on the currency (1974) were also indispensable, since the kings' monetary policy, mainly through devaluation, was one of the most important instruments of financing. As the requests to the kingdom and the currency devaluation were systematically debated in parliamentary assemblies, we closely followed Armindo de Sousa's work (1990).

Beyond these great value sources, we worked with other great contributions already printed. The Portuguese kings' chronicles, written both by Royal chroniclers and noblemen which served those monarchs, of other deeds (Zurara, 1915, 1942, 1978, 1997) and related to each of those reigns were of great use. In fact, many of them served as primary sources in several sections quoted by the sources' collections cited earlier, and some "originals" were elaborated by Rui de Pina (1977, 1989), Garcia de Resende (1973, 1991) and Damião de Góis (1905, 1949), chroniclers of the reigns of Afonso V, João II and Manuel I, respectively.

Another initial and unavoidable reference was Vitorino Magalhães Godinho's essay on public finances and State structuring (2009: 123–173), as well as the studies that João Cordeiro Pereira (1991, 2003) devoted to the state's first budgets known for the 1500s. Moreover, as useful work material, we used Teresa Rodrigues's studies on the Royal Treasury's administration (1982) during the reign of Afonso V, as well as Jorge Faro's manuscript (1965), which not only brings a precious set of documents regarding a set of State revenues and expenditure between the 1380s and 1460s, but engages the analysis of some of those. For the subtopics, we followed Maria José Ferro Tavares' Ph.D. thesis on the Jews in Portugal during the fifteenth century (1982), as well as Virgínia Rau's studies on several foreign merchants' families (1968), mainly Italians who were present in Lisbon, and António Dias Farinha's work on a Portuguese Jewish banker (1994).

From the abundant foreign bibliography, and regarding economic and fiscal background, our central references were the studies coordinated and edited by Richard Bonney (1995, 1999) and other scholars (Ormrod, Bonney & Bonney, 1999) at the European level, essential for the perception of theories, concepts and technical terminology, as well as the understanding of different realities within medieval Western Europe, in order to properly construct a solid comparative view. We have joined to this benchmark set the studies of Antoni Furió (1999), along with essays directed by Denis Menjot & Sánchez Martínez (2006), Manuel Sánchez Martínez, both alone or co-edited with other scholars (1996, 1997, 2008, 2009) and Miguel Angel Ladero Quesada (1982, 1991, 2009, 2011) that accurately scrutinized the fiscal phenomena in the Hispanic kingdoms.

Regarding Portuguese taxation, and without forgetting the essential contributions of Costa Lobo (1903) and Gama Barros (1945) for the early 1900s' historiography, Iria Gonçalves' baseline studies (1964a, 1964b, 1987), written between the 1960s and 1980s, were fundamental, in addition to contributions from Luís Miguel Duarte (1988) and Maria Helena da Cruz Coelho, in co-authorship with Duarte (1996). For more specific aspects, such as the Church's role in taxation, we followed José Marques (1989). The Royal officials' prosopographic study written by Armando Luís de Carvalho Homem (1990), was an important point of departure and provided the most useful information to comprehend how the Royal Treasury was centrally organized. Moreover, the three recent biographies of Afonso V (Gomes, 2006), João II (Fonseca, 2005) and Manuel I (Costa, 2005) were also instruments of constant consultation.

It is worth highlighting a prominence within the bibliographical body compiled, including the recent studies of António Castro Henriques (2008), which was a conducting wire and one of the essential elements of dialogue, points of emphasis and argumentation for our work and widely cited in the course of this book. Furthermore, and as important as the former, we include the work previously done and cited earlier by José Mattoso and Oliveira Marques, with their *History* and *New History of Portugal*, respectively, given the importance of its scientific content for economic and fiscal history studies related to the Portuguese perspective.

1.4 Sources' criticism: what do the acquittance letters offer?

As previously stated, the empirical basis that supports the research that underpins this book was based on a type of documentation that was not fully explored – and of enormous potential – by Portuguese historiographers, as well as by the historians and researchers of Portuguese economic history in a more generic way. Few studies have used systematically this type of source, either to produce a serial study or even a joint work dealing with state finances and taxation more broadly, credit or local organics regarding tax collection, although it is known that there is some scientific production (Rodrigues, 1982; Duarte, 1995; Nunes, 2010) that went through these documents, even if they did not deal directly with fiscal issues.

In any case, here we have a fundamental function as a historian, which is the questioning of the possibilities of analysis that the sources allow us to reach. First, to understand what is and what is meant by an acquittance, what can be deduced from a letter of this kind, what are its constituent elements, how the source itself developed in the period treated and what kind of perspective it can offer for the study of finances.

The very term "acquittance" is already indicative of its importance for this economic study, that is to say, an act by which the creditor declares himself satisfied with his right, exempting the debtor from the commitment. In practical terms, it constitutes a receipt, it is a document or an annotation, by means of which the creditor acknowledges having been paid.[4] In legal terms, it ends a relationship between the two, regarding the disinvestment of a charge, a legal or conventional debt release, obligation or charge.[5] In this specific case study, it is a king's liberation to those responsible for financial affairs, generally and a key player in that process: the *almoxarifes*.[6] Also, all those responsible for collecting taxes or royal rights, in any other specific and localized manner – receivers, accountants, tenants, factories, handlers or moneychangers – who had to deal directly with the amounts raised, and were responsible for reporting these resources to their superiors and witnesses designated to cash in that income – whether the central accountant, the county accountants or any other officer.

From the paleographic point of view, this source did not have a very rigid structure or, apparently, it was issued in different forms, more or less complete, and with variations that allow us to make some inquiries. In this sense, rather than defining or determining its authenticity and probative value, we are interested in observing the main elements that constitute them within this period analyzed. First, the initial protocol, which largely eschews the kings' invocation and salute and jumps directly to the king as the central player of the legal act – particularly the letters from late fifteenth and early sixteenth centuries. An important characteristic of these sources is the forgetfulness of devotion, simplifying the instrument's writing to its maximum, often using "etc.", effectively determining an "invoice" profile, unlike the letters produced in the thirteenth[7] and fourteenth[8] centuries, even though they had been produced for different purposes. Second, the exhibition is very uniform with regard to the *almoxarifes'* supervision in particular, trying to immediately inform the addressee about the matter, by means of following a standard form. That could be characterized by the typical phrase *to those who are seen this acquittance letter of ours, we let know that we now send now make accounts from*, indicating immediately the name of the receiver.

Moreover, on several occasions, it also mentioned his social status – knight of the royal household, squire, servant etc. – or the individual's birthplace/hometown – *resident in . . .* – as well as the position he occupies (*almoxarife*, receiver, scribe) and the duration of that function's exercise – *our almoxarife during the years of* – and finally attesting to the total values received and spent.

Regarding the letters' text, the source is reasonably uniform with respect to the total received by the "debtor" and the specification of amounts collected, even being quite descriptive, with the list of all that was collected in each year, in particular, in some situations. However, that designation may vary, depending on the case – an *almoxarife*'s accounting procedure, for example or a tax farming contract verification, regarding the king's rents in a certain locality, as well as the extraordinary revenues' collection. On top of that, those differences may interfere with the analysis, positively or negatively, in view of the elements that it reports: the typology of the rates that are indicated in the revenues' list, how much each specific tax can yield in particular places and during determined periods, how much can the state collect with the extraordinary *requests* and *loans* in different places. Alongside with these variables and from these values, it is possible to think about regional estimates and national projections.

As for revenues, as we passed mid-fifteenth century, the letters were written more frequently only mentioning global values, without being properly detailed as they were before 1450. This specific fact highlights the lack of care with every penny, as it was before, essential for royal accounting. Moreover, from then on, it reveals a degree of unconcern for both who owns and the ones who should receive the payments. In the following century, this trend continues and even worsens, with little attention to the collection's details.

Pertaining to the sources' another essential component, expenditure is meticulously noted in the mid-fifteenth century's letters, apart from a few exceptions, where it is not possible to identify them by writing or conservation failures, which reinforces the thesis of a government very careful when spending and always concerned about maintaining a positive balance. In any case, fundamentally from the 1480s onwards expenditure ceases to be meticulously reported, being repeatedly pointed out in its reports that *the amount of money that the said almoxarife, had been spent by our letters and orders, contained in their accountings that shall remain in our treasury.*[9] In terms of structure, what the sources conveyed is that there is no disquiet about this fiscal element, at least on the part of the major stakeholder, that is, the principal creditor: the monarch. He invariably released them *free as said by our guard and we sent our acquittance letter, signed by us and sealed by our pendant seal.* This may imply that, at that time, the king's income was more than sufficient to force him performing a more active control of what was spent both by his officers, as well as by the tax farmers or by the extraordinary aids' receivers.

Even not having elements in quantity and series that allow us to draw a complete profile of Portuguese finances, especially expenditures from the late fifteenth and early sixteenth centuries, there were enough elements that have indicated some possible ways of analysis. One of them was to define the budget's profile and its revenue's evolution within this crucial period of overseas' expansion and definition of a new administrative organic. What would predominate in the collection: manorial taxes of direct character, or indirect taxation, aiming on consumption? On top of that, the effective role of the extraordinary revenues in the royal "budgets" and their importance within the state's accounts is another aspect that we try to elucidate from the information gathered. In addition, it was possible to compare the amounts received by renting leases in various localities, with the numbers raised on these same procedures in Lisbon, for example, so that a notion of relevance and scale of these amounts could be established, as well as the role of each local unit to the Portuguese economy.

Credit is also another topic to be explored through this type of source, which can be revealing either implicitly or explicitly. That is, they can reveal in their content resources lent to the monarch or, on the other hand, can offer indications on tenants, whether if they are important or not, who they are, where they act, what values are involved in the negotiations, and, in the cross referencing of information, whether or not they are capable of providing credit, even if short term, but essential, in which the kingdom lived. The warehouses' and customs' acquittances can also give us some hints as to what went into the Portuguese market, how much they paid, where they went and where the consumer goods purchased by the monarch went.

Furthermore, royal officers' payments, the products that circulated within the kingdom and the wealth scattered in a double way between Portugal and its commercial outposts conquered can be analyzed through these sources, which are able to offer information of particular products, prices, quantities imported and exported, addressees and persons involved in those transactions. On top of that, the military component can also provide clues to the finances' analysis, given the acquittance letters that account for the amounts collected to the fortresses' maintenance,[10] as well as war equipment bought and received[11] for the various campaigns carried out in the period, which serve as a baseline to size, albeit to some extent, this expenditure's component within the total spending estimate, owing to the lack of serial documentation for further analysis.

In any case, the acquittance letters still are a rich source of information that could – and should – be greatly explored by historians dedicated to the history of finance, taxation and economics, not only regarding Portugal but also in a broader way.

Notes

1 The Fernandine Wars were a sequence of three military conflicts in 1369–70, 1372–73 and 1381–82, opposing the Kingdom of Portugal under Ferdinand I (1367–83) and Castile under Enrique II (1369–79), fighting over the Portuguese sovereign's claim to the Castilian crown after Pedro I's death in 1369.

2 In order to organize the Portuguese Royal Archives, Manuel I ordered the scribes copies of the most important documents, compiled in a collection entitled "Leitura Nova" ("New Reading"), which began in 1504, preserving the documents which were excessively damaged or whose reading was no longer accessible.

3 All the Portuguese kings and noblemen are identified in this book through their original spelling names, with the exception of *Infante* D. Henrique, cited hereafter as *Henry, the Navigator*, as one of the most prominent and known figures of the Portuguese medieval nobility within the English-language literature and historiography.

4 Definition found at the *Dicionário Houaiss da Língua Portuguesa*, online version – http://houaiss.uol.com.br/ [accessed in 2013/06/12].

5 Definition found in Silva (1813: 543). Available Online in the Brazilian Studies' Digital Library, at the University of São Paulo (Brasiliana USP): www.brasiliana.usp.br/dicionario [accessed in 2013/06/12].

6 The designation does not exist in Latin; it does come from the Arabic *al-muxrif*, which means "treasurer, inspector, intendent", or "the one responsible for Royal income". Indeed, Old Portuguese dictionaries depict the term as "the Royal income collectors in the counties, having that officer the same designation in Castille". Bluteau (1728, v. 1: 276). Available Online in the Brazilian Studies' Digital Library, at the University of São Paulo (Brasiliana USP): www.brasiliana.usp.br/dicionario [accessed in 2018/08/08].

7 Acquittance letter granted by Afonso III to the Master and the Monastery of Avis, with reference to payments in kind, in 1242, concerning the Castle of Albufeira's maintenance. ANTT, *Ordem de Avis e Convento de S. Bento de Avis*, mç. 2, n° 188. Quoted in Cunha (2009: 228).

8 Acquittance letter granted by the Order of Christ to Dinis I, regarding all the property that the king received from the Templars' patrimony, which the Pope donated to the Portuguese Military Order. ANTT, *Gavetas*, gav. 7, mç. 2, n° 6.

9 Acquittance letter granted to Vasco Carneiro, *almoxarife* of Vila Real. ANTT, Leitura Nova, *Além-Douro*, liv. 1, fl. 138v-139.

10 ANTT, *Chanc. D. Afonso V*, liv. 27, fl. 5v-6v; Leitura Nova, *Além-Douro*, liv. 1, fl. 26–26v.

11 ANTT, Leitura Nova, *Estremadura*, liv. 5, fl. 99–101v.

Bibliography

Primary sources

ANTT, Chanc. D. Afonso V, liv. 27.
ANTT, Gavetas, gav. 7, mç. 2, n° 6.
ANTT, Leitura Nova, Além-Douro, liv. 1.
ANTT, Leitura Nova, Estremadura, liv. 5.

Secondary sources and dictionaries

Azevedo, P. de. (1915–1934). *Documentos das chancelarias reais anteriores a 1531 relativos a Marrocos*, 2 vols. Lisbon: Academia das Sciências de Lisboa.

Bluteau, R. (1712–1728). *Vocabulario portuguez & latino: aulico, anatomico, architectonico . . .*, 8 vols. Coimbra: Collegio das Artes da Companhia de Jesus.

Carneiro, M. B. (1818). *Resumo chronologico das leis mais uteis no foro e uso da vida civil publicadas até o presente anno*, vol. I. Lisbon: Impressão Régia.

Dicionário Houaiss da Língua Portuguesa, Online version [http://houaiss.uol.com.br/].

Faro, J. (1965). *Receitas e despesas da Fazenda Real de 1384 a 1481: subsídios documentais*. Lisbon: Instituto Nacional de Estatística.

Freire, A. B. (1903–1916). Cartas de Quitação del rei D. Manuel, in *Archivo Historico Portuguez*, 11 vols. Lisbon: Of. Typographica-Calçada do Cabra.

Góis, D. de. (1905). *Crónica do príncipe Dom Ioam*. Coimbra: Imprensa da Universidade.

Góis, D. de. (1949). *Crónica do Felicíssimo Rei D. Manuel*, 4 vols. Coimbra: Universidade de Coimbra.

Marques, J. M. da S. (1988). *Descobrimentos Portugueses: documentos para a sua História*, 5 vols. 2nd ed. Lisbon: INIC.

Monumenta Henricina. (1960–1974). Comissão Executiva do V Centenário da Morte do Infante D. Henrique, 15 vols. Coimbra: Graf. Atlântida.

Pina, R. de. (1977). *Crónicas de Rui de Pina: introdução e revisão de M. Lopes de Almeida*. Porto: Lello & Irmão.

Pina, R. de. (1989). *Crónica de D. João II*. Lisbon: Publicações Alfa.

Resende, G. de. (1973). *Cancioneiro Geral*, 5 vols, New ed. Lisbon: Centro do Livro Brasileiro.

Resende, G. de. (1991). *Crónica de D. João II e Miscelânea*. Prefácio de Joaquim Veríssimo Serrão. Lisbon: Imprensa Nacional-Casa da Moeda.

Silva, A. M. (1813). *Diccionario da lingua portugueza – recompilado dos vocabularis impressos ate agora, e nesta segunda edição novamente emendado e muito acrescentado, por Antonio de Moraes Silva*. Lisbon: Typographia Lacerdina. [Available Online in the Brazilian Studies' Digital Library, at the University of São Paulo (Brasiliana USP): www.brasiliana.usp.br/dicionario].

Zurara, G. E. de. (1915). *Crónica da Tomada de Ceuta por El Rei D. João I*. Publicada por ordem da Academia das Sciências de Lisboa, segundo os manuscritos nºs 368 e 355 do Arquivo Nacional, por Francisco Maria Esteves Pereira. Lisbon: Academia das Sciências de Lisboa.

Zurara, G. E. de. (1942). *Crónica dos feitos da Guiné*. Prefácio, seleção e notas de Álvaro Júlio da Costa Pimpão. Lisbon: Livraria Clássica Editora.

Zurara, G. E. de. (1978). *Crónica de D. Duarte de Menezes: edição diplomática de Larry King*. Lisbon: Universidade Nova de Lisboa – Faculdade de Ciências Sociais e Humanas.

Zurara, G. E. de. (1997). *Crónica do Conde D. Pedro de Meneses*. Edição e estudo de Maria Teresa Brocardo. Lisbon: Fundação Calouste Gulbenkian – Junta Nacional de Investigação Científica e Tecnológica (Colecção Textos Universitários de Ciências Sociais e Humanas).

Studies

Barros, H. da G. (1945). *História da Administração Pública em Portugal nos Séculos XII a XV: 2ª edição dirigida por Torquato de Sousa Soares*, 11 vols. Lisbon: Livraria Sá da Costa Editora.

Bonney, R. (ed.). (1995). *Economic Systems and State Finance*. Oxford: Oxford University Press.

Bonney, R. (ed.). (1999). *The Rise of the Fiscal State in Europe c. 1200–1815*. Oxford: Oxford University Press.

Coelho, M. H. da C., & Duarte, L. M. (1996). A fiscalidade em exercício: o pedido dos 60 milhões no almoxarifado de Loulé, Revista da Faculdade de Letras: História, série II, 13, 205–230.

Costa, J. P. O. e. (2005). *D. Manuel I: um príncipe do Renascimento*. Mem Martins: Círculo de Leitores.

Cunha, M. C. A. e. (2009). *Estudos sobre a Ordem de Avis (séc. XII-XV)*. Porto: FLUP, Biblioteca Digital.

Duarte, L. M. (1988). Um rei a reinar: algumas questões sobre o desembargo de Afonso V na segunda metade do século XV, Revista de História, 8, 69–82.

Duarte, L. M. (1995). A actividade mineira em Portugal durante a Idade Média, Revista da Faculdade de Letras: História, série II, 12, 75–112.

Farinha, A. D. (1994). *O primeiro banco em Portugal*. Lisbon: M.P.A.T., Secretaria de Estado da Ciência e Tecnologia.

Ferro, M. J. P. (1974). *Estudos de História Monetária Portuguesa (1383–1438)*. Lisbon: (n.p.).

Fonseca, L. A. da. (2005). *D. João II*. Mem Martins: Círculo de Leitores.

Furió Diego, A. (1999). Deuda pública e intereses privados. Finanzas y fiscalidad municipales en la Corona de Aragón, Edad Media: revista de historia, ISSN 1138–9621, 2, 35–80.

Godinho, V. M. (2009). *Ensaios e Estudos: uma maneira de pensar*, vol. I, 2nd ed. Lisbon: Sá da Costa Editora.

Gomes, S. A. (2006). *D. Afonso V: o Africano*. Mem Martins: Círculo de Leitores.

Gonçalves, I. (1964a). *O Empréstimo concedido a D. Afonso V nos anos de 1475 e 1476 pelo almoxarifado de Évora*. Lisbon: Cadernos de Ciência e Técnica Fiscal – Centro de Estudos Fiscais da Direcção-Geral das Contribuições e Impostos – Ministério das Finanças.

Gonçalves, I. (1964b). *Pedidos e empréstimos públicos em Portugal durante a Idade Média*. Lisbon: Cadernos de Ciência e Técnica Fiscal: Centro de estudos fiscais da direcção-geral das contribuições e impostos – Ministério das Finanças.

Gonçalves, I. (1987). *As finanças municipais do Porto na segunda metade do século XV*. Porto: Câmara Municipal do Porto.

Gonçalves, I. (1999). Estado Moderno, Finanças Públicas e Fiscalidade Permanente, *A génese do Estado Moderno no Portugal tardo-medievo: séculos XIII-XV/ciclo temático de conferências org. pela Universidade Autonoma de Lisboa; coord. Maria Helena da Cruz Coelho, Armando Luís de Carvalho Homem; Palavras prévias de Justino Mendes de Almeida*. Lisbon: Universidade Autónoma de Lisboa, 95–110.

Henriques, A. M. B. de M. de C. (2008). *State Finance, War and Redistribution in Portugal (1249–1527)*. Ph.D. Thesis. Department of History, University of York.

Homem, A. L. de C. (1990). *O Desembargo Régio (1320–1433)*. Porto: Junta Nacional de Investigação Científica.

Ladero Quesada, M. A. (1982). *El Siglo XV en Castilla: Fuentes de renta y política fiscal*. Barcelona: Editorial Ariel.

Ladero Quesada, M. A. (1991). Fiscalidad regia y génesis del Estado en la Corona de Castilla (1252–1504), Revista Espacio, Tiempo y Forma, Série III, História Medieval, 4, 95–135.

Ladero Quesada, M. A. (2009). *La Hacienda Real de Castilla (1369–1504): estúdios y documentos*. Madrid: Real Academia de la Historia.

Ladero Quesada, M. A. (2011). *Fiscalidad y Poder Real en Castilla (1252–1369)*, 2nd ed. Madrid: Real Academia de la Historia.

Lobo, A. de S. S. C. (1903). *História da Sociedade Portuguesa no Século XV*. Lisbon: Imprensa Nacional.

Marques, J. (1989). O Príncipe D. João II e a recolha das pratas das igrejas para custear a guerra com Castela, *Actas do Congresso Internacional Bartolomeu Dias e a sua época*, vol. I. Porto: Universidade do Porto – Comissão nacional para as comemorações dos descobrimentos portugueses, 201–219.

Menjot, D. & Sánchez Martínez, M. (dir.). (2006). *Fiscalidad de Estado y fiscalidad municipal en los reinos hispánicos medievales: estudios dirigidos por Denis Menjot y Manuel Sánchez Martínez*. Madrid: Casa de Velázquez.

Nunes, D. G. (2010). *A comenda de Noudar da Ordem de Avis no final da Idade Média*. M.A. Thesis. Porto: Faculdade de Letras da Universidade do Porto.

Ormrod, W. M., Bonney, M., & Bonney, R. (eds.). (1999). *Crises, Revolutions and Self-Sustained Growth: Essays in European Fiscal History, c.1130–1830*. Stanford: Shaun Tyas.

Pereira, J. C. (1991). *O resgate do ouro na Costa da Mina nos reinados de D. João III e de D. Sebastião*. Lisboa: Studia.

Pereira, J. C. (2003). *Portugal na Era de Quinhentos: estudos varios.* Cascais: Patrimonia.

Rau, V. (1968). *Estudos de História: mercadores, mercadorias, pensamento económico,* vol. 1. Lisbon: Editorial Verbo.

Rau, V. (2009). *A Casa dos Contos: os três mais antigos regimentos dos contos.* Lisbon: Imprensa Nacional-Casa da Moeda [re-edition of 1951 and 1959 original prints].

Rodrigues, T. F. (1982). Para a História da Administração da Fazenda Real no Reinado de D. Afonso V (1438–1453), in *Homenagem a A. H. de Oliveira Marques,* vol. I (sécs. X-XV). Lisbon: Editorial Estampa, Separata de Estudos de História de Portugal, 273–289.

Sánchez Martínez, M. (ed.). (2009). *La Deuda Pública en la Cataluña Bajomedieval.* Barcelona: CSIC.

Sánchez Martínez, M., Furió, A., & Sesma Muñoz, A. (2008). Old and New Forms of Taxation in the Crown of Aragon (13th-14th Centuries), in *Actas La fiscalità nell'economia europea (sec. XIII-XVIII),* 39th Settimana di Studi dell'Istituto "Francesco Datini" di Prato. Firenze: Firenze University Press, 99–130.

Sánchez Martínez, M., & Ortí Gost, P. (1997). La Corona en la génesis del sistema fiscal muncipal en Cataunya (1300–1360), *Actas Col·loqui Corona, Municipis i Fiscalitat a la Baixa Edat Mitjana.* Lleida, 233–278.

Sánchez Martínez, M., Ortí Gost, P., & Turull, M. (1996). La Génesis de la Fiscalidad Municipal en Cataüna, *Revista d'Història Medieval,* Universitat de València, 7, 115–134.

Sousa, A. de. (1990). *As cortes medievais portuguesas: 1385–1490,* 2 vols. Porto: INIC.

Tavares, M. J. P. F. (1982). *Os Judeus em Portugal no Século XV,* 1st ed. Lisbon: Universidade Nova de Lisboa.

2   Toward a fiscal model
Building a framework

A good analysis and perception of fiscal studies is mainly due to the assimilation of basic and essential definitions, or "pre-conceptions", in the sense that their knowledge is necessary before we think about any kind of study. Even because, to a large extent, some principles that we bring with us, in what concerns a contemporary way of thinking would not apply in a late medieval or early modern times' context. A current budget's outline, or a simple inventory, passes, first, by a simple credit and debit's signification and observation, that is, a balance check regarding what was collected and the expenditures that were made in function of revenues gathered. In short, you do not spend more than you collect. Any contemporary basic finance guide will be explicit in these instructions. However, this view becomes a false premise when it comes to finances in the late Middle Ages or early modern times. As a rule, the tendency was to spend first, that is, to consume before and pay later, to carry out the transaction or expense and, stimulated by that, to seek the necessary resources to clean up the respective expenditure.

First, it is fundamental to draw a central line in the notebook and separate the budget into two columns, "outputs" (expenditure) and "inputs" (revenues). With regard to the first point, unlike modern and contemporary times, when everything else adapts to revenues collected, expenditure must be understood as the central pillar of finances within an early modern perspective. The reader might wonder: why is that so? Fundamentally, it is due to the state's constant pursuit to increase its levels of revenues' collection to equalize costs. It is this dynamic which constitutes kingdoms and republics driving force to seek for profits that were not available initially which, as a rule, defines the real nature of public finances, whether municipal or national level (Furió Diego, 1999: 64). It is interesting to highlight the fact that terms such as "manage" or "management" do not even appear in older Portuguese language dictionaries.[1] The concept is modern, almost contemporaneous, and the idea of "good management" in early modern times necessarily runs through regular initiatives that aim to raise revenues proportionally to the expenditure's growth (Bonney, 1995b: 426–427), keeping it equal or, preferably, higher than expenditure. If the balance between inputs and outputs were stable, it could be considered a success. The administration/management is, then, in a great deal, a vessel for the resources' redistribution.

To this purpose, the monarch will seek resources among his peers and subjects, and the Crown could organize this demand in various ways: first, trying to analyze and understand how the state's economic dynamics works and, if possible, to conceive the best way to tax the wealth produced by the country, in a way that does not generate conflicts and hence, based on the kingdom's characteristics, in terms of tax collection, set up a fiscal machine and fine tune it for a regular, constant and stable collection. Second, if more resources were required, for urgent or unexpected situations, that is, not being part of expenses' frequent role, an extraordinary tax collection is then initiated. Regarding Portugal's case, that extraordinary income, from the state management's perspective, was based on two initiatives: the *requests* and *loans*, both already well studied.[2] At the municipal level, this type of additional income could be cashed as a collection of poll taxes, that is, the total sums that were distributed and divided among the population through evaluations and previously established criteria.

Essentially, taxation "is the manifestation of the government's power to coerce, to take money out of individuals" (Bonney, 1995b: 472), a power that has been enshrined as a divine right (Bonney & Ormrod, 1999: 16). The so-called "regular" taxes, that is, those which maintain a habitual incidence on the people were, fundamentally, royal rights over what was produced in the monarch or his entourage's lands; on the facilities' utilization by the general public in their daily life, such as ovens and mills; tolls' rights regarding the use of roads, as well as the entry and exit of people and goods in major cities; and houses' rents in urban centers, regardless of their use, that is, to enjoy it fully or partially (could be a single room), as an establishment for their craft's performance or live. It is important to highlight that this particular type of tax focused on key items in people's everyday lives, essential elements for survival: there was no escape. The extra municipal taxes were levied, to a large extent, to cope with sudden increases in expenditure, caused by infrequent royal demands: defense needs, wages' payments or of a municipal representative's maintenance in the parliamentary assemblies, for example. That extraordinary collection could be launched as a direct tax, charged *per capita* among the subjects. However, this varied according to the degree of urgency with which these resources are needed. Still in relation to this mode of taxation, it is convenient to perceive the outpouring under the conditions and context in which it was launched, although generally these extraordinary "contributions" did not reach the ends for which they were intended (Gonçalves, 1999: 103). In many instances, this collection bumped into a lack of permission from the people. Additionally, on several occasions, the collection system was not very effective (Gonçalves, 1999: 103–104).

However, with markets and diplomatic developments in the early fourteenth century, new tax dynamics naturally prevailed (Sousa, 2006: 193–194). An increase in trade, primarily at the regional sphere and, later, in intercontinental level, triggered a new tax collection form in Portugal, aimed on the buying and selling process of goods purchased, as in the case of neighboring Castile, which had intense business activity by mid-fifteenth century (Menjot, 2008: 705). This form of taxation did not burden the individual obligatorily, according to the state's needs, that is, the tax was levied only if the person buys or sells something, i.e., it characterizes an indirect tax. In this sense, the Portuguese case study emphasizes on the *sisas* – 10% of everything that was bought and sold within kingdom's fiscal jurisdiction, divided equally between buyer and seller (5% each) – and customs' tithes. The fact that it was charged in percentage, rather than in absolute value previously fixed, has an objective: to safeguard the collector from inflationary effects and currency debasement. Still regarding the *sisas*, this would become the fundamental fiscal tool, appropriated by the royal financers in a major moment of crisis, as the central pillar of tax collection in Portugal (Gonçalves, 1999: 105–106). Through the economic progress, it is possible to observe another phenomenon: *fiscal buoyancy*, that is, that the forms of collection and the evolution of collection were directly associated with the economy's fluctuations. This idea was previously discussed and dissected by Henriques (2008). The importance of this concept, according to him, lies in the fact that, "on many occasions, political conjunctures have been used to adapt the fiscal system to the kingdom's economic dynamics" (Henriques, 2008: 170–181). Since the late fourteenth century onwards, a new form of relationship has existed between the kings and these Portuguese economy variations. It is important to highlight that the *sisas* were, until the crisis of 1383–85, an extraordinary local (municipal) contribution, of an indirect nature, charged on specific commodities (wine, meat, bread, etc.). And, by the time João I of Avis assumed the kingdom's rule, he asked the people at the Parliamentary assemblies between 1385 and 1390 to grant him those tax revenues, so that he could carry out the war against Castile and provide for the new Avis' household. From that moment onwards, it would never cease to be collect (Sousa, 1990: vol. I, 295–300), and approached becoming ordinary toward to the sixteenth century. Moreover, the *pedidos*, as an extraordinary money request, became so trivialized that they could almost be included among the state's customary income (Duarte, 2006: 437). The same frequency with which they were requested, alongside with payments related to habitual taxation, had the natural effect of excessive tax burden on the population.

With so many different ways of raising taxes, it is not unusual for protests to arise. The grievance upsurges mainly due to a more intense sense of burden, even when accompanied with justifications. This weight, pressure, or fiscal "burden" placed on "taxpayers" is something that, in normal situations, referred to a regular contribution capacity but, on the other hand, also depends on the analytical approach and may suffer variations due to the resulting conjuncture. It is susceptible to influences and/or unusual, exceptional conditions like wars. For example, we can consider a sequence of military campaigns, as well as potential economic difficulties derived from these events as something atypical for a kingdom that has historically lived in perpetual peace. However, from another point of view, we can consider this same circumstance as "routine" in other situations, as in more belligerent provinces, with conflictive border regions, due to clashes of different cultural beliefs, or areas of intense dynastic/families' conflicts, like the cases of the Southern Hispanic kingdoms of Murcia, Valencia and Aragon (Lafuente Gómez & Martínez García, 2011: 109–142).

However, all these elements contribute to compose a *tax culture* or *constitution*. It should be noticed that, regarding those definitions, both terms go in the same anthropological sense, that is, a complex of initiatives, institutions, social patterns linked to the creation and diffusion of a system or way of life.[3] And it is for this composition of a fiscal identity that we will turn to later. For now, we will deal with the theoretical models used in this study's framework, which will help us to continue clarifying other concepts that are also important to comprehend both Portuguese and European fiscal development.

2.1 Fiscal models: a comparative

An archetype or model can be seen from various points of view, from its structure and design, to its application and consideration as an element and/or an integral part of something even greater. According to the Houaiss dictionary of the Portuguese language, the term "archetype" means, among other things, a "model or pattern that can be reproduced in simulacra or similar objects", similar to what the Cambridge dictionary brings, as "a typical example of something, or the original model of something from which others are copied".[4] Moreover, as a complement, can also be defined as a philosophical concept as a "model or original copy, of a transcendent nature, which functions as the essence and explanatory principle for all objects of material reality".[5] In a meaning extrapolation, we might consider this same archetype as an essential element of something, a matrix, the basis of an identity in constant training process. In this sense, one of the ideas, also taken from the same Portuguese dictionary, has to do with a "set of characteristics and circumstances that distinguish a person or a thing and through which it is possible to individualize it".[6]

Some scholars use Braudel's statement to note that

> there is a natural tendency of governments to spend excessively and that the maximization of revenues has been, since the late Middle Ages and early modern times, a necessity as well as a central aspect of the fiscal policies of European countries since then.
>
> (Körner, 1995: 393)

However, from the 1450s onwards, in order to maximize state revenues in many cases it was necessary to take a step forward, fiscally speaking, to complete the transition from a "seigneurial, domain state" condition, to a tributary or "tax state". This transition, studied by Joseph Schumpeter in the 1920s, gave birth to a model that would undergo several readjustments (Bonney & Ormrod, 1999: 19–20). We seek to accomplish something that also interested several experts when using Castile as one of the examples to observe and analyze fiscal structures' changes (Ormrod, 1995: 123–125) in Western European states: to test the validity of J. P. Genet's theory for the Portuguese case, about this transition process – also defined as *fiscalité féodale* – to a *fiscalité d'État*. We will return to the model's definitions and these terms ahead.

To reach that goal at European level, studies have recently been published and organized on the examples of other medieval Western monarchies and Europe's Modern National States, and on the authors and precepts of classical economics, mainly on the ideas of Smith, Ricardo, Stuart Mill and Malthus, "which does not necessarily mean an anachronism or even a pre-judgment of medieval theories and methods as rudimentary" (Isenmann, 1995: 21). From the scope of other studies already published and mentioned earlier, ranging from the early Middle Ages (in some cases) to the end of the eighteenth century, it is not unusual to use the eighteenth-century Enlightenment ideas as a central pillar and even as a common support for a logical analytical connection, which also saw this transition process and whose consolidation and effectiveness varied from kingdom to kingdom, as well as from region to region within these same European states, according to their own conditions. By observing this passage from one condition to another, liberal economists, in producing their ideas and theories, to some extent, "made themselves available for these concepts to be applied to other times, such as the transition to indirect taxes collection" (Bonney, 1995b: 488–489), although reservations are always made about the specificities and conditions of each historical period, even though many periods of late Middle Ages and early modern culture and institutions persisted until the seventeenth and eighteenth centuries, whether in the economic, fiscal, social, political or juridical fields.

Returning to the Bonney-Ormrod theoretical framework, the definitions of "domain state" and "tax state" are embedded in a larger context of a model structured by Schumpeter (1954) in the years following the First World War, which would be responsible for inexorable changes in European nations' taxation. Subsequently, this classic model was challenged and criticized by Petersen (1975) and Krüger (1987), until it was finally retrofitted by Bonney and Ormrod in the late 1990s, mainly due to the previous one to be considered "of excessive specificity", that is to say,

> limited to a particular era – transition between the Middle Ages and modernity – and to specific areas of Europe, and for that reason could not explain important elements such as relations dynamics between expenditure, revenue and credit, possible causes of instability, as well as the emergence of catalysts for change in systems. An innovative, broader and more refined model was therefore sought.
>
> (Bonney & Ormrod, 1999: 2)

According to that model, there would be four prevailing types of tax system: tribute, domain, tax and fiscal. Still following this archetypal, this concept revision is based on three essential points:

1) crises occurring within the tax systems do not alter their natural essence, but depending on the type of crisis, and if out of control, these can lead to a "fiscal revolution";

2) revolutions have a global impact on all main elements of a fiscal system (Bonney & Ormrod, 1999: 9) and move them forward, or force the transition

from one system to another, and that "revolution" arises from a quantitative increase of revenues total amount, coupled with a qualitative transmutation of the type of revenue collected (Moss, 1999: 38);

3) that the concept of "self-sustaining growth" is a model of development within the modern "Fiscal State", in which a proper and "postmodern" system would have been hypothetically achieved. Bottom line, it exists due to several forms of socio-political-economic pressure and, at the same time, should be distinguished when observed and compared against the first tax states that had modernity as a premise – especially when the revenue base and credit structures are observed – but which failed precisely because they were not self-sustaining (Bonney & Ormrod, 1999: 9–10).

Furthermore, there is a fifth type, the "financial" (finance) state, following a discussion based on the periodization developed by Gerhard Oestreich on the states' formation and evolution (Schulze, 1995: 263; Oestreich & Koenigsberger, 1982), where it establishes three phases: first, the prototype of a dualistic political system in the fourteenth and fifteenth centuries; second, a first evolution toward the modern state in its first steps (finance state); and, finally, another development already in the late seventeenth century called "military, administrative and bureaucratic" (fiscal military states). However, according to the model proposed, this category would be nothing but a less-developed phase of a tax state characterized by increasing governmental dependence on short and mid-term loans, without a adequately solid and sophisticated financial structure to support them (Bonney, 1995b: 13), in order to be able to repay loans with other loans (public debt mechanism).

Tax systems do not have a single feature of their own. Rather, each of them is composed of a variety of elements and/or resources of various types. Moreover, a kingdom or country can effectively have different particularities of the various systems in question (Bonney & Ormrod, 1999: 10). On top of that, there is the possibility of a "temporary fiscal condition", that is, a state may, due to conjuncture, have some type of interest – private or public – or to achieve a concrete objective or goal, convert itself to a type of taxation and, subsequently, reverse this process.[7] It is also necessary to observe the absence of a mandatory "chronological sequential evolution". For example, the tax state may not necessarily be the subsequent evolutionary stage of a tribute state in a country. It may possibly be, but it is feasible to "skip" steps in this process (Bonney, 1995a: 364–368), just as it is also possible for a State to be "advanced" in relation to other contemporary tax systems (Bonney & Ormrod, 1999: 12–13; Wickham, 1997).

Within the analyzed model, it is also important to differentiate two key terms: *tribute* and *taxation*. We may think that both, starting from an etymological presupposition, serve to designate the same thing. However, in this context, there are different paths: tribute is associated with the idea of periodically collecting payments as a sign of dependence, that is, the offer of spoils, money or goods in a situation of protection or annexation in some situations, military conflicts or not, such as in the Roman Empire and even in the Carolingian Empire (Ormrod &

Barta, 1995: 54–56). Taxation, on the other hand, is related to something more systematic and regular, to evaluations' basis, to a collection mechanism, and must include a very reasonable degree of subjects' consent (Bonney & Ormrod, 1999: 15–16).

For this comparative approach, we will limit ourselves to two types of tax system that, chronologically, interest us most: domain and tax state. With respect to the former, to sum it up in a few words, it would be the system in which the sovereign "extracts revenues from the exercise of royal rights" (Bonney & Ormrod, 1999: 15). Thus, an assumption arises immediately, albeit arbitrarily (Bonney, 1995b: 491): the predominance of revenues from direct taxes lays as the central idea and support of this category of analysis, i.e., income from land and landlords, as well as taxes levied directly on the peasantry, tolls, customs and monopolies on products and money-minting must be greater or equal to at least half of the total collected. Using a reference from Moreau de Beaumont, French finance manager in the eighteenth century, Bonney sets the French state as an example of a domain state, given that real wealth was mainly derived from revenues on land property and forest yields; of occasional manorial income, including confiscations, and of specific rights in each dominion (Bonney, 1995b: 447).

Somehow all Western European monarchies individually made this transition from the tribute system to the domain system at some point in the Middle Ages, whose transformative essence would be the abandonment of collection based on taxing agricultural surpluses or other forms of wealth extortion by using force, toward to the formation of more sophisticated political and institutional structures that would allow easier access to this same income. However, there are two approaches (Bonney & Ormrod, 1999: 13) to the tax state, which cannot be reconciled to a large extent: firstly, the 'constitutional' view of the transition from a domain system – as a manifestation of the exercise of royal authority, defined by the French as *fiscalité féodale* – for a system in which these same powers, in a situation of transition to the tax state, would be subject to the exercise of fiscal authority by the sovereign over his subjects, and this power needed to be bargained in representative assemblies, resulting in a *fiscalité d'état*; and the economic perspective, which observes the tax system in a diametrically opposed way, as the unfolding of an economic policy based on the taxation of State's renewable economic resources, which serve as a collection base.

Direct taxes conceived *a priori* as a subjects' "voluntary donation" to the sovereign may take various forms, such as contributions levied on landownership and patrimony, for example. In its earliest form, individual taxation is the most common form of direct tax. Designed and collected in different ways in different locations (*contado* in Siena in the fourteenth century; the *capitation* in Russia, the *Golden Penny* in the Holy Roman Empire, the *taille* in France, among others), served as a collection base for many states until the end of the eighteenth century (Bonney, 1995b: 475). Another alternative method for direct collection was the wealth evaluation as the basis of collection for a tax on possessions: the *alliramento* in Siena in the twelfth century is an example of a tax levied on movable property; another hypothesis was the assessment and tax collection on real estate, whose *Tavola delle Possessioni* ("table of possessions") was the entity responsible for this evaluation (Bonney, 1995b: 475–476). This taxation backbone is ultimately composed by extraordinary contributions. In the case of Florence, they were called *prestanze*, which were nothing more than "forced" loans; in Portugal, the *pedidos*, that is to say, the aid to make up the revenues and to balance the kingdom's accounts fall within this definition (Gonçalves, 1964: 13–18), which could also assume various forms of collection, already mentioned earlier.

In an even more refined analysis, we can still see four other development stages within this same category of domain state: primitive, less primitive, entrepreneurial and colonial. A primitive state would be characterized by the monarch's condition of using directly the product of his domains; a less primitive state presupposes a central structure combined with local branches that guarantee the collection of these products and their organization, storage and consumption of this collection, paid in kind; the enterprise or entrepreneurial state only has a part of its income in kind, already moving to a monetized economy, along with an aggressive foreign policy and without necessarily owning colonies to alleviate the fiscal burden (Bonney, 1995b: 460); and finally the colonial domain state, whose wealth exploitation of foreign territories serves to increase spending capacity and to balance the accounts between revenues and expenditure of European "metropolises".

As for the tax state category, this can be apparently defined by two key points: a real and complete actual and imposition of control over subsidies and extraordinary taxes, as well as the transition to an economy whose revenue base comes from indirect taxation, that is, those whose payment is voluntary, to the extent that the individual is not coerced to pay and chooses to do so by consuming or not certain products when he wishes and can pay them. Additionally, there is another fundamental aspect to be highlighted: a regular, almost permanent tax collection system, albeit of different species. Supposedly, this collection category would give the taxpayer more "freedom", since he is free to decide, and would also have an element of "equality", since the tax was levied on the rich and the poor according to their respective consumption levels (Bonney, 1995b: 489, 495).

It is important to emphasize that the model developers follow a historiographical line characterized as *Military Revolution*, that is, that taxation derives more from occasion than from a manifestation form of a right. Likewise, within these occasions – weddings, household constitution of a royal heir etc. – the most frequent and convincing of all: war. According to them, the origin of the tax state must be perceived as a consequence of military development. The central motivation of a taxation mechanism is to extract revenue. However, this extraction is a reactive phenomenon, since this search for resources is motivated by expenditure previously incurred, especially those related to military conflicts, where concepts like "rational taxation" and "fair war" are interrelated (Bonney & Ormrod, 1999: 16). Hence, the idea of justice, discussed by other scholars (Isenmann, 1995: 21–23) and dissected later, gains strength: the Holy Roman Empire's fiscal legislation text is emblematic in this sense (Bonney & Ormrod, 1999: 16).

Within this system type, we are drawn to a collective model: leased and collected by private individuals, i.e., the *tax farming*. That leasing process can be subdivided in general, encompassing the entire State or fiscal system; regional (encompassing only one city or region); or a special situation, characterized by an exceptional occasion, regarding the leasing of a tax on a particular product or a collection concession in a particular tax unit.

Indirect taxes can coexist with direct taxation, that is, they can complement and/or replace the states' fiscal base. Its 'libertarian' character is less aggressive to taxpayers and can be divided – always with a risk of oversimplification – in three types: the tolls' collection, either internally or externally, on agricultural and live-stock origin products' circulation, in which the English (Ormrod, 1999a: 31–33) and Castilian (Bonney, 1995b: 490–492) cases in the late Middle Ages and early modern period would be symptomatic of the collection base created on the wool and cloth exports, following their agro-pastoral vocations; taxes on consumption and/or commercial transactions, always subject to demographic and economic fluctuations; and the taxes on monopoly of specific commodities – such as salt in many regions, including Portugal – which may be under state control or under an individual or corporations control,[8] being also other examples of indirect taxation.

Another situation concerns the indirect taxes' burden, which may vary according to the regions, i.e., how much can it be worth and how important is each incident rate on a particular product, in a kingdom's particular area within the overall budget; and what was the degree of competence and corruption intrinsic to each collection system, which in some cases was offset by the increase in direct taxation, such as the French provinces at the dawn of the early modern period (Bonney, 1995b: 495). For a large part of the later Middle Ages, indirect taxes provided or accounted for the bulk of taxpayers' contribution and because of the sporadic nature of direct taxation they made up as much as 100% of revenues in England (Bonney, 1995b: 502).

2.2 Building a fiscal culture

In the *Cortes* (parliamentary assembly) gathered at Lisbon-Évora, in 1460, Afonso V, once again, persuaded all representatives on the pending matters, namely the annuities paid to the nobility, which remained to be solved and left the royal decrees at parliamentary meetings suspended a year earlier (Sousa, 1990: I, 386–387). There, support was required to meet its financial obligations and maintain his strategy of acquiring political support by granting endowments, graces, housing and other benefits that clearly burdened the treasury. Then the people agreed to offer the monarch an extraordinary contribution of 150,000 gold doubloons, paid in three installments over three years. However, a couple conditions were required to materialize this aid: the king would not take those aids for granted, of such a heavy cost, to the nobility; moreover, he would no longer grant benefits to anyone, for any reason. Although there was an attempt of dialogue and negotiation through an institutional mediation made by the *Cortes*, this is all to say that the king, after all, acted according to his will and right to offer whatever he wanted, to whomever he wanted and when he wished and those his subjects would be called to support his decisions, i.e., even with all the bargaining and counseling, the final decision belonged to the monarch. The central framework on which the fiscal principles of the medieval Western monarchies were based, without exception, is that of the divine royal right, of which that enlightened sovereign figure holds the power to impose taxes and extraordinary revenues' collections, an aspect which, in Portugal's case, must be observed very cautiously, due to particular circumstances of consolidation of the political power (Mattoso, 2001: 899–903). In fact, two biblical references are pointed out by theologians for this context: Christ's response to the Pharisees and the Epistle of St. Paul to the Romans, although here is clearly privileged the spiritual question rather than financial, and issues such as justice and over taxation are relativized by this type of explanation (Isenmann, 1995: 22–23).

Apart from the right to collect, there was the right to collect money when requested. The subjects had an obligation to pay the taxes with no objection or redress whatsoever. The theoretical bases for this were grounded on the writings of both St. Augustine (354–430) and St. Thomas Aquinas (1225–1274). We shall dwell on the ideas of the latter: the tax payment should be in accordance with human laws, i.e., it was morally obligatory only if it was fairly collected; otherwise such impositions should not be observed (Isenmann, 1995: 24–26), and those who do not follow these precepts would be disobeying divine laws. Here, justice as a fundamental concept is already inserted so as to safeguard the Church's position, as well as the kingdoms that follow the Christian precepts. In any case, this same idea of fairness remained relative and not always manifest. The establishment of a standard about what should be "fair", facing a concept of Aristotelian "distributive justice", became necessary. The precepts of *munera honesta* ("fair money") and *munera sordida* ("dirty money") arise, referring primarily, to a merely legal point of view and relative distancing from the economic questions themselves. Our main focus here is to define the first one: any form of collection that involves some predictability to a certain degree of regularity. Despite the fact that concepts such as periodicity and expectedness fit better into discussions of modern finance and taxation, both were used by theologians in the Middle Ages, regarding the elaboration of justifications, but were taken only by the legal sense of the terms. However, any argument to support tax collection will lie between the claims and royal needs on the one hand, and the "common good" on the other (Isenmann, 1995: 30).

In this sense, and returning to the question of "moral obligation", another important issue remains: under what circumstances this condition is defined? The purpose or *causa finalis*, the effectuation or *causa efficiens*, and the measure/ scale or *causa formalis* are the three parameters of this conjuncture. Cause and purpose, that is, the search for the 'common good'; sovereignty, or authority, that is, the monarch's power to levy any tax he deems worthy, grounded in the idea of the *suprema potestas* of canon law; as well as the proportion of taxes levied, which must be relativized by the payer and the main intent, together with the idea that no subject should ever be overburdened, is what clarifies and underpins the principles of tax collection and the organization of royal finances (Isenmann, 1995: 31–37).

It is important to highlight here the fact that this debate of a "tax culture" goes toward the definition of an essence, i.e., as a set of elements that compound something, as previously discussed in this chapter. Regarding the difficulties to compose a structure, a "bedrock" for raising resources in a lasting way, there are a number of key elements to consider: administrative capacity; resources allocated for general or specific purposes; the collectors and taxpayers' level of commitment concerning the social contract established; the levels of corruption intrinsic to the system – which may be directly or inversely proportional to wages paid to tax collectors and royal officers – penalties imposed on defaulters and corruptors, as well as the revenues' redistribution by the state (Bonney, 1995b: 427–428). This idea of a "fiscal constitution", though it has arisen as a plea for political change in later times,[9] as a historical concept, needs adaptations and care when used in this way (Henriques, 2008: 68). It serves to describe how a prevailing type of a tax system takes specific forms and contours in a particular country at a given point in its history (Bonney & Ormrod, 1999: 2–3). It is the balance between "the principles, practices and attitudes of the monarchs and subjects in what concerns the State's finances" (Henriques, 2008: 67). However, the central issue is the need for external regulator over the sovereign's fiscal power. Control exercised, in those times, by the peoples' representatives in the parliamentary meetings: the *Cortes* (Sousa, 1990: I, 182–183). There, theories and arguments find the beacons, the legal references, the legitimacy of certain procedures and an effective support for the discourse's materialization in daily practices. Hence the creation of institutions, triggered by the direct stakeholders – the king, noblemen, merchants and other economically privileged groups – responsible for getting the money to their coffers and, on the other hand, to provide economic support to the state by paying taxes, begins to take shape. The exercise of this authority will be the catalyst element to establish fiscal dynamics in the realms that will use this legal support. However, the political fragmentation of the ninth, tenth, and eleventh centuries left sequels that would remain for a long time. Even with the rise of modern states, this phenomenon would still affect them, by experiencing a moment of change, with the separation of "state finances" and "royal treasuries" which, regarding the Portuguese case, until the eleventh century, were managed by their respective royal households and coordinated by an itinerant chamber attached to the king and, later, to have an office of their own, fixed points of revenue collecting and resource transferred to a central point (Ormrod & Barta, 1995: 62–63).

It should be noted that the pillars of the resources' collection, as well as state finances' institutions in early modern Portugal and Iberia were based on the *Fuero Viejo*, i.e., the medieval Castilian law, which established a set of revenues: justice, currency and royal rights (Gonçalves, 1999: 98), including the *Fossadeira*[10] and *Jantares*.[11] However, it can be said that the *reconquista* would be a milestone in terms of a tax culture in Iberia. Not by chance Afonso III a few years after the process was concluded in Portugal, in 1249, proposes *to break*[12] the currency, in order to stabilize the finances, which no longer lived only from the spoils of wars (Duarte, 2006: 435). In this period, the inquiries carried out by him showed signs of a policy aimed at preserving the Crown's sources of income, that is,

maintaining its economic and financial capacity, in order to consolidate its autonomy of action toward centralization and political strengthening (Mattoso, 2001:
904). In any case, some evidence points to that it will be only with the customs
unification (Henriques, 2008: 130–146), combined with the establishment of the
almoxarifados, as local institutions responsible for the preservation of royal economic rights, later integrated to the *Casa dos Contos*[13] that begins to carve the
fundamental institutional pieces of the Portuguese state fiscal apparatus. None-
theless, it will be the strengthening of this last central office, in particular, which
already had its own accounting books since Afonso IV's reign (1325–1357), but
which would only have regiment and organization defined at the end of the fourteenth century (Costa, 1996: 74), which will provide the necessary support for the
fiscal administrative developments that would come afterwards. The end of this
process would come with the institution of the *contadores* ("accountants"), which
firstly appeared during Dinis I (1279–1325) (Homem, 1990: 148–150), inspired
by the figure of the Castilian *Contador Mayor* (Ladero Quesada, 2011: 228) –
and later instituted in the second half of the fourteenth century – along with the
financial administration's separation in *Contos do Rei* (Royal Treasury), which
managed the royal household revenues and accounting, and the *Contos de Lisboa*
("Lisbon's central fiscal office"), that centralized the management and verification of the *almoxarifados* scattered by the kingdom. Entering the fifteenth century, the creation of the *Contador-Mor* ("chief accountant") and *Contadorias das
Comarcas* (Gomes, 2006: 121) ("counties' accounting branches") would end this
process. This new intermediary controlling mechanism (Rau, 2009: 25–26) was
supposed to ensure central authority's local representation and, therefore, accurate management, avoiding waste and corruption among tax agents. They usually
grouped two or more units and responded directly to the *Vedores da Fazenda*
("top fiscal officers"). Here, it is possible to observe a "decentralizing centralization", i.e., the King seeks to strengthen his own political power by guaranteeing
that the state's sources of income will be preserved by assigning functions to
local delegates with power to work in their conferred jurisdictions, except in
seigneurial influenced lands – queens' lands, military orders' properties, duchies, counties and others with specific jurisdiction, such as the churches' estates
(Gomes, 2006: 123).

Altogether with this fiscal device, the judicial structure provided the necessary legal support to keep the central administrative fiscal mechanism fully operational. Within each district structure, the *contador* himself often could exercise
the function of a judge, assisted by ombudsmen, scribes, clerks and a battalion of
officials that could vary by each circumscription (Gomes, 2006: 123), regarding
taxation conflicts. Above the fiscal apparatus was the kingdom's superior courts:
first, the *Audiência da Portaria* ("Audience of the Ordinance"), which was shut-
tered by Dinis I in 1321, composed by the ombudsmen of the King's deeds – the
porteiros ("doormen") – and the ordinance, responsible for judging matters concerning the Royal Treasury, the Jews and the Moors, which in many occasions
obliged the officers "to repair by their own means the damage that, by duty's performance mistake, could cause to the executed, and to impose this charge to the

office" (Barros, 1945: III, 240–244; Homem, 1990: 124–125). Second, the *Casa da Suplicação* ("House of Appealing"), which was derived from the *Ouvidores das suplicações* ("top ombudsmen officers") (Barros, 1945: III, 264) and, being the kingdom's highest court, those officials had to follow the King in his itinerancy (Costa, 1996: 75). Third, the *Casa do Cível* ("Civil-Criminal Court"), with the attribution of civil and criminal appeals in Lisbon (Gomes, 2006: 123). As far as fiscal matters are concerned, the *ouvidores da portaria* (ombudsmen regarding the doormen officials) would give place to the *Vedores da Fazenda*, whose institution would have been shaped during the reign of Pedro I (1357–1367) (Homem, 1990: 129), formalized in 1369,[14] beginning a new phase of Portuguese taxation: the permanence and generalization of consumption taxation, with the massive collection of indirect taxes on products and goods traded, that is, the institutionalization of *sisas* (sales taxes) as a source of ordinary revenue. From that moment onwards, there would be a greater concern regarding tax matters than with pensions, donations, and sentences (Homem, 1990: 131), which would be added to the inquiries about rents and royal rights, as the central concern of the *Juízes dos Feitos do Rei* ("King's deeds judges"), responsible for judging all conflicts in which the monarch was involved, regardless of being fiscal, criminal or administrative affairs (Homem, 1990: 136–138).

The judicial system itself was capable of generating revenues. As the forensic institutions gained more definitive contours, the fiscal mechanism matured, so that the evolution of these two fundamental elements of Portuguese society occurred simultaneously. The relationship between justice and taxation lies in two points: first, in the people's right to a trial with judges and not by landlords imposing their particular will; second, the values collected by taxes, fees and emoluments charged, combined with the economic potential of the fines imposed, as well as the possibility of the assets' confiscation and inheritance of those judged as guilty. It is also assumed that a large bulk of the Crown's revenues were made, at key moments, of internal dissensions and wars, for example, with the recovery and revocation of donations, combined with a policy of redistribution, especially concerning land and positions within the officialdom, through private denunciations (Duarte, 2006: 434).

Regarding monetary policy, it is true that the royal right to coinage and its control is a source of large profits, but also required great care not to destabilize the economy on a large scale. However, it seems that the process of making money was an interesting issue due to the many variables involved in this area of royal revenues because the amount of precious metals available for this implies a prevaluation or debasement of the currency, which could occur by varying the alloy content that coinage was issued, with more or less precious metal, by increasing the face value or decreasing the absolute weight. In addition, the *monetagium* or "money breaking", that is, the king's right to demand financial compensation from the subjects so that the money was not "broken". This procedure consisted in collecting old currency in circulation, to be re-minted with less precious metal, and the metal surplus was collected, as an extraordinary resource, to the monarch. This procedure could be used as a resource to obtain income, albeit in an unusual way. By definition,[15] this was the basis of a secondary protocol, that is, of an exceptional income and, escaping from predictable reserves, not being foreseen, not frequent or outside the established, and that was not part of the Crown's regular set of revenues. Those earnings were being manipulated by the monarchs, according to the conjunctures and their needs, with particular emphasis during the second half of the fourteenth century, mainly due to the acknowledged and serious financial difficulties that were ravaging the Portuguese finances (Gonçalves, 1999: 99–100).

2.3 European economy and fiscal systems at the dawn of modern times: some milestones and state of the art

Although an excellent balance of taxation in the European economy between late medieval and early modern times has already been done and edited recently (Grohmann, 2008), we dare to leave some notes and hints about what has been done so far in this line of study, handing some indications on initiatives, with which we had contact and knowledge through this research. Nowadays, the development of late medieval and early modern fiscal studies, regarding the Iberian Peninsula, has had a great appeal in several centers, mostly Spanish, with large associated transdisciplinary research groups, among which we can highlight, in Barcelona, the Milá y Fontanals Institute[16] (IMF) in Barcelona, whose scientific production is very relevant. Within the line of research *The Mediterranean: a space of exchanges and power relations* is the subgroup of *Taxation and public finances in the genesis of the Modern State: the case of the Crown of Aragon (XIII-XV centuries)*, under the supervision of Manuel Sánchez Martínez and Pere Verdés Pijuan, which focuses on social beginnings, economic development and taxation and public finance policies, analyzing various social groups (noblemen, peasants, tax collectors, bankers, moneylenders etc.) and the progress of the different tax system's levels (regional, municipal or national), which helped shaping central aspects of society and the state in the Catalan-Aragonese Crown, but never neglecting their private interests. The many publications[17] edited by this center are fundamental for the development of studies in this area, highlighting the thematic about the creation and evolution of public debt mechanisms. His counterpart in Madrid also plays a central role regarding research on this subject, through investigations at the Center for Social and Human Sciences. Still in the Spanish capital, scientific production has at the Universidad Complutense de Madrid another center of excellence with regard to late medieval and early modern Castilian taxation.[18] Further north of the peninsula, the Universities of Valladolid,[19] of the Basque Country[20] (UPV) and of Cantabria[21] have centers of relevance to early modern fiscal studies, whether local or regional investigations, although the latter gives greater emphasis to the economy and taxation in modern times.

Still in the peninsula, another center of great importance is located in Malaga, whose research in fiscal history is quite widespread, with a strong department of economic and business sciences in contact with that of archeology and medieval and early modern history, with several research projects developed and others on taxation and society in the Castilian Crown south of the Tagus, within the *Andalusia*, including researchers from other nearby centers in southern Spain, such as Seville, Granada and Murcia, with a consistent scientific production,[22] as well as the Universities of Valencia, Zaragoza and Girona further east, which also continue to make a significant contribution to studies in this area, focusing on credit institutions and mechanisms within the Crown of Aragon, Barcelona County and the Balearic Islands.[23] And, last but not least, the *Arca Comunis* research network, which plays the fundamental role of integrating all Spanish research projects concerning the history of Spanish taxation and finances, acting integrated and cooperatively with the Spanish Institute of Fiscal Studies,[24] promoting congresses, publications and other projects.

In France, since the pioneering work of Jean Favier (1966, 1971) in the 1960s and 1970s, fiscal studies have been central to Paris's EHESS (École des hautes études en sciences sociales), from where other research projects and groups, whether on this particular theme or whose themes are cross–cutting and/or organized and aggregated. Also at the University of Paris 1 – Sorbonne, the LAMOP (Laboratoire de Médiévistique Occidentale de Paris) operates with various lines of research ranging from prices (Feller, 2011), revenues and wages in the Middle Ages/early modern times, through the formation of communities and villages, to issues related to the circulation of wealth and taxation, supported by the Law School of University of Paris 2–Panthéon-Assas, with solid research in the medieval fiscal area, under the prism of royal right to impose taxes (Rigaudière, 2003a, 2003b, 2003c, 2008). Other key centers in fiscal studies from the legislative perspective have been the University of Auvergne/Clermont-Ferrand, focused on fiscal analysis from the point of view of the legal mechanisms that governed and govern the construction and consolidation of taxation structures (Garnier, 2008, 2009), as well as the University of Perpignan, with relevant research developed also in institutional history (Larguier, 2000, 2008a, 2008b). On other subjects, the University of Lyon 2–Lumière, have a very active research group in fiscal history since the mid-1990s, when the working group of history and archeology of the Christian and Muslim worlds in the Middle Ages (CIHAM-UMR 5648) was created, with several lines, among which stands out the one that works under the theme of money, exchanges and taxation dynamics (Menjot & Sánchez Martínez, 2004). With regard to Normandy, the Universities of Caen/Basse-Normandie and Rouen, acting in partnership through the *Center de recherches archéologiques et historiques anciennes et médiévales*, as well as the GRHIS (Groupe de Recherche d'Histoire), respectively, also have research and production in the area of medieval and early modern history, focusing on the political effects produced by the regional and state fiscal dynamics (Lalou, 2010). In addition, other works on the French public debt have arisen and raised several research initiatives in this line (Boureau, 2006; Hamon, 2006).

However, it must be emphasized that since 1986 there has been a strong committee on the economic and financial history of France, which supports publications and joint venture initiatives, with researchers and centers in the organization of research and conferences (Contamine, Kerhervé & Rigaudière,

2002). Furthermore, this committee, by law, has been associated, since 2006, with an institute of public management and economic development (IGPDE),[25] being directly subordinate to the French Ministry of Economy, Finance and Foreign Trade.

With regard to scientific production on economic and fiscal history in Italy in the Middle Ages and early modern times, there are a large number of centers that produce research in this area with concrete results. One of these centers is at the University of Cassino and Southern Lazio, whose research is directed at studies on taxation, particularly on public debt and economic structuring of the Church and the Pontifical States, both in the Middle Ages and in the Modern Age (Piola Caselli, 1987, 2001, 2008). Although more linked to the modern period, but with some important references to the sixteenth century, the University of Rome 3, with investigation that refer to localities within Central Italian peninsula region. Moreover, they also engage other topics, such as the importance of private credit and public finances (Sabatini, 1997, 2005, 2008) in the context of the Spanish monarchy and Latin America economic development between the sixteenth and seventeenth centuries. In the North, several centers such as Milan, Venice, Siena, Florence, Perugia, Bologna and Pisa are also noteworthy, with a scientific production that turns its attention to multiple themes, ranging from credit and its relationship with debt management in Tuscany city-states (Ginatempo, 2000), to public-private credit networks in the transition from the Middle Ages to modernity, as well as the origins of fundraising in Italy (Carboni, 2008, 2009),[26] the dynamics of direct taxes and public debt in the northern kingdoms,[27] even the association of wine and taxation (Nigro, 2008).

Furthermore, in Italy, we always remember the Fondazione Istituto Internazionale di Storia Economica Francesco Datini, based in Prato, which encourages and organizes a week of studies on various topics of economic history, with more than 40 years of tradition[28] and several published conference proceedings on an enormous variety of subjects, which also cooperates and publishes works together with researchers of several universities of the North, particularly in Tuscany.

As far as England is concerned, it can be said that the development of studies in this topic and regarding this period, has already taken a long time, from the great pioneering syntheses of the 1960s and 1970s,[29] which favored the production relations, the goods produced and traded, as well as the agents involved, until the most recent and specific ones on the economy and taxation (Yun-Casalilla, O'Brien & Comín Comín, 2012) in particular. Nowadays, economic and fiscal history, as much as its cross-cutting themes continue to have great appeal in Britain, whether in older or younger research centers.

Regarding the first situation, Cambridge, with a strong and consolidated department, whose production on the Middle Ages and early modern times is related to transdisciplinary themes that touch fiscal and economic issues, is an example. In addition, there is a line of research in economic and social history,[30] with a varied academic staff and chronology, supported by the Center for Financial History at Newnham College, combined with the faculty of economics, the Judge Business School and the Center for Quantitative Economic History (CQEH), which seek to encompass the various streams of research possible in a long-run approach. Several topics, such as the development of credit in rural areas (Briggs, 2008, 2009) and its social implications, numismatic studies, comparative economic history, statistical analyzes and political-constitutional work are some examples. In Oxford, there is also a line of research that follow the same pattern, with a multidisciplinary team and associated with Saïd Business School and the Faculty of Economics,[31] which promote regular seminars and workshops for undergraduate students to present their studies and research proposals supported by the Winton Institute for Monetary History, with interesting studies on the price indexes of properties in the Middle Ages.[32] York also follows the same path, with the Center for Medieval Studies and the Center for Historical Economics and Related Research at York (CHERRY).[33] At the London School of Economics there is a Department of Economic History,[34] where the study of taxation, particularly in the late Middle Ages, is not much in evidence, but other chronologies are also privileged in this area with British colonies, in addition to the medieval economic policies of the English kingdom (Gardner, 2008) and the economic origins of English political institutions. Other themes, such as the financial and credit market in the late Middle Ages (Chilosi & Volckart, 2011), their integration in the context of the formation of the kingdoms of Central Europe and monetary studies also appear as lines of ongoing investigations.

On the other hand, more centers are emerging and standing out and, in this sense, the case of University of Reading is emblematic, with a well-developed and shared center[35] between the Departments of History and Economics, supported by Henley Business School and ICMA Center,[36] the latter with foreign sponsorship and a wide range of research lines, ranging from the monastic economy to numismatics, military history and, more specifically, economics and finance, credit to British monarchs (Bell, Alexander, Brooks & Moore, 2011) and interest rates in later Middle Ages and early modern times (Bell, Brooks & Moore, 2008).

In Belgium and Netherlands, respectively, the work at the University of Ghent stands out, with a Middle Ages research center[37] in which the theme of urban history prevails. One of the transversal themes within this context is fiscal history.[38] At the University of Leiden, the Institute of History also has research lines related to economics, commerce and taxation (Blockmans, 1999, 2008).

In Portugal, the association between history and economics, regarding the organization of research centers around research projects on economic-fiscal topics, either related to early modern or other chronologies, or even in a long-run perspective, compared to what has been done elsewhere, is something that still walks on baby steps. There is a lot to be explored on this path with great potential, although there is an Economic and Social History Cabinet in Lisbon, at the GHES-ISEG (School of Economics and Management) at the University of Lisbon where public finances have been explored by investigations in modern and contemporary contexts, both in terms of completed, consolidated research contributions and a few still in progress. Two decades ago, a team of researchers from the IEM (Institute of Medieval Studies), coordinated by Amélia Andrade, integrated a French-Spanish project that resulted in a critical glossary of medieval taxation.[39]

However, little more was added regarding an initiative of fiscal studies in Portuguese scope from their own. In the Nova School of Business and Economics, at the New University of Lisbon, the line of research in economic history is very strong, but more limited to banking history, as well as Portuguese banking system in the nineteenth and twentieth centuries. However, the works of Maria Eugenia Mata, although they contemplate the economic social line, most of its work is oriented to contemporary times, although it has contributed with some writings that touched economy and taxation in the modern era.[40]

In the ICS (Institute of Social Sciences) at the University of Lisbon, within the thematic axes, a research project on prices, wages and incomes in Portugal (PWR) in a long-run approach[41] (between the fourteenth and twentieth centuries), was coordinated by Jaime Reis, which essentially studied living standards and productivity within the Portuguese economy, providing a huge contribution in terms of new data and new data basis. Furthermore, the remaining universities and research centers in the country are dedicating some space to individual, isolated and dispersed initiatives, either through the hosting of M.A. or Ph.D. research projects with their own funding, which was how some researchers in medieval and early modern economics at the faculty of arts of the University of Porto, each one with their own theme in particular, but all with economics and social history in common, which resulted in a set of theses[42] already presented. However, Portuguese taxation *per se*, at least as far as the Middle Ages and early modern era is concerned, still lacks further in-depth, systematic and joint studies.

Notes

1 Bluteau (1712–1728), Silva (1813) and Pinto (1832). All these dictionaries are available for consultation at the Centre of Brazilian Studies' website at the University of São Paulo (USP) – *Brasiliana USP*: www.brasiliana.usp.br/dicionario.
2 We refer to the work of Iria Gonçalves, previously cited.
3 Definition found in 1 March 2018, in the *Dicionário Houaiss da Língua Portuguesa*, online version [http://houaiss.uol.com.br].
4 Definition found in 15 August 2018, in the Cambridge Online Dictionary [https://dictionary.cambridge.org/dictionary/english-portuguese/archetype].
5 Definitions found in 26 September 2011, in the *Dicionário Houaiss da Língua Portuguesa*, online version [http://houaiss.uol.com.br].
6 Definition found in 23 September 2011, in the *Dicionário Houaiss da Língua Portuguesa*, online version [http://houaiss.uol.com.br]. For more ideas about the concepts of identity and difference, as well as their applicability in cultural studies within a Brazilian framework, see Silva (2011).
7 See Barratt (1999).
8 The salt example is emblematic, bearing in mind that in Portugal, such monopoly remained under state's control. In Genoa, the salt monopoly was controlled by a banking institution, the *Casa di San Giorgio*, which obtained large profits and, at the same time, regulated its price according to their wishes. In other Italian city-states there were other examples, as the iron, olive oil and fishery. Bonney (1995b: 493–494); for Portugal, see Rau (1951) and Almeida (2005).
9 The concept of "fiscal constitution" is advanced within a context of "fiscal rebellions" that emerged in California in 1978, due to a tax raise carried by the government. Brennan and Buchanan (1980: 1–10).

10 Tax related to the villagers' military obligations in times of war.
11 Levy related to the villagers' foodstuffs' duties, regarding king and noblemen's passing through a specific region.
12 Procedure related to the currency's collection and reminting process, with a lower percentage of precious metal (either gold or silver) and the surplus returning to the monarch.
13 Portuguese Central Office responsible for fiscal affairs and accounting. Barata and Henriques (2012: 277–279).
14 Homem (2009) [Accessed 5 March 2013].
15 Based on the entry "extraordinário", of the *Dicionário Houaiss da Língua Portuguesa*, online version, accessed on 6 March 2013.
16 www.imf.csic.es/.
17 Sánchez Martínez (1997, 2009), Verdés Pijuan (2004a, 2004b, 2005, 2007) and Marti Arau (2009).
18 Ladero Quesada (1967, 1989), Asenjo González (2006, 2008) and Carretero Zamora (2009).
19 Casado Alonso (2000: 135–156) and Bonachía Hernando and Terán Sánchez (2010).
20 García Fernández (1994, 2012) and Vítores Casado (2009).
21 Gelabert González (1995, 1999, 2002) and Fortea Pérez (1997).
22 Galán Sánchez and Peinado Santaella (2006), Galán Sánchez (2012), González Arce (2010, 2012), Terán Sánchez and Menjot (1996) and Terán Sánchez (2006).
23 Furió Diego (1993, 2009), García Marsilla (2009), Ortí Gost (2000), Cateura Bennasser (2009), Sesma Muñoz (1988, 2001) and Lafuente Gómez (2012).
24 By 18 February 2013, there were eleven ongoing registered initiatives, within research groups in development, projects and complementary actions, under the network's rule.
25 www.comite-histoire.minefi.gouv.fr/.
26 Carboni (2008, 2009).
27 Pezzolo (2003), Pezzolo and Stumpo (2008), Molho (2006a, 2006b) and Barthas (2006).
28 www.istitutodatini.it/.
29 Postan, Rich and Miller (1963), Postan (1972) and North and Thomas (1973).
30 www.econsoc.hist.cam.ac.uk/index.html.
31 www.economics.ox.ac.uk/index.php/groups/economic-history.
32 http://winton.ashmus.ox.ac.uk/index.html.
33 Ormrod (1995a, 1995b, 1999a, 1999b, 2000, 2008, 2011).
34 http://www2.lse.ac.uk/economicHistory/home.aspx.
35 www.reading.ac.uk/economic-history/.
36 www.icmacentre.ac.uk/.
37 Henri Pirenne Institute for Medieval Studies: www.pirenne.ugent.be/.
38 Billen and Boone (2011) and Boone (1997, 2008).
39 www.1minut.info/glosariofiscalidad.org/wp/?lang=en.
40 Mata and Valério (1994, 2011) and Mata (2012).
41 www.ics.ul.pt/Instituto/?ln=p&mm=3&ctmid=1&mnid=1.
42 Ferreira (2007), Marques (2012), Miranda (2012), Sequeira (2012) and Dominguez (2013).

Bibliography

Secondary sources and dictionaries

Bluteau, R. (1712–1728). *Vocabulario portuguez & latino: aulico, anatomico, architectonico . . .*, 8 vols. Coimbra: Collegio das Artes da Companhia de Jesus.
Cambridge Online Dictionary [https://dictionary.cambridge.org/dictionary/english-portuguese/archetype].

Dicionário Houaiss da Língua Portuguesa, Online version [http://houaiss.uol.com.br/].
Pinto, L. M. da S. (1832). *Diccionario da Lingua Brasileira* por Luiz Maria da Silva Pinto, natural da Provincia de Goyaz. Na Typographia de Silva. [Available Online in the Brazilian Studies' Digital Library, at the University of São Paulo (Brasiliana USP): www.brasiliana.usp.br/dicionario].
Silva, A. M. (1813). *Diccionario da lingua portugueza – recompilado dos vocabularis impressos ate agora, e nesta segunda edição novamente emendado e muito acrescentado, por Antonio de Moraes Silva.* Lisbon: Typographia Lacerdina. [Available Online in the Brazilian Studies' Digital Library, at the University of São Paulo (Brasiliana USP): www.brasiliana.usp.br/dicionario].

Studies

Almeida, C. A. B. de. (2005). A exploração do sal na costa portuguesa a Norte do Rio Ave. Da antiguidade clássica à Baixa Idade Média, in *Atas do I Seminário internacional sobre o sal português*. Porto: Instituto de História Moderna da Universidade do Porto, 137–170.
Asenjo González, M. (2006). Los encabezamientos de alcabalas en la Castilla bajomedieval: fuentes de renta y política fiscal, in D. Menjot, & M. Sánchez Martínez (ed.), *Fiscalidad de Estado y fiscalidad municipal en los reinos hispánicos medievales: estudios dirigidos por Denis Menjot y Manuel Sánchez Martínez*. Madrid: Casa de Velázquez, 135–170.
Asenjo González, M. (2008). Ciudades y deuda pública en Castilla. La adaptación fiscal del impuesto de la "alcabala real" a las nuevas exigencias de la sociedad política (1450–1520), in *Actas La fiscalità nell'economia europea (sec. XIII-XVIII)*, 39th Settimana di Studi dell'istituto "Francesco Datini" di Prato a cura di Simonetta Cavaciocchi. Firenze: Firenze University Press, 531–544.
Barata, F. T., & Henriques, A. C. (2012). Economic and Fiscal History, in J. Mattoso (dir.), M. de L. Rosa, B. V. e Sousa, & M. J. Branco (eds.), *The Historiography of Medieval Portugal (c.1950–2010)*. Lisbon: Instituto de Estudos Medievais, 261–281.
Barratt, N. (1999). English Royal Revenue in the Early Thirteenth Century and its Wider Context, 1130–1330, in W. M. Ormrod, M. Bonney, & R. Bonney (eds.), *Crises, Revolutions and Self-Sustained Growth: Essays in European Fiscal History, c.1130–1830*. Stanford: Shaun Tyas, 58–96.
Barros, H. da G. (1945). *História da Administração Pública em Portugal nos Séculos XII a XV: 2ª edição dirigida por Torquato de Sousa Soares*, 11 vols. Lisbon: Livraria Sá da Costa Editora.
Barthas, J. (2006). Le moment savonarolien. Sur le rôle et l'importance de la dette publique dans les difficultés de la république florentine du Grand Conseil (1494–1512), in J. Andreau, G. Béaur, & J. Y. Grenier (dir.), *La dette publique dans l'histoire*. Actes des Journées du Centre de Recherches Historiques des 26, 27 et 28 novembre 2001. Paris: Comité pour L'Histoire Économique et Financière de la France, 63–84.
Bell, A. R., Alexander, C., Brooks, C., & Moore, T. (2011). The Evolutionary Dynamics of the Credit Relationship between Henry III and the Flemish Merchants, 1247–1270. University of Reading, ICMA Centre Discussion Papers in Finance DP2011–25, 1–43.
Bell, A. R., Brooks, C., & Moore, T. (2008). Interest in Medieval Accounts: Examples from England, 1272–1340. University of Reading, ICMA Centre Discussion Papers in Finance DP2008–07, 1–26.

Billen, C., & Boone, M. (2011). Taxer Les Ecclésiastiques: Le Laboratoire Urbain Des Pays-Bas Méridionaux (XIIe – XVIe Siècles), in D. Menjot & M. Sánchez Martínez (eds.), *El Dinero De Dios: iglesia y Fiscalidad En El Occidente Medieval (siglos XIII-XV)*. Madrid: Instituto de Estudios Fiscales. Ministerio de Economia y Hacienda, 273–288.

Bonachía Hernando, J. A., & Terán Sánchez, A. C. de (coord.). (2010). *Fuentes para el estudio del negocio fiscal y financiero en los reinos hispánicos (siglos XIV-XVI)*. Madrid: Ministerio de Hacienda – Instituto de Estudios Fiscales.

Bonney, R. (1995a). The Eighteenth Century. II. The Struggle for Great Power Status and the End of the Old Fiscal Regime, in R. Bonney (ed.), *Economic Systems and State Finance*. Oxford: Oxford University Press, 315–390.

Bonney, R. (1995b). Revenues, in R. Bonney (ed.), *Economic Systems and State Finance*. Oxford: Oxford University Press, 423–505.

Bonney, R., & Ormrod, W. M. (1999). Introduction: Crises, Revolutions and Self-Sustained Growth: Towards a Conceptual Model of Change in Fiscal History, in W. M. Ormrod, M. Bonney, & R. Bonney (eds.), *Crises, Revolutions and Self-Sustained Growth: Essays in European Fiscal History, c.1130–1830*. Stanford, CA: Shaun Tyas, 1–21.

Boone, M. (1997). Stratégies Fiscales Et Financières Des Élites Urbaines Dans Les Anciens Pays-Bas Face à L'état burgundo-Habsbourgeois, in Actes Du XXVIIIe Congrès De La Société Des Historiens Médiévistes De l'Enseignement Supérieur Public, Clermont-Ferrand 30 Mai – 1 Juin Paris, 1998. Paris: Publications De La Sorbonne, Série Histoire Ancienne Et Médiévale 51, 235–253.

Boone, M. (2008). Systèmes fiscaux dans les principautés à forte urbanisation des Pays-Bas méridionaux (Flandre, Brabant, Hainaut, Pays de Liège) au bas moyen âge (XIVe-XVIe siècle), in *Actas La fiscalità nell'economia europea (sec. XIII-XVIII)*, 39th Settimana di Studi dell'istituto "Francesco Datini" di Prato a cura di Simonetta Cavaciocchi. Firenze: Firenze University Press, 657–684.

Blockmans, W. (1999). The Low Countries in the Middle Ages, in R. Bonney (ed.), *The Rise of the Fiscal State in Europe c. 1200–1815*. Oxford: Oxford University Press, 281–308.

Blockmans, W. (2008). Rapport de synthèse: Les Pouvoirs Publics dans des Régions de Haute Urbanisation. 'Flandre' et 'italie' aux XIVe-XVie Siècles, in E. Lecuppre-Desjardin & E. Crouzet-Pavan (eds.), Villes de Flandres et d'italie (XIIIe-XVIe siècle). Les Enseignements d'une Comparaison. Turnhout: Brepols, Studies in European Urban History, 12, 65–74.

Boureau, A. (2006). Le monastère médiéval, laboratoire de la dette publique? in J. Andreau, G. Béaur, & J. Y. Grenier (dir.), *La dette publique dans l'histoire*. Actes des Journées du Centre de Recherches Historiques des 26, 27 et 28 novembre 2001. Paris: Comité pour L'Histoire Économique et Financière de la France, 21–35.

Brennan, G., & Buchanan, J. M. (1980). *The Power to Tax: Analytical Foundations of a Fiscal Constitution*. London: Cambridge University Press.

Briggs, C. (2008). The Availability of Credit in the English Countryside (1400–1480), The Agricultural History Review, British Agricultural History Society, 56, 1, 1–24.

Briggs, C. (2009). *Credit and Village Society in Fourteenth-Century England*. Oxford: Oxford University Press/British Academy.

Carboni, M. (2008). *Alle origini del fund raising: confraternite, predicatori e mercanti nelle città italiane (secoli XIV-XVIII)*, in *Il fund raising in italia. Storia e prospettive*. Bologna: Società Editrice il Mulino, 37–81.

Carboni, M. (2009). *Le reti del credito tra pubblico e privato nella Bologna dell'età moderna*, in B. Farolfi, & V. Melandri (eds.), *Il mercato del credito in età moderna. Reti e operatori finanziari nello spazio europeo*. Milano: Franco Angeli, 145–162.

Carretero Zamora, J. M. (2009). Los desequilibrios de los repartimientos fiscales en la Corona de Castilla: el modelo de "el servicio del reino" en época de Carlos V, iura vasconiae: revista de derecho histórico y autonómico de Vasconia, ISSN 1699–5376, 6, 9–46.

Casado Alonso, H. (2000). Comercio, crédito y finanzas públicas en Castilla en la época de los Reyes Católicos, Actas del Simposio internacional "Dinero, moneda y crédito: de la monarquía hispánica a la integración monetaria europea", Madrid, 4–7 de Mayo de 1999, coord. por Antonio Miguel Bernal Rodríguez, ISBN 84-95379-10-4, 135–156.

Cateura Bennasser, P. (2009). Crédito y fiscalidad en las villas rurales de Mallorca (1315–1410), in R. Vallejo Pousada & A. Furió Diego (coord.), *Los tributos de la tierra: fiscalidad y agricultura en España: (siglos XII-XX)*. Valencia: Universidad de Valencia, 59–80.

Chilosi, D., & Volckart, O. (2011). Money, States and Empire: Financial Integration and Institutional Change in Central Europe, 1400–1520, Journal of Economic History, 71, 3, 762–791.

Contamine, P., Kerhervé, J., & Rigaudière, A. (dir.). (2002). L'impôt au Moyen Âge: l'impôt public et le prélèvement seigneurial, fin XIIe – début XVie siècle. Actes du colloque tenu à Bercy les 14, 15 et 16 juin 2000, 3 vols. Paris: Comité pour L'Histoire Économique et Financière de la France.

Costa, Pre. A. J. da. (1996). A Chancelaria Real Portuguesa e os seus registos, de 1217 a 1438, Revista da Faculdade de Letras: História, série II, 13, 71–101.

Dominguez, R. C. (2013). *O Financiamento da Coroa Portuguesa nos finais da Idade Média: entre o "africano" e o "venturoso"*. Ph.D. Thesis. Porto: Faculty of Arts.

Duarte, L. M. (2006). A memória contra a História: as sisas medievais portuguesas, in D. Menjot & M. Sánchez Martínez (dir.), *Fiscalidad de Estado y fiscalidad municipal en los reinos hispánicos medievales: estudios dirigidos por Denis Menjot y Manuel Sánchez Martínez*. Madrid: Casa de Velázquez, 433–445.

Favier, J. (1966). *Les Finances pontificales à l'époque du Grand Schisme d'Occident, 1378-1409*. Paris: De Boccard.

Favier, J. (1971). *Finance et Fiscalité au bas Moyen Âge*. Paris: Société d'édition d'enseignement supérieur.

Feller, L. (2011). Sur la formation des prix dans l'économie du haut Moyen Âge, Annales, histoire, sciences sociales, ISSN 0395-2649, 3, 627–662.

Ferreira, S. C. (2007). *Preços e Salários em Portugal na Baixa Idade Média*. M. A. Thesis. Porto: Faculty of Arts.

Fortea Pérez, J. I. (1997). Entre dos servicios: la crisis de la Hacienda Real a fines del siglo XVI. Las alternativas fiscales de una opción política (1590–1601), Studia histórica. Historia moderna, ISSN 0213–2079, 17, 63–90.

Furió Diego, A. (1993). Diners i crèdit: els jueus d'Alzira en la segona meitat del segle XIV, *Revista d'historia medieval*, ISSN 1131–7612, 4 (Ejemplar dedicado a: Jueus, conversos i cristians: mons en contacte), 127–160.

Furió Diego, A. (1999). Deuda pública e intereses privados. Finanzas y fiscalidad municipales en la Corona de Aragón, Edad Media: revista de historia, ISSN 1138–9621, 2, 35–80.

Furió Diego, A. (2009). Fiscalidad y agricultura en la Edad Media, in R. Vallejo Pousada & A. Furió Diego (coord.), *Los tributos de la tierra: fiscalidad y agricultura en España: (siglos XII-XX)*. Valencia: Universidad de Valencia, 17–58.

Galán Sánchez, A. (2012). Poder y fiscalidad en el Reino de Granada tras la conquista: algunas reflexiones, *Studia histórica. Historia medieval*, ISSN 0213–2060, 30 (Ejemplar dedicado a: Poder y fiscalidad en la Edad Media hispánica), 67–98.

Galán Sánchez, A., & Peinado Santaella, R. G. (2006). De la Madïna musulmana al concejo mudéjar: fiscalidad regia y fiscalidad concejil en la ciudad de Granada tras la conquista castellana, in D. Menjot & M. Sánchez Martínez (ed.), *Fiscalidad de Estado y fiscalidad municipal en los reinos hispánicos medievales: estudios dirigidos por Denis Menjot y Manuel Sánchez Martínez*. Madrid: Casa de Velázquez, 197–238.

García Fernández, E. (1994). Fiscalidad y niveles de renta de la población de Estella a comienzos del s. XV, Historia, instituciones, documentos, ISSN 0210–7716, 21, 345–366.

García Fernández, E. (2012). La vida política y financiera de Vitoria a partir de las cuentas municipales de fines de la Edad Media, *Studia histórica. Historia medieval*, ISSN 0213–2060, 30 (Ejemplar dedicado a: Poder y fiscalidad en la Edad Media hispánica), 99–127.

García Marsilla, J. V. (2009). La sisa de la carn: Ganadería, abastecimiento cárnico y fiscalidad en los municipios valencianos bajomedievales, in R. Vallejo Pousada & A. Furió Diego (coord.), *Los tributos de la tierra: fiscalidad y agricultura en España: (siglos XII-XX)*. Valencia: Universidad de Valencia, 81–102.

Gardner, L. (2008). *To Take or to Make?: Contracting for Legitimacy in the Emerging States of Twelfth Century Britain*. Discussion papers in economic and social history, 73, Oxford: University of Oxford, 1–32.

Garnier, F. (2008). Fiscalité et finance médiévales: un état de la recherche, Revue historique de droit français et etranger, ISSN 0035–3280, 3, 443–452.

Garnier, F. (2009). La norme fiscale au Moyen Âge: l'exemple des villes du Rouergue, in C. Leveleux, A. Rousselet-Pimont, P. Bonin, & F. Garnier (Textes réunis par), *Normes et normativité, études d'histoire du droit rassemblées en l'honneur d'Albert Rigaudière*, Paris: Economica, 97–123.

Gelabert González, J. E. (1995). The Fiscal Burden, in R. Bonney (ed.), *Economic Systems and State Finance*. Oxford: Oxford University Press, 539–576.

Gelabert González, J. E. (1999). Castile, 1504–1808, in R. Bonney (ed.), *The Rise of the Fiscal State in Europe c. 1200–1815*. Oxford: Oxford University Press, 201–242.

Gelabert González, J. E. (2002). Fisco real y fiscos municipales en Castilla (siglo XVI-XVII), in Historia de la propiedad en España: bienes comunales, pasado y presente: ii Encuentro interdisciplinar, Salamanca, 31 de mayo-3 de junio de 2000, ISBN 84-95240-54-8, 81–100.

Ginatempo, M. (2000). *Prima del debito: Finanziamento della spesa pubblica e gestione del deficit nelle grandi città toscane (1200–1350ca.)*. Firenze: Leo S. Olschki Editore.

Gomes, S. A. (2006). *D. Afonso V: o Africano*. Mem Martins: Círculo de Leitores.

Gonçalves, I. (1964). *Pedidos e empréstimos públicos em Portugal durante a Idade Média*. Lisbon: Cadernos de Ciência e Técnica Fiscal: Centro de estudos fiscais da direcção-geral das contribuições e impostos – Ministério das Finanças.

Gonçalves, I. (1999). Estado Moderno, Finanças Públicas e Fiscalidade Permanente, in *A génese do Estado Moderno no Portugal tardo-medievo: séculos XIII-XV/ciclo temático de conferências org. pela Universidade Autonoma de Lisboa; coord. Maria Helena da Cruz Coelho, Armando Luís de Carvalho Homem; Palavras prévias de Justino Mendes de Almeida*. Lisbon: Universidade Autónoma de Lisboa, 95–110.

González Arce, J. D. (2010). Los precedentes de la fiscalidad extraordinaria de la monarquía hispana: los pedidos reales en la Castilla al sur del Tajo (siglo XIV y XV), in J. A. Bonachía Hernando & A. C. de Terán Sánchez (coord.), *Fuentes para el estudio del negocio fiscal y financiero en los reinos hispánicos (siglos XIV-XVI)*. Madrid: Ministerio de Hacienda – Instituto de Estudios Fiscales, 11–40.

González Arce, J. D. (2012). De conjunto de rentas a impuesto aduanero. La transformación del almojarifazgo durante el siglo XIV en el reino de Murcia, Anuario de Estudios Medievales, ISSN 0066–5061, 42, 2, 669–696.

Grohmann, A. (2008). La fiscalità nell''economia europea, secc. XIII-XVIII, in *Actas La fiscalità nell'economia europea (sec. XIII-XVIII)*, 39th Settimana di Studi dell'istituto "Francesco Datini" di Prato a cura di Simonetta Cavaciocchi. Firenze: Firenze University Press, 5–50.

Hamon, P. (2006). Les dettes du roi de France (fin du Moyen Âge-XVIe siècle): une dette "publique"? in J. Andreau, G. Béaur, & J. Y. Grenier (dir.), *La dette publique dans l'histoire*. Actes des Journées du Centre de Recherches Historiques des 26, 27 et 28 novembre 2001. Paris: Comité pour L'Histoire Économique et Financière de la France, 85–97.

Henriques, A. M. B. de M. de C. (2008). *State Finance, War and Redistribution in Portugal (1249–1527)*. Ph.D. Thesis. Department of History, University of York.

Homem, A. L. de C. (1990). *O Desembargo Régio (1320–1433)*. Porto: Junta Nacional de Investigação Científica.

Homem, A. L. de C. (2009). Os oficiais da Justiça central régia nos finais da Idade Média portuguesa (ca. 1279-ca. 1521), *Medievalista* [online]. Ano 5, 6, July, IEM [Accessed in 2013/03/05]. Available at http://www2.fcsh.unl.pt/iem/medievalista/. ISSN 1646–740X.

Isenmann, E. (1995). Medieval and Renaissance Theories of State Finance, in R. Bonney (ed.), *Economic Systems and State Finance*. Oxford: Oxford University Press, 21–52.

Körner, M. (1995). Expenditure, in R. Bonney (ed.), *Economic Systems and State Finance*. Oxford: Oxford University Press, 393–422.

Krüger, K. (1987). Public Finance and Modernisation: The Change from Domain State to Tax State in Hesse in the Sixteenth and Seventeenth Centuries: A Case Study, in P. C. Witt (ed.), *Wealth and Taxation in Central Europe: The History and Sociology of Public Finance*. Warwickshire: Leamington Spa, 49–62.

Ladero Quesada, M. A. (1967). *La Hacienda Real castellana entre 1480 y 1492*. Valladolid: Universidad de Valladolid.

Ladero Quesada, M. A. (1989). Estado y Hacienda en Castilla durante la Baja Edad Media, in *Estado, Hacienda y Sociedad en la Historia de España*. Valladolid: Instituto de Historia Simancas-Universidad de Valladolid, 11–43.

Ladero Quesada, M. A. (2011). *Fiscalidad y Poder Real en Castilla (1252–1369)*, 2nd ed. Madrid: Real Academia de la Historia.

Lafuente Gómez, M. (2012). La incidencia de la fiscalidad real extraordinaria sobre las villas y comunidades de la Extremadura aragonesa: Calatayud, Daroca y Teruel (1309–1362), in F. García Fitz & J. F. Jiménez Alcázar (coord.), La historia peninsular en los espacios de frontera: las "Extremaduras históricas" y la "Transierra" (siglos XI-XV). Cáceres-Murcia: Monografías de la Sociedad Española de Estudios Medievales, 2, 153–177.

Lafuente Gómez, M., & Martínez García, S. (2011). Ejército y fiscalidad en la encomienda santiaguista de Montalbán (Aragón) durante la guerra de los dos Pedros (1356–1366), Revista Espacio, tiempo y forma. Serie III, Historia Medieval, ISSN 0214–9745, 24, 109–142.

Lalou, É. (2010). Les finances et le rôle de l'État dans l'économie de la Normandie royale, in M. Arnoux & A. M. Flambard Héricher (dir.), La Normandie dans l'économie européenne (XIIe-XVIIe siècles). Actes du Colloque de Cerisy-la-Salle, 4–8 Octobre 2006. Caen: Publications du CRAHM, 2010, 9–18.

Larguier, G. (2000). *Fiscalité et institutions à Perpignan (XIIe-XVIIIe siècles)*. Perpignan: Presses Universitaires de Perpignan.

Larguier, G. (coord.). (2008a). Les Communautés et l'Argent: Fiscalité et finances municipales en Languedoc, en Roussillon et en Andorre XVe-XVIIIe siècle – Journées d'Histoire et Histoire du Droit et des institutions de l'Université de Perpignan Via Domitia. Perpignan: Presses Universitaires de Perpignan, col. Études, 2.

Larguier, G. (2008b). Fiscalité municipale, fiscalité royale, fiscalité provinciale en Languedoc (France), XIVe-XVIIIe siècles. Nature, poids, évolution, in *Actas La fiscalità nell'economia europea (sec. XIII-XVIII)*, 39th Settimana di Studi dell'istituto "Francesco Datini" di Prato a cura di Simonetta Cavaciocchi, Firenze: Firenze University Press, 351–370.

Marques, A. E. de O. (2012). *Paisagem e povoamento: da representação documental à materialidade do espaço no território da diocese de Braga (séculos IX-XI): ensaio metodológico*. Ph.D. Thesis. Porto: Faculty of Arts.

Marti Arau, A. (2009). Endeutament censal i crisi financera en una vila senyorial: Castelló d'Empúries (1381–1393), in M. Sánchez Martínez (ed.), *La Deuda Pública en la Cataluña Bajomedieval*. Barcelona: CSIC, 153–217.

Mata, M. E. (2012). From Pioneer Mercantile State to Ordinary Fiscal State: Portugal, 1498–1914, in B. Yun-Casalilla, P. K. O'Brien, & F. Comín Comín (eds.), *The Rise of Fiscal States: A Global History, 1500–1914*. Cambridge: Cambridge University Press, 215–232.

Mata, M. E., & Valério, N. (1994). *História Económica de Portugal*. Lisbon: Ed. Presença.

Mata, M. E., & Valério, N. (2011). *The Concise Economic History of Portugal*. Coimbra: Edições Almedina.

Mattoso, J. (2001). O triunfo da monarquia portuguesa: 1258–1264. Ensaio de História Política, Análise Social, 35, 157, 899–935.

Menjot, D. (2008). Les enjeux de la fiscalité directe dans les systèmes financiers et fiscaux des villes castillanes aux XIVe et XVe siècles", in *Actas La fiscalità nell'economia europea (sec. XIII-XVIII)*, 39th Settimana di Studi dell'istituto "Francesco Datini" di Prato a cura di Simonetta Cavaciocchi. Firenze: Firenze University Press, 699–729.

Menjot, D., & Sánchez Martínez, M. (ed.). (2004). *La fiscalité des villes au Moyen Âge (Occident méditerranéen) 4 – La gestion de l'impôt*. Toulouse: Privat.

Miranda, F. (2012). *Portugal and the Medieval Atlantic: Commercial Diplomacy, Merchants, and Trade, 1143–1488*. Ph.D. Thesis. Porto: Faculty of Arts.

Molho, A. (2006a). *Firenze nel Quattrocento: I – Política e Fiscalità*. Roma: Edizioni di Storia e Letteratura.

Molho, A. (2006b). La dette publique en Italie au XIVe et XVe siècles, in J. Andreau, G. Béaur, & J. Y. Grenier (dir.), *La dette publique dans l'histoire*. Actes des Journées du Centre de Recherches Historiques des 26, 27 et 28 novembre 2001. Paris: Comité pour L'Histoire Économique et Financière de la France, 37–61.

Moss, V. (1999). The Norman Fiscal Revolution, 1193–8, in W. M. Ormrod, M. Bonney, & R. Bonney (eds.), *Crises, Revolutions and Self-Sustained Growth: Essays in European Fiscal History, c.1130–1830*. Stanford: Shaun Tyas, 38–57.

Nigro, G. (2008). Vino, fiscalità e vinattieri in Prato nelle carte di Francesco Datini, in Lunedì chomincerà lo Schiavo nel nome di Dio a vendemiare. Tracce di vino nelle carte e sui colli pratesi, a cura di Giampiero Nigro. Prato: Fondazione istituto internazionale di Storia Economica "F. Datini", ISBN: 9788895755007, 7–41.

North, D. C., & Thomas, R. P. (1973). *The Rise of the Western World: A New Economic History*. Cambridge: Cambridge University Press.

Oestreich, G., & Koenigsberger, H. G. (eds.). (1982). *Neostoicism and the Early Modern State*. New York: Cambridge University Press.

Ormrod, W. M. (1995a). Royal Finance in Thirteenth-Century England, in P. R. Coss & S. D. Lloyd (eds.), *Thirteenth Century England V*. Woodbridge: Boydell Press, 141–164.

Ormrod, W. M. (1995b). The West European Monarchies in the Later Middle Ages, in R. Bonney (ed.), *Economic Systems and State Finance*. Oxford: Oxford University Press, 123–160.

Ormrod, W. M. (1999a). England in the Middle Ages, in R. Bonney (ed.), *The Rise of the Fiscal State in Europe c. 1200–1815*. Oxford: Oxford University Press, 19–52.

Ormrod, W. M. (1999b). Finance and Trade under Richard II, in A. Goodman & J. L. Gillespie (eds.), *Richard II: The Art of Kingship*. Oxford: Oxford University Press, 155–186.

Ormrod, W. M. (2000). The English State and the Plantagenet Empire, 1259–1360: A Fiscal Perspective, in J. R. Maddicott & D. M. Palliser (eds.), *The Medieval State*. London: Hambledon Press, 197–214.

Ormrod, W. M. (2008). Poverty and Privilege: The Fiscal Burden in England (XIIIth-XVth Centuries), in *Actas La fiscalità nell'economia europea (sec. XIII-XVIII)*, 39th Settimana di Studi dell'istituto "Francesco Datini" di Prato a cura di Simonetta Cavaciocchi. Firenze: Firenze University Press, 637–656.

Ormrod, W. M. (2011). Government Records: Fiscality, Archives and the Economic Historian, in *Actas Dove va la storia economica? Metodi e prospettive, secc. XIII-XVIII*, 42th Settimana di Studi dell'istituto "Francesco Datini" di Prato a cura di Francesco Ammannati. Firenze: Firenze University Press, 197–224.

Ormrod, W. M., & Barta, J. (1995). The Feudal Structure and the Beginnings of State Finance, in R. Bonney (ed.), *Economic Systems and State Finance*. Oxford: Oxford University Press, 53–79.

Ortí Gost, P. (2000). *Renda i fiscalitat en una ciutat medieval: Barcelona, segles XII-XIV*. Barcelona: Institución Milá y Fontanals.

Petersen, E. L. (1975). From Domain State to Tax State. Synthesis and Interpretation, Scandinavian Economic History Review, 23, 116–148.

Pezzolo, L. (2003). The Venetian Government Debt, 1350–1650, in M. Boone, K. Davids, & P. Janssens (eds.), *Urban Public Debts: urban government and the market for annuities in Western Europe (14th-18th centuries)*. Leuven: Brepols, 61–74.

Pezzolo, L., & Stumpo, E. (2008). L'imposizione diretta in italia dal Medioevo alla fine dell'ancien régime, in *Actas La fiscalità nell'economia europea (sec. XIII-XVIII)*, 39th Settimana di Studi dell'istituto "Francesco Datini" di Prato a cura di Simonetta Cavaciocchi. Firenze: Firenze University Press, 75–98.

Piola Caselli, F. (1987). L'espansione delle fonti finanziarie della Chiesa nel XIV secolo, in Archivio della Societa' Romana di Storia Patria, 110, 63–97.

Piola Caselli, F. (2001). Tax Systems and Fiscal Drag in the Papal State (16th-18th centuries), in *Quaderni del Dipartimento Economia e Territorio*. Cassino: Università degli Studi di Cassino, 1–22.

Piola Caselli, F. (2008). *Government Debts and Financial Markets in Europe* (ed.). London: Pickering & Chatto.

Postan, M. M. (1972). *The Medieval Economy and Society: An Economic History of Britain, 1100–1500*. Berkeley and Los Angeles: University of California Press.

Postan, M. M., Rich, E. E., & Miller, E. (1963). *The Cambridge Economic History of Europe – vol. III: economic organization and policies in the Middle Ages*. Cambridge: Cambridge University Press, 1963.

Rau, V. (1951). *A exploração do comércio do sal de Setúbal: estudo de história económica.* Lisbon: Bertrand.

Rau, V. (2009). *A Casa dos Contos: os três mais antigos regimentos dos contos.* Lisbon: Imprensa Nacional-Casa da Moeda [re-edition of 1951 and 1959 original prints].

Rigaudière, A. (2003a). L'essor de la fiscalité royale, du règne de Philippe le Bel (1285–1314) à celui de Philippe VI (1328–1350), in *Penser et construiré l'État dans la France du Moyen Âge (XIIIe-XVe siècle).* Paris: Comité pour L'Histoire Économique et Financière de la France, 523–589.

Rigaudière, A. (2003b). La répartition de l'impôt royal en Auvergne sous les règnes de Charles VI et de Charles VII, in *Penser et construiré l'État dans la France du Moyen Âge (XIIIe-XVe siècle).* Paris: Comité pour L'Histoire Économique et Financière de la France, 591–620.

Rigaudière, A. (2003c). Le contrôle des comptes dans les villes auvergnates et vellaves aux XIVe et XVe siècles, in *Penser et construiré l'État dans la France du Moyen Âge (XIIIe-XVe siècle).* Paris: Comité pour L'Histoire Économique et Financière de la France, 621–660.

Rigaudière, A. (2008). L''assiette de l''impôt direct dans les villes du Midi français au bas Moyen Age d''après leurs livres d''estimes, in *Actas La fiscalità nell'economia europea (sec. XIII-XVIII),* 39th Settimana di Studi dell'istituto "Francesco Datini" di Prato a cura di Simonetta Cavaciocchi, Firenze: Firenze University Press, 425–482.

Sabatini, G. (1997). *Il controllo fiscale sul territorio nel Mezzogiorno spagnolo. Le province abruzzesi.* Ricerche di Storia Economica. Napoli: Istituto Italiano per gli Studi Filosofici.

Sabatini, G. (2005). Entre Hacienda Real y poderes locales: los intentos de reformar las finanzas municipales del reino de Nápoles en los siglos XVI y XVII, *Studia Historica – Historia Moderna,* XXVII, 223–239.

Sabatini, G. (2008). From Subordination to Autonomy: Public Debt Policies and the Formation of a Self-ruled Financial Market in Southern Italy in the Long Run (1550–1850), in F. Piola Caselli (ed.), *Government Debts and Financial Markets in Europe.* London: Pickering & Chatto, 97–114.

Sánchez Martínez, M. (1997). Fiscalidad y finanzas municipales en las ciudades y villas reales de Cataluña, in Finanzas y fiscalidad municipal: actas del V Congreso de Estudios Medievales. León: Fundación Sánchez-Albornoz, ISBN 84-923109-0-1, 207–238.

Sánchez Martínez, M. (ed.). (2009). *La Deuda Pública en la Cataluña Bajomedieval.* Barcelona: CSIC.

Schulze, W. (1995). The Emergence and Consolidation of the 'Tax State'. I – The Sixteenth Century, in R. Bonney (ed.), *Economic Systems and State Finance.* Oxford: Oxford University Press, 261–279.

Schumpeter, J. A. (1954). The Crisis of the Tax State, International Economic Papers, n° 4, New York, 5–38 [translation of 'Die Krise des Steuerstaates', Zeitfragen aus dem Gebiet der Soziologie, 4, 1918].

Sequeira, J. I. R. (2012). *Produção têxtil em Portugal nos finais da Idade Média.* Ph.D. Thesis. Porto-Paris: Faculty of Arts-EHESS.

Sesma Muñoz, J. A. (1988). Fiscalidad y poder: La fiscalidad centralizada como instrumento de poder en la Corona de Aragón (siglo XIV), Espacio, tiempo y forma. Serie III, Historia medieval, ISSN 0214–9745, 1, 447–464.

Sesma Muñoz, J. A. (2001). Fiscalidad de estado y comercio exterior en Aragón, *Acta histórica et archaelogica mediaevalia,* ISSN 0212–2960, 22 (Ejemplar dedicado a: Homenatge al Dr. Manuel Riu i Riu (vol. 2)), 459–468.

Silva, T. T. da (org.). (2011). *Identidade e diferença: a perspectiva dos estudos culturais*, 10th ed. Petrópolis: Ed. Vozes.

Sousa, A. de. (1990). *As cortes medievais portuguesas: 1385–1490*, 2 vols. Porto: INIC.

Sousa, A. de. (2006). 1325–1480, in J. Mattoso (dir.), *História de Portugal – vol. IV: A Monarquia Feudal*. Mem Martins: Circulo de Leitores, 8–89.

Terán Sánchez, A. C. de. (2006). Fiscalidad de Estado y concejos en el reino de Sevilla durante el reinado de los Reyes Católicos (1474–1504), in D. Menjot & M. Sánchez Martínez (ed.), *Fiscalidad de Estado y fiscalidad municipal en los reinos hispánicos medievales: estudios dirigidos por Denis Menjot y Manuel Sánchez Martínez*. Madrid: Casa de Velázquez, 113–134.

Terán Sánchez, A. C. de., & Menjot, D. (1996). Hacienda y fiscalidad concejiles en la Corona de Castilla en la Edad Media, Historia, instituciones, documentos, ISSN 0210–7716, 23, 213–254.

Verdés Pijuan, P. (2004a). La gestión de los impuestos indirectos municipales en las ciudades y villas de Cataluña: el caso de Cervera (s. XIV-XV), in D. Menjot & M. Sánchez Martínez (coord.), *La fiscalité des villes au Moyen Âge (Occident méditerranéen): La gestion de l'impôt*. Toulouse: Ed. Privat, 173–189.

Verdés Pijuan, P. (2004b). *Per ço que la vila no vage a perdició: la gestió del deute públic en un municipi català (Cervera, 1387–1516)*. Barcelona: CSIC-Institución Milà i Fontanals.

Verdés Pijuan, P. (2005). Politiques fiscales et stratégies financières dans les villes catalanes aux XIVe et XVe siècles, in *Colloque: L'impôt dans les villes de l'Occident méditerranéen (XIIIe- XVe siècle)*. Comité pour l'histoire économique et financière, Paris, 155–171.

Verdés Pijuan, P. (2007). Barcelona, capital del mercat del deute públic català, Barcelona. Quaderns d'Història, 13, 283–311.

Vítores Casado, I. (2009). Durango y sus gentes a través del impuesto: repartimientos, libros de estimas y fogueraciones como fuente para el estudio de la sociedad urbana en la baja Edad Media, Sancho el sabio: Revista de cultura e investigación vasca, ISSN 1131–5350, 31, 23–53.

Wickham, C. (1997). Lineages of Western European Taxation, 1000–1200, in M. Sánchez Martínez & A. Furió Diego (eds.), *Actes del col•loqui: Corona, Municipis i Fiscalitat a la Baixa Edat Mitjana*. Lleida: Institut d'Estudis llerdencs, 25–42.

Yun-Casalilla, B., O'Brien, P. K., & Comín Comín, F. (eds.). (2012). *The Rise of Fiscal States: A Global History, 1500–1914*. Cambridge: Cambridge University Press.

3 European fiscal panorama during the later Middle Ages and early modern times

Comparisons

The indebtedness of municipal, regional and national finances was a common feature among European kingdoms dating back to the dawn of the Modern Age. What is the significance about municipal or regional finances? Originally, they were the financial substrate of Western European monarchies. From that point of view, the kings in general would serve themselves from the revenues generated in the urban centers, and this was especially true from the fourteenth century onwards (Sánchez Martínez, 2010: 43–44). They are the starting point of an evolutionary process. It is from this conjuncture that we move toward a state finances' regime. And its evolution represents, to a great extent, one of the cornerstones to the so-called modern state (Terán Sánchez & Menjot, 1996: 247). However, it is important to note the path taken by each kingdom regarding economic and fiscal choices, so that the consequences of each case can be understood, as well as the political consequences of these same options. To a large extent, it was the tacit application of the Roman principles of *sovereignty* and *nature* as justification elements for an authority with which the political power, that is, royalty, imposed the taxes and, thus, created a fiscal system for the whole country and its inhabitants, even if in some occasions old or customary formulas have been preserved (Ladero Quesada, 2011: 15–16).

This taxation system, which at first emanated from noble rights on royal patrimony was managed by official representatives (Sánchez Martínez, 2010: 45), and progressed in the sense of perceiving the economic evolution and the growth of the urban centers that, little by little, saw flourishing among its inhabitants a feeling of unity, and a rather vague "awakening" of a collective consciousness. The idea of *universitas* on fiscal issues – and, consequently, of responsibilities' division in governance, that is, in the city's headings, such as its defense, conflict management, and the supervision of fees collected for buildings and services' maintenance that benefited the community (Sánchez Martínez, 2010: 45–46). From a certain perspective corroborated by other scholars, then, cities had *finances* but not a *taxation system* (Sánchez Martínez, 2010: 46).

As urban centers developed, with the usufruct of royal patrimony ceded to the collectivity by the monarchs – larger or smaller, varying from case to case – as means to obtain their own revenues, taxation instruments became more sophisticated. It is possible to identify this phenomenon from the poll taxes collected in

Aragon at the end of the twelfth century, through the establishment of a "common coffer", which would serve as a transition identifier (Sánchez Martínez, 2010: 47) of a collective determination that prevails over the individual spirit, a fundamental step for the configuration and consolidation of a municipality (Turull Rubinat, 1996: 581–610). Later on, they would reach another level, while the military campaigns and new royal necessities derived from expeditions of conquest and warfare equipment created a situation of pressure for more income, pushing the monarchs to tax in an extraordinary and equal way their subjects: cities' inhabitants, peasants, the Church and the nobility (Sánchez Martínez, 2010: 50–53). Finally, an even higher level of sophistication arose with the implementation of rents/pensions' sales in exchange for financial contributions, which were widely negotiated, as in Aragon's cities and towns, since 1340. The public bond/debt market was beginning to emerge as well.

In general, the public debts' percentage within the state's finances, as well as in municipalities' indebtedness reached extraordinary levels, and it was necessary to counteract this tendency. It seems interesting to note that there are common features regarding the search for financial solutions; right off the bat, an even stronger fiscal pressure on all realms' subjects – with some occasional exceptions – and not only on those who rendered direct vassalage to the monarchs, as well as the verification of municipalities and counties as passive subjects of a more active royal taxation. Therefore, they were used to financially underpin the respective crowns, as instruments of revenue extraction of a so-called "state budget" that arises as a result of these practices, as well as the development and consolidation of municipal finances (Furió Diego, 1999: 36). It is known that this panorama includes, in all the cases examined, ecclesiastical revenues, the *decimas* in Castile and Aragon and tithes in other cases in Northern Europe. That type of income could be granted to the monarchs in crusade contexts or in military campaigns that were appropriate to this premise, or even other types of earnings, which in many cases would definitively be incorporated into the regular revenues of these kingdoms, constituting important amounts within their respective finances,[1] deserving a separate chapter, perhaps another research work. However, we have assumed that this type of collection, since it is not a regular income stream in the first place, and the Church would not always contribute. It was on the contrary, as they even claimed privileges and tax exemptions, and we have made an option not to deal with this in this chapter, and even in the study as a whole, the Churches' taxation/revenues and focus on the essential aspects that mainly surrounds the constitution and development the state's fiscal elements in each of the cases discussed later, particularly in Portugal, which relates to the composition of their revenues and expenditure.

Portugal, as well as Castile, would not follow the Aragonese option of selling life annuities in exchange for resources. Rather both with a similar state finance structure in many respects, had revenue organization structured, in essence, on sales taxes, which relied on the people's necessities (goods), not on the productions' means and, on account of this, favored the wealthier (Terán Sánchez & Menjot, 1996: 246). And it would be precisely this overdependence on indirect taxation that would divert them from the public debt's path, unlike Aragon's municipalities. The worsening of the fiscal pressure on the subjects, which was derived, to a large extent, from the tax collection leasing system, a combination of both *private* and *public* strategy, which in turn favored only a few people (Terán Sánchez & Menjot, 1996: 246–247), particularly the noblemen. The resources' final destination was a social group that benefited from redistribution phenomenon, as did the tax leaseholders, merchants and businessmen with investment capacities, who acquired the right to collect fees, in most cases, at derisory prices. They made large profits, while crowns would gather almost stabilized values and, in many moments, watched their revenues remain almost stagnant.

In any case, a feature that seems common to all cases analyzed, and which will be dissected individually are the remnants of a feudal structure still very present and rooted, whose rights would not yet be completely subordinated to the state's public authority (Ormrod & Barta, 1995: 79), struggling to extend its fiscal scope to a fuller range of economic activities.

3.1 Castile

The Castilian case is, in fact, the closest to the Portuguese example in comparative terms. Its fiscal development, following some references (Ladero Quesada, 2011: 17–18), is characterized by two very distinct moments and very particular conjunctures: first, from the mid-thirteenth century until the 1366–69 civil war, characterized by a strong initial impulse provided by Alfonso X's visionary conduction (1252–1284), both in doctrinal and practical terms of royal power; second, followed by his great-grandson, Alfonso XI (1312–1350), laying the foundations of a new economic and political situation within the Iberian peninsula.[2] That new context was directly related to a solid development of commercial activity, increased consumption and monetary circulation, as well as a clear attempt to forcefully enhance tax collection, as well as to streamline both the fiscal mechanism and the income flow, so as to try not to let anything escape from tax authorities' range. Regarding the first moment, we can see and subdivide it in some particular contexts: first, under the aegis of Fernando III (1245–1250), which characterizes a peak of fiscal pressure resulting from the efforts to conquer Andalusia, modifying, in the sense of a simplification (Ladero Quesada, 2011: 16–17), the Castilian taxation's traditions and system, by virtue of specific conditions during times of war; secondly, already under the reign of Alfonso X *the wise*, as was previously described. Through this point of view, it is possible to notice how indirect taxes constituted more than 90% of Castile's ordinary revenues since the 1320s (Ladero Quesada, 1991: 97–98). It should also be pointed out that, by the way collection methods, alongside the actors involved, this taxation approach was supposed to effect mainly the city's population rather than peasants, although it should be, by principle, a flat rate effecting everyone (Asenjo González, 2008: 532).

A second moment corresponds to the period which covers the Trastámara dynasty (1369–1516), where the collection profile does not change, but the legislative and institutional apparatus about the treasury management that would sustain this mechanism was consolidated. Furthermore, this structure would be configured for a more favorable redistribution across the Castilian nobility that, at the same time, enlarged its domains and jurisdictions. In addition, the increase in fiscal pressure was felt by the military campaigns maintained between the 1370s and 1420s, and these developments would eventually lead the system to a condition of weakness, only contained by the rise of the Catholic kings during the 1470s. They would control the situation through the collection of extraordinary revenues (Ladero Quesada, 1991: 102) and, later, with the consolidation of the public debt and the issuance of bonds, known as *juros al quitar* ("titles"), which would constitute the central element of Castilian long-term debt and a primary consolidation item (Álvarez Nogal, 2009: 15–17). The earliest *juros* in Castile were, in the first place, not exactly public credit titles, but rather payments and annuities offered by the monarch in large part to the nobles, as means for raising popular support, much like the Portuguese case. However, this gratification mechanism, used in an uncontrolled way mainly during the reign of Enrique IV of Castile (1454–1474) caused serious damage to the economy and the fiscal system, a scenario that would change only with the Catholic kings' strong fist to review and override many of these benefits (Asenjo González, 2008: 533).

The bedrock of Castilian ordinary revenues were composed from the times of Alfonso the wise, by direct elements such as landlords' rights, which already yielded very little at the end of 1200s, except for the *fonsadera*.[3] This was subsequently supplemented by the creation of extraordinary revenues and the application of indirect tax collection, with the exception of local tolls granted to municipalities, first temporarily and thereafter on a permanent basis. This would lead to the foundations of a new tax system (Ladero Quesada, 1999: 177–178) in which tax farming was generalized (Ladero Quesada, 2009: 243–244), and had as its fundamental element the widespread and lasting collection of the *alcabala*, i.e., sales taxes equivalent to the Portuguese *sisas*, throughout the kingdom around the 1340s, together with the salt mines' revenues, customs, and the *servicio y montazgo* (Ladero Quesada, 2009: 149–180) charged on the nomadic cattle and herds that traveled through the kingdom. In addition, the 10% customs duty on imported and exported products passing through the northern kingdoms ports (Ladero Quesada, 2009: 117–122), i.e., Cantabria, Asturias and Galicia – the *diezmos de la mar de Castilla* (customs of Castilian Sea) – tributes that, as well as in Portugal, supposedly represent an innovation within a process of a tax system renovation in Castile, plus what was collected from the clergy. The frontier with Islam added this possibility to the Castilian kings, to be able to use and justify the incorporation of ecclesiastical revenues to the others, although it was a very variable type of revenue (González Arce, 1992: 73–78; Menjot, 2008: 707). In times of emergency, such as wars, they also used short-term loans (Ladero Quesada, 1991: 100–101) and extra revenues, such as the *Bulas de Cruzada* ("Pope's acquiescence to collect churches' taxes locally"), *préstamos* ("loans") and *servicios* ("extraordinary resources") granted by the *Cortes* (Ladero Quesada, 2009: 245). The cooperation between the urban oligarchies, the population (confraternities and corporations), and the monarch would be fundamental to establish the *encabezamiento* system (poll tax), which would ensure a more efficient collection. It is also important to emphasize that, as the tax system "professionalized", the influence of clientelism diminished (Asenjo González, 2008: 537).

With regard to ordinary expenditure and redistributive process, a large part of ordinary revenue was converted into automatic annual gratification payments to noblemen, which were located in the royal accounting book, known as *situados*, which rose from 26 to 85% of regular expenditure between 1429 and 1474, and retroceded to 35% during the Catholic kings' reigns, rising again due to the *juros'* negotiation and the organization of public debt. Add to this the *libranzas*, that is, payment orders by letter which could also be used as bills of exchange, intended for various military purposes, royal house and chamber's expenses, as well as payments for "public administration", that is, payments of rations and officers' wages, among others. The extraordinary expenditure had elementary motivators: wars, fundamentally against Granada,[4] Aragon (Valdeón Baruque, 1966, 2002) and, later, the assembly of an army and organization of the foreign relations within a new approach (Ladero Quesada, 1991: 103–104, 2009: 419).

In any case, the Castilian crown, through its representatives in *Cortes*, has never been able to adequately deal with its finances, in particular the revenue's control. In parallel, their spending would also follow the same path, uncontrolled, and without adequate supervision. At this juncture, on many occasions, the monarchs were forced to give ground and to bargain with the nobility, for the maintenance of its political and legal autonomy regarding all economic and financial affairs (Ladero Quesada, 1999: 196). On the other hand, the newly implemented tax system would provide a solid political support base that would allow the rise of Catholic kings and the formation of an absolute monarchy.

3.2 Aragon

If we could characterize or define the guiding lines of Aragon's taxation in a few words, two would be rather sufficient: public debt. The sale of rental contracts and rights was the central axis, while at the same time, the dividing line of a process of fiscal transformation dating back to the late thirteenth and early fourteenth centuries. This change happened in parallel and was bolstered by the Crown's increasing financial demands and needs, as well as the slow corrosion of the traditional revenues (Sánchez Martínez, 1995: 419). Until then taxation was underpinned by a municipal system based on direct taxes, supported essentially by the local *taille* to pay obligations to the monarch, the *questia* – a personal contribution based on a quantity of resources on the part of all community inhabitants. On top of that, vassalage rights collected from Jews, Christians, and Muslims, wherein the short-term credit provided by Jews and merchants, or the forced loans to the municipalities' neighbors (Furió Diego, 1999: 38), roughly generated the kingdom's revenues. This taxation system derives and emanates, first, from a collective desire and need – the idea of *universitas* – without waiting for the construction of a municipal system. Despite the community's needs, this tax (*questia*) must be understood both as a source of income and as instrumentation of implicit authority, an element of monarchical demand. Although extraordinary, this levy was the focus of cities' finances (Ortí Gost, Sánchez Martínez & Turull Rubinat, 1996: 119–120) during the eleventh and twelfth centuries. In regard to the process of consolidating the Aragonese tax system, even before the public debt mechanism's adoption, the tax system was constituted to organize the tax collection in accordance with local needs; its dismantling was automatic, once the objectives were achieved, i.e., there was no definite and lasting structure. Supposedly, this is one of the arguments to assert that there was no permanent tax system before 1350 (Ortí Gost, Sánchez Martínez & Turull Rubinat, 1996: 123–125).

In terms of extraordinary direct taxation, Aragon also had an equivalent tax to the royal right to demand financial compensation from the people for not breaking the currency: the *bovatge* (Ortí Gost, 2001) in Catalonia and the *monedatge* or *monedaje* (Orcástegui Gros, 1983) in Valencia and Majorca failed to comply with its objectives for two reasons. First, precisely because they were not regular; second, because they were later "negotiated" to the municipalities and the nobility, i.e., the king exchanged his right to collect for a fixed amount, losing "efficiency" as an income source (Furió Diego, 1999: 42). While the king needed more resources, extraordinarily indirect taxation took shape, by means of Catalan *sisas* and by the *imposicions* or *imposiciones*, that is, sales taxes collected at municipal level, which would be indispensable due to a cycle of military campaigns (Turull Rubinat & Verdés Pijuan, 2006) on several fronts since the first decades of the fourteenth century. Aragon needed money, and this requisition was distributed and organized (Mira Jódar, 2003: 696–700) between its "administrative units": Valencia, Majorca and Catalonia, and its intermediary fiscal instances: the *Diputaciones del General*, and by the mid-1400s, this source of revenue earned configuration and strength. The titles were divided into two categories of *censals morts* (annuities) edited by the Provincial Council – the *censales* ("census"), or perpetual instruments, and the *violarios* ("lifelong annuities"), which could be paid with the proceeds of indirect taxes on imports and exports, the *dret d' entrades i exides* ("entries and exits' toll rights"). Those issuances, whose issuing centers, collectors and payers were the municipalities, had different interest rates ranging from 7.14% in the case of the former to 10%, 10.71%, 12.14% or 14.28% regarding the latter. The first type was more successful than the second, mainly due to longer repayment terms and lower interest rates, which were interesting for municipal governments that would pay less and save money. The amounts collected were delivered to bankers and money changers in Barcelona, responsible for the management, or applied directly to the purpose for which they were issued – repairing of walls, sanitation works etc. – while the pension amounts to be paid to bondholders (the interest rates were stipulated in each contract) were secured by indirect taxes, together with new bond issuances. In a short time, the process embodied a snowball effect (Sánchez Martínez, 2009: 229–230), which had to be contained. For this purpose, it was necessary to regulate the extraordinary subsidies for the issuance and sale of income securities (Sánchez Martínez, 2009: 232–233). From then on, the payments would be made with the distribution between extraordinary regional indirect taxes (*generalities*) and direct extraordinary taxes – in the Catalan case, the *fogatge*, that is, a tax levied on the amount of *fuegos*[5] in each territory. However, the role of titles was not affected. As a direct consequence of extraordinary taxation, prices soared – the textiles, mainly – due to the tariff rates' adjustment (Sánchez Martínez, 2009: 235–236).

Regarding Aragon's case, the development process of the Aragonese fiscal bureaucratic mechanism transformed the municipalities into managers and administrators of a relevant part of the taxes granted to the king (Sánchez Martínez, 1995: 421), the main actors of a "fiscal state", and this two way, interdependent process has to do with the growing need of states for more money, on one side, and a strengthening and institutional development of the municipalities themselves (Furió Diego, 1999: 37) on the other hand.

3.3 France

When it comes to the exercise of taxation within French territory, it is important to note that it permutated in several forms, and state finance was only one of them. In this chapter, from the beginning, we are dealing with it, although it is known that the king is only one of the great secular lords and not necessarily the wealthiest or most powerful. During the later Middle Ages, the monarchy never exerted effective control over the different zones of what today corresponds to the current borders of the country, and its fiscal jurisdictions, as well as the respective evolution of royal finances suffered with the retractions and expansions in this same period (Henneman Jr., 1999: 101). Thus the use of the concept or the idea of "king's land" or "royal domain" over certain districts must be carefully observed, especially when we notice the territory's political fragmentation, which was superseded as the monarchy became a synonym of state, uniting the several counties and duchies more by means of political alliances concretized by marriages (Henneman Jr., 1999: 102–103) but also by military conquests in some occasions. Yet, this fiscal and financial evolution is, of course, a parallel process to the landlords' overcoming by the Crown in jurisdictional, economic and military terms.

However, this evolutionary process, in terms of ordinary revenues, originated in certain types of resource that in the 1200s were, essentially, feudal rights supplemented by manorial income (Rigaudière, 2003: 523), that is, direct taxation that ranged from monopoly income, fines and emoluments collected by the courts, and even the profits on the minting. The indirect taxation came from the 1270s onwards, with the establishment of customs, created to protect the French economy, containing the exit of certain products, but having little impact on the revenue increase, basically for taxing only the exports and due to the fact that France did not have valuable commodities to export at the time (Ormrod, 1995: 134). In the 1300s, the sales taxes was of great relevance, and at first took the form of extraordinary subsidies: the *aide* (assistance), whose percentage charged varied on the product to be taxed, and the *gabelle*, that is, a levy regarding the monopoly on salt decreed by Philip VI (1328–1350), and which produced a fruitful yield (Ormrod, 1995: 134–135; Henneman Jr., 1999: 113).

As for the fiscal system itself, it evolved from the need to respond *ad hoc* to emerging urgencies in terms of revenue management that already existed, and to seek new sources of income (Henneman Jr., 1999: 103). In addition, between the 1270s and 1320s, at a time of kingdom's territorial expansion, as well as economic activity development, the growth of fiscal resources would be inevitable and mandatory. For this purpose, an indispensable requirement would be a permanent fiscal mechanism, especially with the military campaigns conducted by Philip III (1270–1285), in Languedoc region and against the Crown of Aragon (Henneman Jr., 1999: 105; Rigaudière, 2003: 537–538). Furthermore, in this sense, the Hundred Years' War and the Black Death would be, at the same time, milestones for French taxation, particularly the ransom's payment of Jean II *le bon*, in 1356, which led the kingdom to a serious economic crisis and an inexorable reform in the tax system, especially in the way in which extraordinary taxes were collected and managed (Henneman Jr., 1999: 112–115), which at the beginning of 1300s had a significant weight in total revenues.

On the other hand, the credit development from the 1250s onwards would lead to a notable increase in royal indebtedness, through a series of loans contracted (Hamon, 2006: 85–87) and combined with soaring expenditures which, according to the "military revolution" historiographical line,[6] were largely related to war. This context would be the backdrop for even greater fiscal pressure on the subjects in the following centuries, who would feel the weight of taxes which, in some cases, would increase up to twenty-one times their original value in forty years (Henneman Jr., 1999: 116). Other direct taxes, such as the *taille* (originally indirect) and the *fouage* – similar to the Catalan *fogatge* – first collected with some regularity and permanently afterwards, meant a strong impulse in the royal revenues (Ormrod, 1995: 131). Indeed, in the French case, internal and external military conflicts largely conditioned both the genesis and the consolidation of an effective "state taxation" (Contamine, 2002: I, 33–39), in addition to its political-administrative problems and the absence of a representative political assembly (Ormrod, 1995: 130) capable of voting subsidies until the 1310s.

The unfolding of the Hundred Years' War had a massive impact on the French financial situation, as many regions were under British control, causing an expected decline in revenues, which was partially recovered by Charles VI (1380–1422). Thanks to the Valois, and a new emphasis on taxation devices, a fiscal balance was reached through the adoption of permanent subsidies, combined with a strong monarchical control over that income (Ormrod, 1995: 148–149). Nevertheless, the great French upturn would come with the conversion of extraordinary taxes into permanent ones, as the *aides*, *gabelles* and the *taille*, during the 1460s (Ormrod, 1995: 154), similar to what happened in Portugal some decades before with the sales taxes, the *sisas*. Furthermore, the internal battles regarding the realm's unification under Louis XI (1461–1483), despite reflecting the political divergence, helped to promote the "superposition of state over the realms" toward more stable taxation routine, as well as to a tax state condition (Kerhervè, 2002: II, 372–373; Schulze, 1995: 265). Clearly, France took the chance offered by the wars to promote a shift in institutional policy, and capitalized upon it with the assembly of a permanent and profitable taxation mechanism, which enabled the kingdom to achieve earlier a better financial situation rather than its rivals Britain, Spain and Portugal (Ormrod, 1995: 154–155; Henneman Jr., 1999: 119–120; Bonney, 2012: 93) as they entered the early modern times.

3.4 England

The British state finances, as well as those of other kingdoms, owe their expansion and development to a situation of increasing tax pressure on the subjects, derived from a systemic policy of dynastic, territorial expansion (Ormrod, 1995: 124) based, above all, on good diplomatic relations, as well as on the pragmatism of war actions. In both situations, the demand for more resources, in addition to ordinary revenues, was felt, fundamentally, from the 1200s, with the increase in the warfare costs (Ormrod, 1995: 125). As a direct consequence of this situation, Parliament was strengthened[7] and the balance of power, especially with regard to extraordinary taxation in times of war, would change from then on. This state of conflict made collection more effective (Ormrod, 1995: 142–144) in the north rather than south of the English Channel.

At the same time, ordinary royal revenues were composed, to a large extent, of royal rights and rents on what was produced on the king's land – which is not to say that the revenue was exclusively agricultural – along with the exercise of justice, something mostly lucrative. It is noteworthy that, unlike most Western European kingdoms, the English Crown has not enjoyed, until then, currency and coinage breaks as a source of revenue (Ormrod, 1999a: 25–27). The arbitrary taxation (*tallages*) imposed on the Jews – until their expulsion in 1290 – as well as the impositions on the king's land and on the towns complements this English revenue collection framework. This scenario would drastically change with increased spending, a gradual increase in inflation, a retreat from agricultural production combined with the effects of the Black Death, and Parliament's stronger action to contain abuses and review seigniorial rights which underpinned the monarchical collection previously established, providing what other scholars call the "fiscal revolution" of the later Middle Ages and early modern times (Ormrod, 1999a: 27).

In terms of expenditure, up to the time of the Hundred Years' War, it is difficult to detail Crown expenditure, since most of the existing records privileged revenues. However, the sources that survived after the conflict outbreak account for an exponential increase in what was spent, especially in military terms, and this management difficulty led to an organization of "budgets", even to be able to assess the necessity or not of requesting extraordinary revenues, which were widely used between 1350s and 1450s – ranging from direct taxes collected from the clergy, increased indirect taxation on exported and imported products, increased customs duties and taxes on the central English commodity: wool. On top of that, the loans contracted by Edward III (1327–1377), especially with the Italian bankers (Ormrod, 1999a: 36) created a potentially dangerous debt for the English exchequer (Ormrod, 1995: 142). During the fifteenth century, particularly in its second half, the exports decrease of this raw material, combined with the increase in exports of woolen cloths, altered the revenues' pattern, causing a sharp decline due to the difference in taxation: 33% over the former, while only 2 to 6% affected the latter, redirecting the tax system less to indirect taxation and more to direct taxation (Ormrod, 1995: 150–151, 1999a: 41–43). This explains, to a large extent, why England was struggling to become a tax state, in order to be able to provide the necessary resources during the war with France and, by its end in 1453, the political-institutional conjuncture within a king's lands proved inadequate for this model to continue, which allowed the following dynasties to retake a fiscal model based on seigniorial relations.

Another source of income, although irregular, came from the collection in the other territories that comprised the British islands, such as Ireland and Wales, Normandy and the French territories governed by the British Crown, which were not subordinated to the English tax system (Thornton, 1999: 97–109). In these cases, these revenues could be incorporated, depending on who the landlord was. The king would eventually access these resources if other members of royal family ruled those lands, which on some occasions and simultaneously was able to preserve some regional autonomy in these areas, particularly in fiscal terms.

Regarding the taxation structure, the English fiscal mechanism basis dates back to the twelfth century, controlled by the *Exchequer*, a kind of treasurer who received and supervised the accounts of the king's local agents, the *sheriffs*. This format would survive the power loss of King John (1199–1216), in front of the Barons at the signing of the Magna Charta, remaining until the late thirteenth and early fourteenth centuries, when the adoption of fees and charges would pass directly through the scrutiny of Parliament, especially in times of war, constituting an important element of its identity (Ormrod, 1999a: 20) as a *dominium politicum et regale*.

However, the cornerstones of modern fiscal mechanism would be settled during the Tudor period, especially under Henry VIII (1509–1547), less by any restructuring process, but more by the ecclesiastical revenues and properties expropriated and added to the Crown's estates and set of resources (O'Brien & Hunt, 1999: 60–61). Structural changes would only be implemented after the Glorious Revolution, despite all the controversy regarding Geoffrey Elton's work on the "Tudor Revolution" in government (Cunich, 1999: 120–121). Until then the main focus was at the improvement of direct taxation, which delayed the complete and urgent development of a solid fiscal mechanism (O'Brien & Hunt, 1999: 61).

3.5 Italy

In the Italian case, first of all, it should be noted that the peninsula was made up of several city-states, each with its own economic, political and cultural characteristics. Although generally characterized as "mercantile republics" by Jean-Claude Hocquet (Hocquet, 1995: 85), it is necessary to observe cautiously the differentiation between them: there are cases, as in the principalities of Lombardy – Verona and Milan, for example – the Duchy of Savoy and Naples, dominated by an aristocratic ruling elite, and in others more classical, in Tuscany – like Florence

and Siena – in Liguria, with Genoa, and in Venice, where in fact this mercan
Republican picture fits. And it is precisely this difference between them that v
guide the respective options regarding fiscal policies (Mainoni, 1999: 163–16
whether through direct taxes, indirect taxation or by the structuring and issua
of public debt. In any case, an element that remained the common guiding thre
and central reference of these policies since the twelfth century was the *estii*
that is, a tabulation of families' assets and wealth for the verification of finan
capacities (Mainoni, 1999: 151–152). From then on, both direct taxes – as
fodro, based on property estimates – or such as the issuance of bonds (by t
ing into account a survey of possible investors), and even extraordinary taxat
would have this estimate as a direction for whatever option was made.

Within this framework, there were marked differences in taxation in the m
important and developed urban centers of these territories, in nearby smal
towns and in the countryside would be noticeable: direct and individual ta:
tion was particularly prevalent in rural areas, while citizens in urban areas w
exempt from this type of excise, paying only indirect taxes on consumption a
trade (Pezzolo, 2012: 267–268) – customs duties, tolls and *dazi*, that is, a levy
goods circulating between the city-states – while the inhabitants of the "capita
enjoyed a special system of taxation. Unusually, landowners in urban areas pe
fewer taxes on their plantations than rural inhabitants and owners.

In more specific terms, the taxation of foodstuffs – from meat, salt, olive oi
wine, grains, barley, wheat, rye – was categorized as primary necessities. Ti
increase the profitability of this collection, other forms of negotiation were implemented, notably the salt monopoly. Customs operated selectively in regard to
the origin of the products and merchants who traded. In Venice (Hocquet, 1995:
85–86), the rate could vary between 2.5 and 20%, if the merchandise came by
land or sea, respectively; other two rates could still be applied if the article in
question arrived by sea and was re-exported by water or land: in both cases, if the
merchant were Venetian, he paid only 1.25%.

Direct taxation experienced a period of expansion, as political-military pressures increased, and underwent some changes (Pezzolo, 2012: 268–269) in the
same period when Genoa and Venice lost their bylaws of unavoidable commercial outposts due to Constantinople's takeover by the Turks in 1453. Before that,
the fiscal weight was all based on foreign merchants and consumers, thanks to
heavy taxes on goods. With the decline of those ports, this same burden was
transferred to the locals. The *avaria mobili* collected in Genoa, a tax on the profits
of movable property – with the exception of the silk weavers and sailors' guilds,
which were exempt from this charge – is an example of such taxation. In Venice,
initially in the fourteenth century, the government option was for forced loans,
the *impositiones* – such as the *gravezze* charged on the Venetians' houses and
properties, then replaced by direct taxes collected from those who did not participate in regular loans or *prestiti*, as they were known (Hocquet, 1995: 87; Molho,
2006a: 83–87).

Regarding public credit and states' debts, two different models were present⁴
according to the most recent research (Pezzolo, 2012: 277): the long-term pur'ⁱc

debt bonds, typical of the Republics, and the short-term debt titles, associated with the principalities, although this distinction is not very clear and not without exceptions. In Venice (Hocquet, 1995: 87–89; Pezzolo, 2012: 277–278), conflicts with other city-states led to a debt restructuring and the issuance of income securities. Each loan raised from investors was followed by a rise in consumer taxes – a guarantee regarding the payment of rents to creditors. This led to an inflationary process (of salt in particular), which, coupled with the frequency of wars, triggered a crisis in the debt service due to the *moratorium* by the Venetian government in some occasions, raising the associated interest and, at the same time, devaluing the bonds in the market. Even with various interventions, the amount of debt kept growing, which led Venice to levy direct taxes to cover the financial losses, already in the 1450s, with the collection of *decimas* on all social groups – including clergy.

On the other hand, in the case of Genoa (Hocquet, 1995: 89–91), especially since the 1400s, its structure has always sought to defend creditors and protect the whole financial and debt service mechanism, but for a long time also followed the option of short-term loans with high interest rates. In the thirteenth century, the government implemented a "privatization" of revenues through a "tax auction" that guaranteed a relationship of trust with potential investors each time the state needed money and needed partners, as in the case of military campaigns. All loans, *a posteriori*, were consolidated and restructured by Guglielmo Boccanegra, and its payments secured by revenues from the salt monopoly – from which the term that would denominate the Genoa debt management unit (*compera salis*) arises, and also named the famous *Casa di San Giorgio* (Felloni, 2010), which would then govern the debt and, at the same time, would become the "state bank".

In Florence, around 1430, ordinary revenues were no longer sufficient to cover the whole debt service (Molho, 2006b: 37). The *Monte delle doti* – originally created as a fund for the management of Florentine brides' dowries – began to manage public debt (Molho, 2006a: 79–80, 2006b: 47–50), issuing bonds to support military campaigns. Those papers also circulated in a "secondary" market, that is, the first carriers could resell their obligations to third parties, generating a greater flow of wealth and slightly diminishing the effects of an "inelastic" economy. On the other hand, profit could be reached by relying less on the metallic content of their currency, on their strength in kind and more on their ability to circulate and more on their titles.

The Milanese duchy (Pezzolo, 2012: 277–278) would not have a consolidated public debt mechanism until the sixteenth century. Under these circumstances, credit came either through forced or short-term loans, often defaulted. Those resources normally came from local financiers to cover the costs of military conflicts, pushing away their wealthy bourgeoisie, which often preferred to invest in Genoese or Venetian institutions (Chittolini, 2002: 170–172). In this respect, the Kingdom of Naples was very similar, in view of the preparation required to defend the realm in the midst of the conflicts between the House of Anjou and Pedro III of Aragon, between 1280 and 1282, for the King of Sicily title, which dragged on for years, resulted in the Aragonese conquest – both of Sicily and Naples – as early as the 1430s, which overburdened the treasury too much and further weakened an already very fragile economy and finances (Pezzolo, 2012: 278–279).

3.6 Netherlands

Like the jurisdiction of the dukes of Burgundy and later the kings of France, the region of the Netherlands also tried to carry out a process of fiscal unification, partially achieved by the end of fifteenth century. This intention, however, was frustrated at the beginning of the following century, largely due to the conflicts within the representative institutions, dominated by the most important cities – such as Ghent, Bruges, Antwerp, Ypres, Lille and Middelburg, among others – triumphing thus the regional and local elites, who were able to maintain each of their fiscal systems, with its peculiarities.

Up to that time, the so-called "seventeen provinces" had experienced the ups and downs caused by the houses of Valois and Habsburg, which were submitted to the *recette générale de toutes les finances*, created by Philip II in 1387, which audited the receipts collected by the *Chambres des Comptes'* receivers in Burgundy and Flanders (Blockmans, 1999: 281–282). Despite the high degree of specialization, finances were heading toward a regional unification, but not for the Netherlands as a whole, and this did not mean unity in administrative practices either. In any case, scholars (Blockmans, 1999: 282–283) affirm the importance of observing in detail in the case of Burgundy comparatively to the other counties, that is to say, there is no clear distinction between manorial revenues (as part of the ordinary revenue of the *recette générale*) and extraordinary or other means of irregular income (as an element of the extraordinary income in the general accounts). Particularly because the *receveur géneral* pointed out as "ordinary" the collections made by its subordinate officials, the local *receveurs généraux*, who handled both the manorial income and the aids, while that what was referred to as "extraordinary" concerns late payments, which the main *receveur* normally did not expect to receive. This distinction is fundamental for anyone using the Flemish tax sources for other approaches and studies, and at the same time demonstrates some disorder in their accounting and explains the difficulty of having a broader and clear view of the revenues.

This particularization would be largely responsible for the income's difficulty in accessing the central coffers because of their fragmented and insufficiently systematized profile: some estimates (Coutiez, 1980) point to 53% of ordinary revenue and 52% of aid in the Hainaut region that effectively reached the *recette générale* in the 1400s. Segmentation of revenues can probably also be cited as a cause for steady improvements in management since the end of the previous century. In addition, the excessive exploitation of certain forms of taxation was constantly opposed by local representative assemblies (Blockmans, 1999: 286–287), such as indirect taxes on consumption, trade or property, particularly in the major cities of Flanders – Ghent, Bruges and Ypres. They were responsible for almost 40% of the duchy's income (Boone, 2002: 327), and in the Netherlands, mostly because they also survived essentially off of trade income. The desire of local merchant elites was to maintain their autonomy and control over the imposition of new taxes, conditions and forms of distribution and collection so as not to over-burden a population that was already constantly under pressure from the weight of extraordinary aid collected during periods of military conflict.

As for the form of taxation, two systems coexisted during the later Middle Ages and early modern period: a system of local taxation, for military and related purposes, and another of general taxes, which were subdivided into fixed amounts to be paid by the various regions. The first – similar to the French *fouage* and the Catalan *fogatge* – consisted of ordinary *per capita* contributions based on elaborated lists containing the number of residences, more common in rural areas; in Zeeland and the Netherlands, listings were also organized based on the com-pulsory military service that each city should provide. The second included an "abstract" distribution plan, which tended to favor larger cities and overburden the countryside inhabitants, varying from region to region (Blockmans, 1999: 288–290). Areas such as Brabant, Flanders, Zeeland and the Netherlands together contributed with most of the duchy's general revenue in the late fourteenth and early fifteenth centuries, largely because of the excessive fiscal pressure exerted particularly in Zeeland and Netherlands (Blockmans, 1999: 297–304). However, permanent indirect taxes would not avenge in the long run, excessively demanded to meet heavy maintenance of an army for external wars, and resolution of inter-nal conflicts between counties – each with its own defensive apparatus – always counting with the collection of extraordinary taxes.

The corruption of the collecting officers, the local powers' strength, and the lack of objective information on the actual capacity to evaluate and tax the wealth pro-duced generated constraints in the empirical knowledge of the economic potential of each territory. This would result in an imbalanced fiscal pressure exerted on each county (Blockmans, 1999: 304–305) and, in the future, a political fragmenta-tion (Boone, 2002: 339–341) that would remain thereafter.

On the other hand, entering the sixteenth century, credit mechanisms and public debt services were consolidated as the most trustworthy in Europe. The Dutch success in managing their own debt was able to attract foreign investors, convert-ing Amsterdam into the European financial center, being eclipsed by London only in the 1700s ('t Hart, 1999: 309–310). Their fiscal mechanism combined with a "domestic tranquility" underpinned by a solid and diligent government, capable of balance multiple economic interests and colonial determinations, paved the path to what some scholars calls the "Golden Age" (1580–1670).[8] However, war-fare and its financing became the driving force behind fiscal development, trigger-ing the competition with France, Spain and England regarding the trade control in the Baltic and Mediterranean, as well as to overtake the Portuguese colonial trade in South America during the 1590s (Fritschy, 't Hart & Horlings, 2012: 39–42).[9]

3.7 Portugal

Squaring Portugal within the framework proposed by Bonney and Ormrod is nei-ther linear nor simple, given the many constraints and variables. Perhaps that is exactly why it is worth pursuing an identity for the Portuguese case and understanding the dynamics of taxation. Historically, state finances in Portugal and political and administrative issues remained circumscribed by the authors in the 1980s and 1990s from an "essentially institutional point of view, that is, as a chapter within a long running narrative the creation of a centralized state and the organization of a royal bureaucracy" (Barata & Henriques, 2012: 277). According to recent authors, an intense debate between historical Portuguese scholars as José Mattoso, Armando Luís de Carvalho Homem, Vitorino Magalhães Godinho and Oliveira Marques marks the discussion about the inflection point for the creation of an organized tax system, which, according to some, occurred in the fourteenth century, during the reign of Ferdinand I (1367–1383). Before this, some of these historians have classified it as a "not very coherent" system (Homem, 1990: 129). According to Carvalho Homem, the establishment of a central officer responsible for the supervision of finances – the *Vedor da Fazenda* – in the 1350s, combined with the use of taxes on commercial transactions – were a game changer for the Portuguese tax system organization. On the other hand, following the arguments of José Mattoso, the reforms implemented by Afonso III (1248–1279), together with the creation of a nationwide complex of fiscal districts, the *almoxarifados*, and the foundation of the first local district in Guimarães, would be the reference for a system no longer controlled by the court nobility (Mattoso, 2001: 904–905).

This same active discussion about this pivotal point for the Portuguese fiscal development, and the choice of an institutional way as the guiding principle of the same debate, serves to illustrate another fundamental aspect: that the study of taxation has not always competed, at least first place, to people of pure formation in history or social sciences, but to those who better perceive this dynamic, that is, who creates and regulates them. In other words, this task fell to law scholars, the history of law and, apparently, economists, doctors, civil servants, among others who were interested in tax matters, with a better economic background than historical. At the very least, it demonstrates the "uncomfortableness" caused by taking the researcher/writer out of his comfort zone, being forced to master scientific work tools and concepts that are unfamiliar to him and which were not even taught to him originally. The "evidence" of this phenomenon lies in studies published since the 1870s with Oliveira Martins (1972), and 1880s with Gama Barros and his studies on public administration, Costa Lobo in the 1900s, or Alberto Sampaio (1979), Paulo Merêa (2006), Mário Júlio Brito de Almeida e Costa (1961) and Marcello Caetano (1963); regarding the people with economic formation, the examples of João Lúcio de Azevedo[10] and Braamcamp Freire[11] – although of incomplete instruction in the economic area – give the tone of a change in the historiographic panorama that, from then on, would still pass through the hands of historians of other such as António Sérgio (1973) and Jaime Cortesão (1964), who would not pay particular attention to the fiscal issues themselves, but to aspects of the economy that somehow relate to each other.

Portugal's Fiscal History would only see its first pages written by historians "of craft and formation" in the 1940s and 1950s, with Virginia Rau[12] – still quite marked by the institutional bias in its beginning; Vitorino Magalhães Godinho,[13] more devoted to the phenomenon of oceanic expansion, prices and currencies, although his information about the wealth circulation within the Portuguese Empire are still of the greatest relevance for the global perception of an extraordinary revenue to which the Crown had access and guided the institutional paths followed; and Oliveira Marques (1980), who sought to rethink the routes followed by a historiographical production that was essentially focused on production and distribution, thus suggesting a new "agenda" and pointing out possible new itineraries and research topics and techniques.

From this new wave, already in the 1960s, important milestones would emerge from the point of view of taxation studies in the Middle Ages in Portugal and, not by chance, edited by the Portuguese Center for Fiscal Studies: essays on requests and loans in the kingdom (Gonçalves, 1964b), and a case study on a particular loan granted to king Afonso V on the eve of the Battle of Toro, in 1478 (Gonçalves, 1964a). At this point, we would then have the first aspect of medieval finances – the extraordinary revenues – analyzed on the basis of numbers and data collected from original documentation. In addition to those, another fundamental study would emerge in this same decade, completing the "essential tripod" of Portuguese medieval and early modern taxation bibliography for those who wanted to follow this path: documentary subsidies analyzing revenues and expenditure of the Royal Treasury between the fourteenth and fifteenth centuries (Faro, 1965). After this, we would have a hiatus of more than a decade until the creation of the Portuguese Association of Economic and Social History – APHES,[14] in July 1980, by the hands of Magalhães Godinho and his disciples. The post-Carnation Revolution (1974), would testify the emergence of a new academic context, stimulated by the great student demand. However, the fiscal and economic history did not take advantage of this occasion, not inspiring the historians, even less the medievalists and modernists, in which primordial elements of the Portuguese economy were at that time unknown and still largely forgotten: Portugal had fallen in a pitfall, that is, had been seduced by the siren song of the second generation of the *Annales* and their "history of mentalities".[15]

The 1980s and 1990s witnessed an inhibited and confused recovery of this topic, still very marked by the "institutionalism" as a legacy left to the historians who, consciously or unconsciously, "drank" in those sources to produce fundamental studies that, in fact, would mark the Portuguese historiography. But what was essential was – and still is – to be done, that is, the overall perspective is valid, no doubt about that, as long as the evidence of many pieces missing in the medieval and modern taxation puzzle is not ignored. Collective works of larger wingspans, without a more precise reconstruction of the concrete conditions in which revenues were collected and expenses were processed, mean little or nothing in the study of this subject in the face of what has not yet been done. Therefore, an aggregate and quantitative vision is essential, without taking into account the inertia of institutions and practices, especially local ones.

The most recent historiographical production on this subject "has challenged this point of view, based on new concepts and models" (Henriques, 2008: 8). However, the difficulties with primary sources and the use of relatively new conceptual models are some of the difficulties to overcome. Moreover, the phenomenon of enshrinement, the real impact of minting and monetary devaluation,[16] and the controversy over the true potential of Portugal's sales taxes (*sisas*) as an instrument for accommodating the tax burden on the population are themes discussed by the authors with some doubts and reluctance.

Recent research seeks the sociology of finances,[17] the effects of the First World War on the transformation of states and the basis for the effect of military conflicts on taxation policies. According to their findings, the countries involved engaged the battle by resorting to *capital* and, as a consequence, neglected services and goods provided by *labor* or by their own *tax base*, that is, by everything that could generate revenue through taxes. By following this way, they became indebted and began to exert more pressure on the "taxpayers" in order to pay the creditors, from whom they became dependent. Moreover, the argumentation basis is that tax collection and expenditure are closely intertwined, and that the "redistribution" of revenue was, arguably, the rationale for the preservation and permanence of the state's fiscal powers.[18] According to this view, "the field of history devoted to economic-fiscal problems is much more complex and broad than the concept or idea of "public finances" might suggest" (Henriques, 2008: 13). The chaining of these two currents will give us the central problems and the starting point for our argumentation development.

The impact of military effort is undoubtedly one of the decisive factors of the Portuguese economic and fiscal situation. Unlike the cases previously mentioned – England, Castile, France and Venice, in particular – notably concerning territorial and demographic dimensions, Portugal did not have the same conflicting scenario as these examples. But in its own measure, it developed a group of military campaigns that overburdened a state, which, at the beginning of the fourteenth century, had no expansionist aspirations or, rather, had them "under control". On the other hand, in the space of a century, this country would be a protagonist on the European scene, appearing "as an expansionist state, and . . . this dramatic change provides and intriguing testing ground for the transition between fiscal models" (Henriques, 2008: 19–20). The whole situation would change from then on due to a sequence of campaigns triggered by the Fernandine Wars[19] (1369–1382) and which would follow in sequence the succession crisis of 1383–85, the kingdom's defense that continued until the beginning of the following century, the conquest of Ceuta (1415), the Tangiers' disaster (1437), the expedition to Castile in 1445 against the Infants of Aragon, the short civil wars, culminating at the Battle of Alfarrobeira (1448), the advances in North Africa and the maintenance of those outposts, the litigation with Castile and the unfolding of oceanic expansion would dredge up the treasury mercilessly.

From the fiscal point of view, Afonso V would receive a heavy inheritance from his ancestors. However, he himself has a large share of the contribution in the difficult context created. The military campaigns southwards were, according to some scholars, "an option in which reasons of faith, strategy and money voluntarily converged". After the first victories,

> he returned to the kingdom a month later, crowned with prestige, as king of Portugal and of the Algarve, lord of Ceuta and *Ksar-es-Seghir* in Africa. Famous, but not rich – and with new burdens to deal with, so impoverished

was the treasury that it was impossible to make ends meet, whether old or new: the kingdom's administration, the Crown's lands, the maintenance of outposts conquered in Africa, the payment of 'rewards to those who served us in the acts referred'.

(Sousa, 1990: I, 379–380)

This was the prelude of difficulties to come.

The solution could be found in the decentralization imposed by *the African*, both in fiscal and administrative terms. The attempt to reform the state would not loom, and the bureaucracy increased. The creation of the *Contadorias das Comarcas* ("counties' regional accounting branches") is an example of this phenomenon, resulting in an extra burden to the Royal Treasury. Furthermore, there was still the necessity to fill in positions and to reward the monarch's pairs, endowing them not only with important spots within the administration but also with fiscal annuities and privileges: exemptions and favors in tax collection leasing procedures were symptomatic of this redistributive framework.

However, the expansion's first economic results appeared only in João II's reign (1481–1495). *The Perfect Prince* would benefit from the wealth coming overseas, which would force the Crown to a re-centralization in order to control this new source of revenue, creating monopolies and exploiting them through temporary concessions to wealthy individuals or private partnerships. One of the aspects that we will notice through this analysis is that this phenomenon conceded the Portuguese state the privilege of not having to worry about establishing an adequate tax system – or, rather, restructure it in order to provide an increase in its revenues and a better management of their expenditure. But even so, and since the kingdom had grown largely, becoming an empire in the sixteenth century, an operational collection structure would be complex to implement. Not only because of administrative regions' scope but also mainly due to the difficulty of organizing and implementing rules and human means to efficiently do so in such a vast domain, from Western Europe to Asia's Eastern extreme.

This re-centralization would continue during Manuel I's reign (1495–1521). *The Fortunate*, with his reforming pretensions and a new political project, first applied on a micro-scaled level, in his territories, still as Duke of Beja and, later, to a macro-scale level, i.e., the kingdom and Empire, was able to set a fast pace of growth to the royal household, enriched by the overseas' business (Costa, 2005: 100–101). With a demesne increased by the Military Order of Christ's income overseas (Costa, 2005: 101), and his control over the nobility, the situation was politically controlled. Such stability came through either by the economic means, with a new redistributive capacity[20] that favored his patrons, and through genealogy, influencing and promoting politically motivated marriages in order to strengthen his supportive political base. Acting within the Portuguese aristocracy's heart, he was able to maneuver the kingdom's destinies in favor of his governance, although the state finances – the *almoxarifados* and counties' regional fiscal branches – were not doing so well, and also in need of revenues coming from the East and Africa.

Furthermore, one last problem is to analyze and respond to a final issue: can kings manage to maneuver their tax systems according to their needs or to the political society that they belong to? Some scholars noted a tendency for fiscal systems to exceed their productivity periods and to serve not the state's interests but their subjects' (Ormrod, 1999b: 186). The phenomenon of redistribution was already analyzed by recent research. However, it should be noted to what extent the regular revenues produced by the Portuguese fiscal mechanism were able or not to support such a policy. After these points, we believe that there is a good dossier here to start our approach on the Portuguese state finances.

Notes

1 Ormrod (1995: 132–133). For more references about the ecclesiastical revenues' importance within general royal finances in some cases, see Lewis (1968), Green (1988), Ladero Quesada (2009) and Sánchez Martínez (2011).
2 Ladero Quesada (1991: 96–97). See also Hernández (1993).
3 *Fonsadera* (in Portuguese, *Fossadeira*) was an assessment that peasants had to pay for those who were missing from the plow. Over time, it became a tribute, paid in kind or cash, which would refer to the performance of military duty, mostly related to the *reconquista* in Castile. See Ladero Quesada (1999: 180–181).
4 Ladero Quesada (2002: 49–121). See also García Fitz (2007) and Coca Castañer (2012). To the introduction of Castilian fiscal mechanism in that realm after the *reconquista*, see Galán Sánchez (2012).
5 *Fuegos* ("Fires", in English, or *Fogos*, in Portuguese) were a demographic measurement unit, which could be used for population statistics or fiscal purposes, despite all the controversy on the reality of those numbers. Normally, a *fuego* is considered as a 4.5 or 5 coefficient, depending on the region. See Ladero Quesada (2013: 174–175).
6 Ormrod (1995: 125–128). About this historiographical approach, see also Roberts (1956) and Rogers (1993, 1995). To the counterpoint, see Black (1991).
7 To engage more details about this balance of power, see Ormrod (2010).
8 For more about the Golden Age of the Dutch Republic, see Van Der Woude and De Vries (1997) and Maddison (1991).
9 Fritschy, 't Hart and Horlings (2012: 39–42).
10 Despite his academic background as an economist, he had plenty of work done related to the history of Portugal. See Azevedo (1929, 1931, 1933, 1973).
11 For more details and a list of financial/accounting books, see Mexia (1904).
12 For a more detailed description of her work, see Rau (1949, 2009).
13 To access more data on the Portuguese oceanic expansion, see Godinho (1962, 1963–1970, 2009).
14 www.aphes.pt.
15 For more of that perspective about Portuguese economic history, see Duarte (2005: 5–6).
16 For more details about money, currency and exchange rates, see Marques (1996).
17 Regarding this historiographic line, see Witt (1987), Backhaus (2002) and Goldscheid (1962).
18 For further developments, see Guéry (1984).
19 Ferdinand I's chronicle, written by Fernão Lopes, clearly illustrates the turning point the wars were to his argumentation and to Portugal's state finances: "When the war began . . . another world was born, new and very opposed to the first one". Henriques (2008: 147).
20 For more details about the Portuguese kings' power origins and doctrines, see Henriques (2008: 12–13).

Bibliography

Secondary sources and dictionaries

Faro, J. (1965). *Receitas e despesas da Fazenda Real de 1384 a 1481: subsídios documentais*. Lisbon: Instituto Nacional de Estatística.

Mexia, A. (1904). Somaryo dos livros da Fazenda tirado por Affonso Mexia, com uma introducção por A. Braamcamp Freire. Separata do Archivo Historico Portuguez. Lisbon, Off. Typ. Calçada do Cabra 7, vol. 2.

Studies

Álvarez Nogal, C. (2009). Oferta y demanda de deuda pública en Castilla. Juros de alcabalas (1540–1740), *Estudios de historia económica*. Madrid: Banco de España, 2009, ISSN 0213–2702, n° 55 (Ejemplar dedicado a: Oferta y demanda de deuda pública en Castilla. Juros de alcabalas (1540–1740)).

Asenjo González, M. (2008). Ciudades y deuda pública en Castilla. La adaptación fiscal del impuesto de la "alcabala real" a las nuevas exigencias de la sociedad política (1450–1520), in *Actas La fiscalità nell'economia europea (sec. XIII-XVIII)*, 39th Settimana di Studi dell'istituto "Francesco Datini" di Prato a cura di Simonetta Cavaciocchi. Firenze: Firenze University Press, 531–544.

Azevedo, J. L. de. (1929). Organização económica, in D. Peres, *História de Portugal*, vol. 2. Porto: Portucalense Editora, 395–444.

Azevedo, J. L. de. (1931). Organização económica, in D. Peres, *História de Portugal*, vol. 3. Porto: Portucalense Editora, 627–664.

Azevedo, J. L. de. (1933). Organização económica, in D. Peres, *História de Portugal*, vol. 5. Porto: Portucalense Editora, 289–316.

Azevedo, J. L. de. (1973). *Épocas de Portugal Económico. Esboços de História*, 3nd ed. Lisbon: Livraria Clássica Editora.

Backhaus, J. (2002). Fiscal Sociology. What For? American Journal of Economics and Sociology, 61, 1, 55–77.

Barata, F. T., & Henriques, A. C. (2012). Economic and Fiscal History, in J. Mattoso (dir.), M. de L. Rosa, B. V. e Sousa, & M. J. Branco (eds.), *The Historiography of Medieval Portugal (c.1950–2010)*. Lisbon: Instituto de Estudos Medievais, 261–281.

Black, J. (1991). *A Military Revolution? Military Change and European Society, 1550–1800*. London: Humanities Press.

Blockmans, W. (1999). The Low Countries in the Middle Ages, in R. Bonney (ed.), *The Rise of the Fiscal State in Europe c. 1200–1815*. Oxford: Oxford University Press, 281–308.

Bonney, R. (2012). The Rise of the fiscal state in France, 1500–1914, in B. Yun-Casalilla, P. K. O'Brien, & F. Comín Comín (eds.), *The Rise of Fiscal States: A Global History, 1500–1914*. Cambridge: Cambridge University Press, 93–110.

Boone, M. (2002). Les ducs, les villes et l'argent des contribuables: le rêve d'un impôt princier permanent en Flandre à l'époque bourguignonne, in P. Contamine, J. Kerhervé, & A. Rigaudière (dir.), *L'impôt au Moyen Âge: l'impôt public et le prélèvement seigneurial, fin XIIe – début XVie siècle*. Actes du colloque tenu à Bercy les 14, 15 et 16 juin 2000. Paris: Comité pour L'Histoire Économique et Financière de la France, II, 323–341.

Caetano, M. (1963). Subsídios para o estudo das Cortes Medievais Portuguesas, *Revista da Faculdade de Direito da Universidade de Lisboa*, XV, Lisbon, 1–36.

Chittolini, G. (2002). "Fiscalité d'État" et prérogatives urbaines dans le duché de Milan à la fin du Moyen Âge, P. Contamine, J. Kerhervé, & A. Rigaudière (dir.), *L'impôt au Moyen Âge: l'impôt public et le prélèvement seigneurial, fin XIIe – début XVie siècle*. Actes du colloque tenu à Bercy les 14, 15 et 16 juin 2000. Paris: Comité pour L'Histoire Économique et Financière de la France, I, 147–176.

Coca Castañer, J. E. L. de. (2012). La Cruzada Particular de un Maestre de la Orden de Alcantara (1394), in *Studia historica. Historia medieval*, ISSN 0213–2060, 30 (Ejemplar dedicado a: Poder y fiscalidad en la Edad Media hispánica), 175–195.

Contamine, P. (2002). Lever l'impôt en terre de guerre: rançons, appatis, souffrances de guerre dans la France des XIVe et XVe siècles, in P. Contamine, J. Kerhervé, & A. Rigaudière (dir.), *L'impôt au Moyen Âge: l'impôt public et le prélèvement seigneurial, fin XIIe – début XVie siècle*. Actes du colloque tenu à Bercy les 14, 15 et 16 juin 2000. Paris: Comité pour L'Histoire Économique et Financière de la France, I, 11–39.

Cortesão, J. (1964). *Os Factores Democráticos na formação de Portugal*. Lisbon: Portugália.

Costa, J. P. O. e. (2005). *D. Manuel I: um príncipe do Renascimento*. Mem Martins: Círculo de Leitores.

Costa, M. J. B. de A. (1961). *Raízes do Censo Consignativo: para a história do crédito medieval Português*. Coimbra: Edições Atlântida.

Coutiez, Y. (1980). La part du comté de Hainaut dans les ressources financières de Philippe le Bon, Mémoires et Publications de la Société des Sciences, des Arts et des Lettres du Hainaut, 91, 105–138.

Cunich, P. (1999). Revolution and Crisis in English State Finances, 1534–47, in W. M. Ormrod, M. Bonney, & R. Bonney (eds.), *Crises, Revolutions and Self-Sustained Growth: Essays in European Fiscal History, c.1130–1830*. Stanford: Shaun Tyas, 110–137.

Duarte, L. M. (2005). A História Económica do Portugal Medieval (Sugestões para uma recuperação), in *Lecture of the VIII Congresso da AEHE (Asociación Española de História Económica)*, Santiago de Compostela, 1–7.

Felloni, G. (2010). A Profile of Genoa's Casa di San Giorgio, a Turning Point in the History of Credit, Rivista di storia economica, Roma, 3, 335–346.

Fritschy, W., 't Hart, M., & Horlings, E. (2012). Long-term Trends in the Fiscal History of the Netherlands, 1515–1913, in B. Yun-Casalilla, P. K. O'Brien, & F. Comín Comín (eds.), *The Rise of Fiscal States: A Global History, 1500–1914*. Cambridge: Cambridge University Press, 39–66.

Furió Diego, A. (1999). Deuda pública e intereses privados. Finanzas y fiscalidad municipales en la Corona de Aragón. Edad Media: revista de historia, ISSN 1138–9621, 2, 35–80.

Galán Sánchez, A. (2012). Poder y fiscalidad en el Reino de Granada tras la conquista: algunas reflexiones, Studia histórica. Historia medieval, ISSN 0213–2060, 30 (Ejemplar dedicado a: Poder y fiscalidad en la Edad Media hispánica), 67–98.

García Fitz, F. (2007). 'Las guerras de cada día': en la Castilla del siglo XIV, *Edad Media: revista de historia*, ISSN 1138–9621, 8 (Ejemplar dedicado a: La crisis del siglo XIV en los Reinos Hispánicos), 145–181.

Godinho, V. M. (1962). *A Economia dos Descobrimentos Henriquinos*. Lisbon: Sá da Costa.

Godinho, V. M. (1963–1970). *Os descobrimentos e a economia mundial*, 2 vols. Lisbon: Ed. Arcádia.

Godinho, V. M. (2009). A Formação do Estado e as Finanças Públicas, in V. M. Godinho, *Ensaios e Estudos: uma maneira de pensar*, vol. I, 2nd ed. Lisbon: Sá da Costa Editora, 123–173.

Goldscheid, R. (1962). A Sociological Approach to Problems of Public Finance, in R. A. Musgrave & A. T. Peacock (eds.), Classics in the Theory of Public Finance. London: Macmillan, 202–213.

Gonçalves, I. (1964a). *O Empréstimo concedido a D. Afonso V nos anos de 1475 e 1476 pelo almoxarifado de Évora*. Lisbon: Cadernos de Ciência e Técnica Fiscal – Centro de Estudos Fiscais da Direcção-Geral das Contribuições e Impostos – Ministério das Finanças.

Gonçalves, I. (1964b). *Pedidos e empréstimos públicos em Portugal durante a Idade Média*. Lisbon: Cadernos de Ciência e Técnica Fiscal: Centro de estudos fiscais da direcção-geral das contribuições e impostos – Ministério das Finanças.

González Arce, J. D. (1992). La política fiscal de Alfonso X en el Reino de Murcia: portazgo y diezmos, Studia historica. Historia medieval, ISSN 0213–2060, 10, 73–100.

Green, V. H. H. (1988). "Taxation, Church", in J. R. Strayer (ed.), *Dictionary of the Middle Ages*. New York: American Council of Learned Societies, XI, 605–611.

Guéry, A. (1984). Le roi dépensier: le don, la contrainte, et l'origine du système financier de la monarchie française d'ancien régime, Annales. Économies, Societés, Civilisations, 39, 6, 1241–1269.

Hamon, P. (2006). Les dettes du roi de France (fin du Moyen Âge-XVIe siècle): une dette "publique"?, in J. Andreau, G. Béaur, J. Y. Grenier (dir.), *La dette publique dans l'histoire*. Actes des Journées du Centre de Recherches Historiques des 26, 27 et 28 novembre 2001. Paris: Comité pour L'Histoire Économique et Financière de la France, 85–97.

Henneman Jr., J. B. (1999). France in the Middle Ages, in R. Bonney (ed.), *The Rise of the Fiscal State in Europe c. 1200–1815*. Oxford: Oxford University Press, 101–122.

Henriques, A. M. B. de M. de C. (2008). *State Finance, War and Redistribution in Portugal (1249–1527)*. Ph.D. Thesis. Department of History, University of York.

Hernández, F. J. (1993). *Las Rentas del Rey: sociedad y fisco en el reino castellano del siglo XIII*, 2 vols. Madrid: Fundación Ramón Areces.

Hocquet, J. C. (1995). City-State and Market Economy, in R. Bonney (ed.), *Economic Systems and State Finance*. Oxford: Oxford University Press, 81–100.

Homem, A. L. de C. (1990). *O Desembargo Régio (1320–1433)*. Porto: Junta Nacional de Investigação Científica.

Kerhervè, J. (2002). Impôt, Guerre et Politique en Bretagne au XVᵉ siècle: L'exemple du Diocese de Saint-Brieuc, in P. Contamine, J. Kerhervé, & A. Rigaudière (dir.), *L'impôt au Moyen Âge: l'impôt public et le prélèvement seigneurial, fin XIIe – début XVie siècle*. Actes du colloque tenu à Bercy les 14, 15 et 16 juin 2000. Paris: Comité pour L'Histoire Économique et Financière de la France, II, 369–443.

Ladero Quesada, M. A. (1991). Fiscalidad regia y génesis del Estado en la Corona de Castilla (1252–1504), Revista Espacio, Tiempo y Forma, Série III, História Medieval, 4, 95–135.

Ladero Quesada, M. A. (1999). Castile in the Middle Ages, in R. Bonney (ed.), *The Rise of the Fiscal State in Europe c. 1200–1815*. Oxford: Oxford University Press, 177–199.

Ladero Quesada, M. A. (2002). La frontera de Granada. 1265–1481, *Revista de Historia Militar. N° extraordinario: Historia Militar: métodos y recursos de investigación*, 49–121.

Ladero Quesada, M. A. (2009). *La Hacienda Real de Castilla (1369–1504): estúdios y documentos*. Madrid: Real Academia de la Historia.

Ladero Quesada, M. A. (2011). *Fiscalidad y Poder Real en Castilla (1252–1369)*, 2nd ed. Madrid: Real Academia de la Historia.

Ladero Quesada, M. A. (2013). Población de las ciudades en la baja Edad Media (Castilla, Aragón, Navarra), *Atas I Congresso Histórico Internacional As Cidades na História: População*, 24 a 26 de Outubro de 2012. Guimarães: Câmara Municipal de Guimarães, 165–202.

Lewis, P. S. (1968). *Later Medieval France: The Polity*. London: Macmillan.

Maddison, A. (1991). *Dynamic Forces in Capitalist Development*. Oxford: Oxford University Press.

Mainoni, P. (1999). Fiscalidad directa e indirecta en la Italia medieval del Centro y del Norte: Algunas orientaciones historiográficas recientes, *Edad Media: revista de historia*, ISSN 1138–9621, 2 (Ejemplar dedicado a: instrumentos de pago y finanzas en la Edad Media), 151–166.

Marques, A. H. de O. (1980). Ideário para uma História Económica de Portugal na Idade Média, in A. H. de O. Marques, *Ensaios de História Medieval Portuguesa*. Lisboa: Vega, 17–50.

Marques, M. G. (1996). *História da Moeda Medieval Portuguesa*. Sintra: Instituto de Sintra.

Martins, J. P. de O. (1972). *História de Portugal*. Lisboa: Guimarães Editores.

Mattoso, J. (2001). O triunfo da monarquia portuguesa: 1258–1264. Ensaio de História Política, Análise Social, 35, 157, 899–935.

Menjot, D. (2008). Les enjeux de la fiscalité directe dans les systèmes financiers et fiscaux des villes castillanes aux XIVe et XVe siècles", in *Actas La fiscalità nell'economia europea (sec. XIII-XVIII)*, 39th Settimana di Studi dell'istituto "Francesco Datini" di Prato a cura di Simonetta Cavaciocchi. Firenze: Firenze University Press, 699–729.

Merêa, P. (2006). Organização Social e Administração Pública, in P. Merêa, *Estudos de História de Portugal*. Lisbon: INCM, 129–231.

Mira Jódar, A. J. (2003). La financiación de las empresas mediterráneas de Alfonso el Magnánimo: Bailía general, subsidios de Cortes y Crédito institucional en Valencia (1419–1455), Anuario de estudios medievales, ISSN 0066–5061, 33, 2 (Ejemplar dedicado a: Expansionismo político y territorial de las potencias occidentales en el Mediterráneo), 695–727.

Molho, A. (2006a). *Firenze nel Quattrocento: I – Política e Fiscalità*. Roma: Edizioni di Storia e Letteratura.

Molho, A. (2006b). La dette publique en Italie au XIVe et XVe siècles, in J. Andreau, G. Béaur, & J. Y. Grenier (dir.), *La dette publique dans l'histoire*. Actes des Journées du Centre de Recherches Historiques des 26, 27 et 28 novembre 2001. Paris: Comité pour L'Histoire Économique et Financière de la France, 37–61.

O'Brien, P. K., & Hunt, P. A. (1999). England, 1485–1815, in R. Bonney (ed.), *The Rise of the Fiscal State in Europe c. 1200–1815*. Oxford: Oxford University Press, 53–100.

Orcástegui Gros, C. (1983). La reglamentación del impuesto del monedaje en Aragón en los siglos XIII-XIV, Aragón en la Edad Media, ISSN 0213–2486, 5, 113–122.

Ormrod, W. M. (1995). The West European Monarchies in the Later Middle Ages, in R. Bonney (ed.), *Economic Systems and State Finance*. Oxford: Oxford University Press, 123–160.

Ormrod, W. M. (1999a). England in the Middle Ages, in R. Bonney (ed.), *The Rise of the Fiscal State in Europe c. 1200–1815*. Oxford: Oxford University Press, 19–52.

Ormrod, W. M. (1999b). Finance and Trade under Richard II, in A. Goodman & J. L. Gillespie (eds.), *Richard II: The Art of Kingship*. Oxford: Oxford University Press, 155–186.

Ormrod, W. M. (2010). *Parliament, Political Economy and State Formation in Later Medieval England*, in P. Hoppenbrouwers, A. Janse, & R. Stein (eds.), *Power and Persuasion: Essays on the Art of State Building in Honour of W. P. Blockmans*. Turnhout: Brepols, 123–139.

Ormrod, W. M., & Barta, J. (1995). The Feudal Structure and the Beginnings of State Finance, in R. Bonney (ed.), *Economic Systems and State Finance*. Oxford: Oxford University Press, 53–79.

Ortí Gost, P. (2001). La primera articulación del estado feudal en Cataluña a través de un impuesto: el bovaje (ss. XII-XIII), Hispania: Revista española de historia, ISSN 0018–2141, 61, 209, 967–998.

Ortí Gost, P., Sánchez Martínez, M., & Turull Rubinat, M. (1996). La génesis de la fiscalidad municipal en Cataluña, *Revista d'historia medieval*, ISSN 1131–7612, 7 (Ejemplar dedicado a: La gènesi de la fiscalitat municipal (segles XII-XIV)), 115–134.

Pezzolo, L. (2012). Republics and Principalities in Italy, in B. Yun-Casalilla, P. K. O'Brien, & F. Comín Comín (eds.), *The Rise of Fiscal States: A Global History, 1500–1914*. Cambridge: Cambridge University Press, 267–284.

Rau, V. (1949). *O Regimento da Casa dos Contos de Goa de 1589*. Separata da Revista do Centro de Estudos Económicos, 9, Lisbon.

Rau, V. (2009). *A Casa dos Contos: os três mais antigos regimentos dos contos*. Lisbon: Imprensa Nacional-Casa da Moeda [re-edition of 1951 and 1959 original prints].

Rigaudière, A. (2003). L'essor de la fiscalité royale, du règne de Philippe le Bel (1285–1314) à celui de Philippe VI (1328–1350), in *Penser et construire l'État dans la France du Moyen Âge (XIIIe-XVe siècle)*. Paris: Comité pour L'Histoire Économique et Financière de la France, 523–589.

Roberts, M. (1956). *The Military Revolution, 1560–1660: An Inaugural Lecture Delivered Before the Queen's University of Belfast*, in *Inaugural Lectures*. Belfast: M. Boyd.

Rogers, C. J. (1993). The Military Revolutions of the Hundred Years War, The Journal of Military History, 57, 258–275.

Rogers, C. J. (ed.). (1995). *The Military Revolution. Readings on the Military Transformation of Early Modern Europe*. Boulder: Westview Press.

Sampaio, A. (1979). *Estudos Históricos e Económicos*, 2 vols, 3rd ed. Lisbon: Vega.

Sánchez Martínez, M. (1995). La evolución de la fiscalidad regia en los países de la Corona de Aragón (c.1280–1350), in Europa en los umbrales de la crisis, 1250–1350: Actas de la XXI Semana de Estudios Medievales, Estella, 18 a 22 de julio de 1994, ISBN 84-235-1392-0, 393–428.

Sánchez Martínez, M. (2009). Las primeras emisiones de deuda pública por la Diputación del General de Cataluña (1365–1369), in M. Sánchez Martínez (ed.), *La Deuda Pública en la Cataluña Bajomedieval*. Barcelona: CSIC, 219–258.

Sánchez Martínez, M. (2010). La Monarquía y las ciudades desde el observatorio de la fiscalidad, in J. A. Sesma Muñoz (coord.), La Corona de Aragón en el centro de su Historia 1208–1458: Actas del congreso La Monarquía Aragonesa y los Reinos de la Corona, Zaragoza, 1 al 4 de diciembre de 2008. Zaragoza: Gobierno de Aragón – Depart. de Educación Cultura y Deporte, ISBN 978-84-8380-198-7, 43–64.

Sánchez Martínez, M. (2011). La participación de la iglesia de Catalunya en las finanzas regias (siglos XIII-XIV), in D. Menjot & M. Sánchez Martínez (eds.), *El dinero de Dios: iglesia y fiscalidad en el Occidente Medieval (siglos XIII-XV)*. Madrid: Ministerio de Economía y Hacienda, Instituto de Estudios Fiscales, 133–165.

Schulze, W. (1995). The Emergence and Consolidation of the 'Tax State'. I – The Sixteenth Century, in R. Bonney (ed.), *Economic Systems and State Finance*. Oxford: Oxford University Press, 261–279.

Sérgio, A. (1973). *Introdução Geográfico-Sociológica à História de Portugal*. Lisbon: Sá da Costa.

Sousa, A. de. (1990). *As cortes medievais portuguesas: 1385–1490*, 2 vols. Porto: INIC.

't Hart, M. (1999). "The United Provinces, 1579–1806", in R. Bonney (ed.), *The Rise of the Fiscal State in Europe c. 1200–1815*. Oxford: Oxford University Press, 309–325.

Terán Sánchez, A. C. de., Menjot, D. (1996). Hacienda y fiscalidad concejiles en la Corona de Castilla en la Edad Media, in Historia, instituciones, documentos, ISSN 0210–7716, 23, 213–254.

Thornton, T. (1999). Taking the King's Dominions: The Subject Territories of the English Crown in the Late Middle Ages, in W. M. Ormrod, M. Bonney, & R. Bonney (eds.), *Crises, Revolutions and Self-Sustained Growth: Essays in European Fiscal History, c.1130–1830*. Stanford: Shaun Tyas, 97–109.

Turull Rubinat, M. (1996). *Arca Communis*: Dret, municipi i fiscalitat, *Initium. Revista Catalana d'Història del Dret*, I, 581–610.

Turull Rubinat, M., & Verdés Pijuan, P. (2006). Gobierno municipal y fiscalidad en Cataluña durante la Baja Edad Media, Anuario de historia del derecho español, ISSN 0304–4319, n° 76, 507–530.

Valdeón Baruque, J. (1966). *Enrique II de Castilla: la guerra civil y la consolidación del régimen (1366–1371)*. Valladolid: Universidad de Valladolid-Secretariado de Publicaciones.

Valdeón Baruque, J. (2002). *Pedro I el Cruel y Enrique de Trastámara: ¿la primera guerra civil española?* Madrid: Aguilar.

Van Der Woude, A., & De Vries, J. (1997). *The First Modern Economy. Success, Failure and Perseverance of the Dutch Economy, 1500–1815*. Cambridge: Cambridge University Press.

Witt, P. C. (1987). Introduction: The History and Sociology of Public Finance: Problems and Topics, in P. C. Witt (ed.), *Wealth and Taxation in Central Europe: The History and Sociology of Public Finance*. Warwickshire: Leamington Spa, 5–18.

4 A Portuguese "Fiscal X-Ray"

One study, two moments

4.1 Two radiographs, one analysis

First of all, it is important to look at some key points about the approach chosen to analyze the data collected. Establishing standards was the first step in structuring the framework. By creating the categories to interpret the numbers found in the sources, I tried to carry out a sequential/serial study of the data obtained and the amounts collected and spent, searching for an evolution line of fiscal traits. This proved idealistic, mainly in view of the huge "gaps" left by the sources available, as well as the ones I was able to collect. The approach had to be different due to the existing documentation. Some important clues were advanced by previous studies (Henriques, 2008: 20–31). A wide-ranging chronological survey – thirteenth to sixteenth centuries – showed me the way to the municipal archives and royal chancery records, in search of tax leasing contracts (tax farming procedures) and acquittance letters produced in the period chosen and treated by me.

It was fundamental to follow the lists left by the *Caderno de Assentamentos* ("Notebook of Settlements"), transcribed and edited in the 1900s (Freire, 1908: VI, 233–240; 443–444). There, we obtained precious indications of the letters' structure, as well as the making of the accounting notebooks that would serve as "indexes", although only from a certain period, from Manuel I's reign onwards. Another important element was to follow the inventories made by Jorge Faro through the documentation he published, where we followed, with particular interest, the list of councils' knights, noble knights, nobles' esquires and nobles' messengers that constituted Afonso V's household (Faro, 1965: 199), which drew our attention by giving the dimension of the Crown's expenditure with its court, together with the *Livro das Tenças* ("Book of Endowments") of 1523 (Freire, 1904: II, 81–157; 201–227). From there, we sought to confirm and measure this high volume of resources between endowments, graces, marriages and mercies. Finally, among the three reigns, a reasonable number of letters was obtained, which relate to the royal accounts, whose distribution by reign is unbalanced yet useful to provide a picture of Portugal's state finances.

Due to the impossibility to follow the path of a serial approach, the option for a comparative study between two moments seemed to be the best solution, due to the characteristics of the data obtained. Two set of sources exist, both with a large amount of information: the first, from 1430s to 1470s, and the second, more substantial one, covering from 1480s to 1540s. Although the chronological beacons enters João III's reign (1521–1557), the data still refers mostly to the previous reign due to the delay (Rodrigues, 1982: 279–281) observed during the whole process. From the making of the accounting books in each *almoxarifado* to its final part of acquittance letters' issuance, there could be a gap of years. Given the methodological choice, we focused on the most refined separation of the data found as possible.

4.2. Revenues

When it comes to revenues, it is convenient to analyze one of the Treasury's main sources of income: the *sisas* ("sales taxes"). First, those were extraordinary taxes and collected at municipal level for local utilization. Later, following the political process of the 1383 crisis, they were made ordinary, offered by the people's representatives to King João I (1385–1433) to finance the kingdom's defense against Castile and incorporated into the Royal Treasury. However, the *sisas* were first placed on Portuguese Jews in 1316, as an increase of the services granted to the monarch (Henriques, 2008: 152–153). Concessions (or services), in fact, were not municipal taxes, but payments granted to the central power, in a kind of "partnership" where there was clearly the favored party and the party prejudiced, similar to the Castilian *servicios*. The change in the sisas' collection, which since 1386 had been applied to all goods sold and bought[1] would change the cities' perspective on this new mode of collection, more burdensome from the point of view of those who consumed and, consequently, more susceptible to complaints. It is worth noting that inflation, at that time, was one of the most relevant factors in choosing indirect (sales) taxes, stipulated and charged in percentage, due to its "immunity", that is, even if there was currency's devaluation, the sums in cash would be safe (Henriques, 2008: 157–161). The *sisas* were also separated into groups: general (charged in the transaction of any product, manufactured or not, in a more extensive way, as footwear, utensils, arms, clothes, etc.) and specific, on the most common commodities sold in Portugal at that time: bread, fruit, cloths, colored cloths, wine, meat, wheat, wood, fish, marçaria (other goods in general, such as clothes, shoes) and real estate.

The central issue to note is that since the beginning of the fifteenth century, the *sisas* are already the flagship of Portuguese tax collection. Between 1398 and 1402, other scholars estimate that they represented about 75% of total revenue, while in 1382, in times of extraordinary needs – urban maintenance, defense, debt settlement or other collective needs – this percentage would be closer to 40% in such years (Faro, 1965: LXXVII; Henriques, 2008: 160, fig. 13). This reversal can and should be explained through the needs of municipalities to repay debts with the Crown, to avoid tax fraud and evasion with the collection of the *talha* within the cities (Duarte, 2006: 442) (similar to the French *taille*) but essentially by the combination between the consumption evolution and, consequently, an increase in the collection of indirect taxes and the decay of royal rights as a central element of this taxation (Henriques, 2008: 160–161). In 1473, to some scholars, the *sisas* occasionally composed about 92% of total revenues, including the royal tenths and toll rights (Faro, 1965: LXXVIII).

However, we do not think it appropriate to state that sales taxes "replaced" the extraordinary revenues, i.e., the *pedidos* ("requests") and *Empréstimos* (loans) (Henriques, 2008: 222–223). The *Sisas* were converted into regular income and, combined with other forms of extraordinary tax resources, provided a "complementation" to the state's earnings. Although recent studies have noted the decline in the frequency those aids were levied and collected,[2] what happened can be summarized in two essential points: first, a misuse and purpose deviation for which those aids were collected; and second, an "anticipation" by the Royal Treasury to collect them and use it later, although for other destinations with some regularity (Henriques, 2008: 231–232).

Those symptoms can be identified in many situations. Perhaps some of the most flagrant was when part of the money used by the Ksar es-Seghir (northern Morocco, between Ceuta and Tangier) campaign in 1458. That money had already been collected by three *pedidos* to the people in 1456, mentioned in the parliamentary assembly held in Lisbon (Sousa, 1990: I, 377–379), intended to attend the Pope's request for help in taking Constantinople back,[3] conquered by the Turks in 1453. Furthermore, the resources advanced for the capture of Asilah (on the Atlantic coast of Morocco) in 1471, and Ceuta's assistance came, in great measure, from extraordinary taxation that was not directly linked with these campaigns. For instance, the *pedidos* approved by the parliament gathered at Torres Vedras in 1441, were meant to buy silver for minting purposes, but the use of this resource at the *almoxarifado* of Lamego, in the same year, as in others, was actually to pay some debts with local residents, who had been "seized", in another occasion, of wine, meat, bread and firewood.[4]

4.2.1 *Ordinary revenues*

From the point of view of the large syntheses produced to cover the entire history of Portugal, it is necessary to observe what has been done so far about tax collection, and the numbers that concern it. The first *History of Portugal* collection, published between the 1920s and 1930s, had in one of the chapters a description of state's revenues sources quite elucidative, but mainly approached by the theoretical point of view (Merêa, 2006: 163–167). That was very likely the starting point for the historians who would study Portugal's economy and finances in the 1950s and 1960s. One chapter demonstrates and explains each of the resources that the king had at his disposal and which mainly derived from rights over his lands, with the respective juridical-institutional justification. It also explains the origins of the *pedidos*, which would derive from the Castilian *pedido* or *petitium*, collected since the 1100s (Ladero Quesada, 2011: 51). It separates well the "general and permanent" contributions from "extraordinary procedures", such as the minting rights and the *sisas*, which were supplementary at the beginning. However, it does not advance with estimates or numbers. On the other hand, another chapter of the same collection goes into the social aspects of the economy (Magal-hães, 2012: 336), in parallel with other disciplines, largely leaving aside the purest economic and statistical data.

Another *History of Portugal*, essentially approached by the political perspec-tive, was published in the 1980s. It brings us some figures already known, espe-cially when describing the extraordinary collection for the marriage of Afonso V's sister, Leonor, with the emperor Frederick III of Germany (Serrão, 1980: 79). Moreover, it reports the necessary resources to defray the king's return from France in 1477, as well as the deal with Fernão Gomes for the Guinea's explora-tion (Serrão, 1980: 99, 174). From the point of view of tax numbers, it does not direct large additions to the historiographical debate, nor great novelties or special archival prospection for taxation purposes.

Oliveira Marques, in one of the volumes of his *New History of Portugal*, edited during the 1990s, mentions that there was little work produced on fiscal themes, either on local or seigneurial finances (Marques & Serrão, 1987: 308). Neverthe-less, some considerations are made, mainly regarding a budgetary point of view. The incessant search of resources to cover negative balances corroborated with other scholars about the prevalence of what is spent on what is collected in terms of importance within "medieval budgets". It is the expenditure that stimulates the state to seek for income that is not available firsthand and which, as a rule, defines the true the nature of public finances in any scope. Moreover, one can summa-rize the kingdom's revenues in the 1390s in eight points: the *sisas*, the tithes, the royal rights and Crown's properties, tolls and anchorages, the notaries' pensions, justice's fines, the chancery's rights and the specific tributes on the Jews (Duarte, 2006: 437). Regarding the relative weight of Lisbon and Oporto vis-à-vis the rest of the country, the author uses as a reference the income report from the coun-ties in 1473. According to him, the country's two largest cities would contribute almost 40% of national revenues (Marques & Serrão, 1987: 311).

An important point is also the analysis and diagnosis proposed by Duarte: that trade is the source of preferential collection, mainly due to a deficient and incom-plete tax structure based mainly on indirect taxes (Marques & Serrão, 1987: 311). In other words, overtaxing consumption derives from system failures. However, would not it be the other way around? Would not the mechanism fail because of the option taken by indirect taxation? Had the state, for example, opted for a fis-cal system administered directly, with state officials duly supervised and audited, instead of leasing its tax collection, tax evasion could be reduced and revenue increased? The option for sales taxes does not necessarily aid economic growth, but it can have the opposite effect (Bonney, 1995: 502; Gelabert González, 1995: 564–565). In his work, Oliveira Marques approaches the significant number of financial reforms implemented between the late fifteenth and early sixteenth cen-turies, influenced by a European tendency for a clearer differentiation between the king's pocket and the "public" coffers (Schulze, 1995: 268–270), which privi-leged the organizations' improvement, in order to increase revenues and untangle the local taxes' network. He also mentions, in particular, the general revision of *Foral* charters,[5] which started with Afonso V but was mainly carried out during

Manuel I's reign (1499–1521). He classified it as a "new list of taxes" to be paid to the sovereign or to the feudal lords in each municipality. Moreover, the new county accountants' and Treasury regiments in 1514 and 1516, respectively, and the restructuring of customs, particularly with regard to overseas revenues, are also seen as this administration upgrading process. The "abundance" of acquittance letters would be symptomatic of a more present state, of a more active and controlling oversight, so as not to let a single penny escape from the coffers. This would also represent the replacement, slowly, of the tax farming or lease regime from private investors, common in the fourteenth and fifteenth centuries, to a centralized and organized system run by the Crown, outlining the traces of a new structure in formation (Marques & Dias, 1998: 249–250).

Other scholars set the tone of a stabilized, wealthy, enshrined, yet indebted state in a different *History of Portugal*, focused on two topics: economic/fiscal organization and the political debate on the fiscal and economic guidelines. In the first part, the economic reorganization implemented by Afonso III is depicted. The direction was to stop the exit of cereals and precious metals, promulgate the *Foral* charters and leasing procedures, with the main objective of streamlining revenues. To reach that goal, the King implemented three key measures: receiving payments in cash; leasing the tax collection; and extensive use of customs rights, as Gaia and Porto were examples. However, this same reordering was largely carried out by the Inquiries of 1258, which served for the king to account for what actually belonged to him or, in other cases, for what he could appropriate (Mattoso, 2006: 148–149). He granted privileges to municipalities and their fairs, trying to boost domestic trade with tax exemptions. However, according to scholars, *the Bolognese* would have turned his attention more to monetary reforms and urban revenues, while his heir and successor, Dinis I (1279–1325), went the opposite way. Through the extension of the *Foral* policy, i.e., circumscribing what he could profit in each village and leasing payments' contracts in the hinterlands, he wanted to increase revenues with a more demanding management from the point of view of economic control, rearranging revenues in rural areas (Mattoso, 2006: 164–166).

The second part is notably focused on his institutional studies on the Portuguese medieval parliamentary assemblies, the *Cortes*. Those reports brought, from 1380s onwards, a treasury eroded by internal successions' conflicts and disputes with the Castilian neighbors, describing, through chronicles, depleted finances, a devalued currency, skyrocketing prices and a suffering population (Sousa, 2006: 199–200). A situation that from the revenues' perspective did not seem so dramatic for the Crown due to the collection of the *sisas* that, according to the royal chronicler Fernão Lopes, provoked "great damage and destruction to the people" (Lopes, 1945: I, 98–99) and would henceforth be part of the Crown's regular revenues. Furthermore, the regulation of its collection, the administrative reforms, as well as the legislation created in order to avoid resource waste, were also signs of a financial shortage (Sousa, 2006: 201). Finally, when dealing with the fiscal mechanisms, the parliamentary assembly gathered in Lisbon, in 1459, used as a guiding line a chronological trajectory of the *sisas* narrated by the debate

within the representatives (Sousa, 2006: 228–231) but did not provide more concrete figures.

The lack of sources, data and statistics for economic historians to approach
Portuguese economic and fiscal history is one of the fundamental questions, for
both medieval and early modern times. In addition, issues about the mispercep-
tion between revenue and expenditure, between pre-designated revenue to cover a
specific expenditure, as well as the nature and conversion of extraordinary taxes in
regular income should also be taken into account. In this case study, we will con-
fine ourselves to dissecting and observing the revenues generated by the state's
fiscal mechanism in a pre-determined chronological framework, as well as the
expenditure also carried out by the Crown in the same period. But first, let's take
a look at the earnings, divided into ordinary and extraordinary.

Regarding ordinary revenues, toward the end of the fourteenth century some
scholars delineated this budget component in a few revenues. For the period
studied by us, the profile of state revenues is already much more robust, and the
creation of accounting procedures is somewhat symptomatic of a structure in an
evolutionary process (Gomes, 2006: 124–125), which had been conceived and
underpinned by fiscal administrative units at the local level – the *almoxarifados* –
and, later, by regional supervisors (*Contadorias das Comarcas*), and a central
office of accounting and management: the *Casa dos Contos*, equivalent to the
English Exchequer.

Following the indications of a budget sketch of 1477–78 (Faro, 1965: 225), we
developed a framework in which we fit these units according to their geographic
region. From North to South, at the beginning of the last quarter of the fifteenth
century, the king withdrew his revenues in the northern part of the kingdom in the
Entre-Douro-e-Minho (between the Douro and Minho rivers) region, the *almoxarifados* of Porto, Guimarães, Ponte de Lima, Porto and Viana's customs and the
rights – tithes and *sisas* – collected from Castile's cloths that entered by Northeast;
in the region of Trás-os-Montes (North-Northeast border), the income came from
the *almoxarifados* of Vila Real and Torre de Moncorvo, as well as from the *portos
secos* (dry ports or borders' customs checkpoints), mostly from Castilian cloths.

Going Southwards, in the Beira province (region limited by four rivers: to the
North by the Douro, south by the Tagus, and west by the Mondego), the monarch
received income from the *almoxarifados of* Guarda, Lamego and Viseu, along
with the profits from the Castilian cloths entering through the Eastern border; in
Estremadura, in the *almoxarifados* of Santarém, Abrantes, Leiria, Óbidos, Sintra,
Alenquer, Coimbra and Aveiro, plus the rents collected from the Castilian cloths.
Further South, in the Entre-Tejo-e-Guadiana (also known as the Alentejo, i.e.,
beyond the Tagus or between the Tagus and Guadiana River, border with Castile),
the *almoxarifados* of Setúbal, Beja, Évora, Estremoz and Portalegre, together
with the cloths' profits; in the extreme south, in the Algarve region, in the *almoxarifados* of Tavira, Faro, Loulé, Silves and Lagos, besides the general customs
of that region, the factory of the almadravas (tuna fishing boats), tolls and rents.

Lisbon was indeed a world apart. Through the kingdom's main port, the king
collected revenues, within the scope of the royal household, from the Chancellery

rights, the Queen's Household rights on land property, the *jugadas* (taxes paid in kind – corn, wine, wheat or flax, in the lands that the king reserved especially for himself when he granted some of the *Foral* charters), the *reguengos* (rights on land property where the lord was the king himself), and the *quarto dos ingleses* ("English Quarter"). Moreover, he also counted on the *sisas* of the normal and colored cloths traded, wine, wood, fish, real estate, wheat, fruit, bread, *marçaria* ("manufactured goods"), meat, *aver-do-peso* ("commodities sold by weight"), minting treasury, chancery rights' on the House of Supplication ("supreme court"), customs, tolls, imposition of salt and wood. For each of those revenues mentioned, there was an *almoxarife* and a receiver who were accountable to Lisbon's central office of accounting.

Each *almoxarifado* was responsible for gathering tax revenues locally. In the documentary survey, the acquittance letters predominantly account for the *sisas* collected within the jurisdiction of each of the tax units. In some areas, such as Entre-Douro-e-Minho, Beira and Estremadura, the collection areas are more grouped, although the mountainous relief would certainly be an obstacle to the displacement of those responsible for the collection. As an example, at the city of Guarda,[6] the fiscal jurisdiction of the collectors would go through a series of smaller villages, such as Castelo Branco and Covilhã, in Beira Baixa, passing through Marialva, Trancoso, Seia, Gouveia and even Guarda, Belmonte, Castelo Rodrigo, Castelo Mendo, Sabugal and Almeida, crossing the border lines, a range of 120 kilometers. In the case of the Entre-Tejo-e-Guadiana region, this area was closer and easier, due to the plain lands, simplifying the work of the collectors, as in the case of Setúbal, where the area of activity is essentially restricted to the Sado River estuary, in places such as Setúbal, Sesimbra, Palmela, Almada, Alcácer do Sal and Benavente, a range of 60 kilometers. Or, literally, from West to East, as in Beja,[7] which the respective *almoxarifado* covers places from Santiago do Cacém and Odemira, on the Southwest coast, through Castro Verde, Ferreira do Alentejo, Mértola, to Serpa, Moura and Noudar, municipalities near the border area with Castile, covering a range of 200 kilometers.

The amplitude of these areas and the difficulty of access to some localities may be one of the factors that could help explain a series of problems related to the collection of those resources. To a great extent, they also explain why the Crown chose to lease the tax collection. Without being sure of what would come, a real notion of what certain zones might yield, or even a simple and objective rationale to understand the cost-benefit ratio of sending a royal official to collect taxes in Torre de Moncorvo (Northeast border with Castile) or Tavira, at the Mediterranean coast, the choice was made for the most practical option, in order to have a fixed and guaranteed income, and to let the leaseholder worry about all the problems related to the logistics of collection.

Income was then separated into ordinary and extraordinary. As far as revenue is concerned, there were no great obstacles in detailing its origin, since the documentation largely proves the Crown's option for indirect taxes. Of the fifty-one acquittances collected by us between 1439 and 1467, fourteen relate to the *almoxarifados'* revenue and expenditure, another ten dealt with the accounting procedures of extraordinary requests raised within the kingdom, nine relate to tax-leasing procedures in Lisbon, regarding *sisas* and *aver-do-peso*, for example, and the remaining eighteen dealt with accounting procedures of warehouses' accounting officers, treasurers of Ceuta's affairs, factories of commercial outposts and royal household's exchequers, among others.

Immediately, it is difficult because of the differing currency mentioned in the documentation. Particularly in the case of *almoxarifados*, of the fourteen documents, three were accounted for in *libras* ("pounds"), while the remainder are in *reais brancos* ("white" reais, due to a higher silver content). We follow, then, the option of converting[8] the first into the second ones, since the overwhelming majority of records account for this form (*reais*), especially from 1442 onwards.

From a broader point of view, there is a manifest evolution of revenues, steadily from 1450s onwards, linked to a number of factors. The fact that taxes, particularly the sales taxes, were collected *ad valorem* rather than fixed nominal value, exempted the kings from the evil effects of currency devaluation and inflation. Furthermore, revenues had actually grown substantially, largely due to the *sisas'* permanent adoption, which demonstrates how much the state finances were thereafter dependent on the market economy. The local perspective shows us, in relation to the collection growth, that this is a proven fact when observed in the long term.

Following the two established chronological benchmarks – 1450s and 1520s – for the first period there is sparse data for most of the local tax jurisdictions. However, data stands out in greater quantity for four *almoxarifados*: Guarda, Lamego, Setúbal and Beja. Let us examine these four examples.

In Guarda's case, there are enough observations to identify a development, especially from 1500s onwards, thanks to many gaps before 1500, especially between the 1440s and 1480s. As an important hallway and checkpoint for all commodities that entered from Castile, largely cloth (both normal and colored), it is possible to observe, in absolute terms, an overall evolution but with some upheavals in the way: some inconstancy (advances and retreats) regarding the values within the last years of Duarte I's reign, a steep upward trend until the conflicts regarding the Castilian succession, a stabilization of these values under João II and a fall followed by a stabilization and later recovery under Manuel I.

It should be noted that Figure 4.1 has some limitations, that is, it has some collection blanks, limitations caused by the gaps that these sources do not allow to fill. There are long periods, whole decades without any reference at all. However, with what has been collected, it is possible to verify a long-term evolution, although it is not possible to verify the precise trajectory of this growth between 1440 and 1480. Nevertheless, it is palpable to associate each point of the line described in the graph with the events within the studied period. It should be noted that these figures refer only to ordinary revenues – considering here already as part of this amount. Requests, loans and extraordinary municipal taxation of a direct nature do not enter into these accounts.

In a more detailed revenue analysis, we can only determine the revenue profile on one occasion, in this case of Guarda, that is, in only opportunity we found the

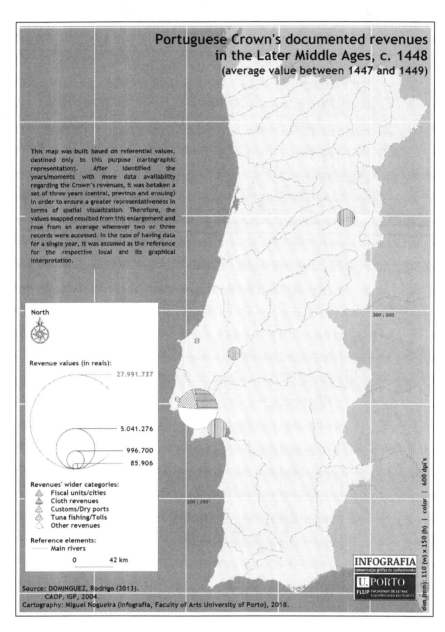

Map 4.1 Portuguese Crown's documented revenues in the later Middle Ages, c.1448 (average value between 1447 and 1449)

Figure 4.1 Guarda's fiscal revenue development (1436–1522)

description of the revenues; in the rest, only the total values are met. However, in this source, we realize that *sisas* constitute the overwhelming majority of the total amount collected. This detailed description will be discussed further ahead, in the section on the type and importance of each revenue in each region (Figure 4.5).

Regarding Lamego's case, we also obtained elements for remarks similar to Guarda's. However, it is important to make a few caveats: first, the fact that the revenue curve evolution in Figure 4.2 is more timid in its course until the 1520s, when the collection takes a considerable leap, explained, in part, by its location in the context of marketing the region's wines.[9] Second, as a bishopric, much of the income of that zone would be associated with the Church,[10] so the monarch would only have access to them with papal authorization, as in the case of tithes for example. Although monarchs have exercised their patronage rights,[11] and the churches' lists that form part of the royal patrimony were extensive (Boissellier, 2012: 233–235), even though they are outside the chronology studied (1350s), these rights influenced accounting in a narrow way in the fifteenth and sixteenth centuries; in total amounts, they did not represent even 10% of what was collected. It will also be an aspect to be properly dissected later. Third, the nominal values collected are about 50% of Guarda.

It should be noted that, in localities such as Lamego, the extraordinary revenues were broken down in the same documentation, together with the regular taxes. It does not happen in other cases observed, where the *pedidos* constitute separate lists and own acquittances. This shows that Portugal's royal finance accounting practices were not yet totally unified. In a quick analysis, we found that this type of extraordinary collection had the power to boost profits by more than 50%, as in 1441,[12] or even to increase several times the amount of available resources.

In Setúbal's case (Figure 4.3), one of the most important Portuguese ports regarding international trade, located in the Sado estuary[13] 45 kilometers south of Lisbon, it is necessary to make some observations: first, the relevance of local economic production, namely salt,[14] wine,[15] fishing[16] and shipbuilding.[17] Second, its geographical proximity to Lisbon, a city with which, for a long time, maintained a condition and a relation of dependence/subordination, as a place to dispose of its production – particularly salt and firewood. This situation has only changed with the establishment of the city's own customs (Andrade & Silveira, 2007: 147–165), symptomatic of an urban and economic growth within a larger context of the kingdom's economic expansion.

In numerical terms, seen in Figure 4.3, the evolution is reasonably balanced and constant, except in two moments: a rapid growth of revenues between the 1450s and 1490s, and a loss in 1513, in which the *almoxarifado*'s revenue collection leasing did not yield the Crown's estimates. Moreover, in the long term, there is a consistent evolution in terms of nominal values.

As far as Beja is concerned, we see a difference here compared to the other *almoxarifados*, made clear by Figure 4.4. The downward curve of the collection shows two distinct moments: a first fall, during the 1430s and 1440s, followed by a dizzying rise during the transition from the fifteenth century to sixteenth century, and thereafter a sharp decline in nominal values in the 1500s and 1510s,

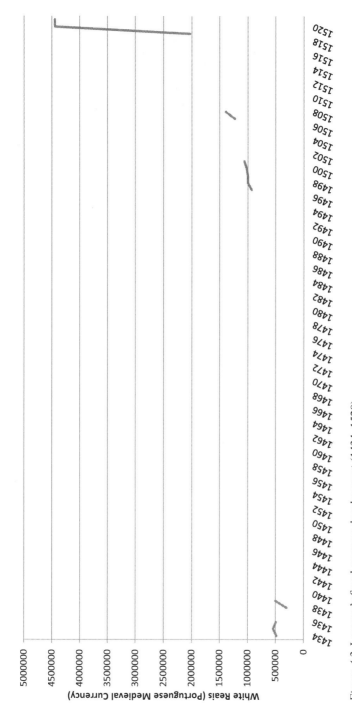

Figure 4.2 Lamego's fiscal revenue development (1434–1520)

Figure 4.3 Setúbal's fiscal revenue development (1439–1523)

Figure 4.4 Beja's fiscal revenue development (1439–1519)

followed by a stabilization in the following years. Since the conquest by Sancho II between 1232 and 1248, most territories and their respective income were associated with Portugal's military orders (Christ, Avis and Santiago). In this case, Santiago controlled much of the income[18] in that area. In addition, the Alentejo hinterlands were not a preferential passage zone for merchants and merchandise. Frontier checkpoints, like Estremoz, raised more significant revenues. However, more isolated villages, lost in between the shore and the Castilian border, usually did not generate a substantial movement in commercial transactions and, consequently, the tax collection related to this traffic was not attractive. As a strong evidence, the amount of *sisas* that did not find interested investors, or leasers, in this area, is relevant. In any case, there is a clear collection evolution in the 1450s onwards, as a result of some economic development largely provided by the cereals cultivation – corn, wheat, rye and barley, essentially – and cattle breeding,[19] which increased the contraband of herds as a side effect due to more favorable prices in Castile. Another source of income exploited was the use of collective equipment – such as ovens and mills – which were part of a context of manufactured production linked to agriculture and other economic activities (Braga, 1998: 182–194) and which appeared in the sources, albeit as a very small part of the total collection.

It is clear that, for other locations, such as Guimarães and Ponte de Lima,[20] Torre de Moncorvo,[21] Viseu[22] and Óbidos,[23] for example, for which we find a couple of references or little more, or even for other important units such as Porto, Coimbra or Évora, with no mention in the sources until at least 1473 (Faro, 1965: 82–85), it is very difficult to reconstruct the state finances' big picture since most of the records that survived has to do with municipal accounting (Gonçalves, 1987: 8), which contains only some of the desired information. From the 1480s onwards, it is easier to perceive the general revenues' oscillation, although without details of each collection in most cases.

As mentioned earlier, there is sparse information for most of local tax units. Accompanying the second chronological reference, it is easier to see this evolution, mainly due to a greater amount of data available in the acquittance letters collected in primary and secondary sources. The overwhelming majority of the records we worked with – 266 out of a total of 325, or about 81% – accounted for the collection from 1480s to 1520s, during João II's and Manuel I's reigns. In this other fiscal context, there are many figures and a more complete picture, albeit with quite a few blanks, but more noticeable in regard to the development of fiscal revenues.

It is evident the difficulty of tracing development profiles. This is explained by the "brevity" or pragmatism of the records collected regarding the description of what was collected. Rare were the cases[24] in which those earnings were carefully detailed. In any case, the overwhelming majority only accounts for the totals accumulated by the respective *almoxarifes*, which shows only how profitable each unit could be depending on the economic potential of each jurisdiction. On the other hand, the massive nominal evolution of those totals is notorious, which gives the overall growth dimension, detached from any conditionality.

4.2.2 Extraordinary revenues

For Portugal, as with other kingdoms, the need for extraordinary revenues is frequent (or almost constant). Extraordinary income derives from the right to assign a value to the coin, create and mint it according to the sovereign's will, as is its prerogative. Such a mechanism would have its legal justification in the customary law of the *monetagium*. However, in Portugal, the need to use arrived when the difference between revenues and expenditure became more visible with the conquest of Algarve in 1249. The spoils of war, loot, court fines and some taxes charged by the king and the privileges granted on the land, in that context, were sufficient for the maintenance of the royal household and the realm's government. Until then, according to other scholars, there was no sign of an organized fiscal apparatus (Gonçalves, 1964: 13–15).

The concept regards the extraordinary contributions discussed and voted on Parliamentary meetings, the *Cortes*. Considering this type of income, they can be classified into two well-known categories, which are the *pedidos* and *empréstimos* ("loans"). The first type of contribution has a particular and central characteristic: it is an additional input of a direct nature, that is, a poll tax distributed among the subjects and collected through a kingdom-wide organization. Operational procedures were set up for evaluation and collection, establishing officers responsible for those functions – in this case, the *avaliadores* ("evaluators"), the *aquantiadores* ("quantifiers") and, finally, the *sacadores* ("draftsmen') and the *escrivães* ("scribes"), albeit at different levels (municipal or regional). The difficulty is to distinguish each one of the multiple expressions used to designate them, since the poll tax could assume different forms, as a *talha* (similar to the French *taille*), or a *sisa* before its integration in ordinary state finances, as mentioned by other scholars. Regarding the differences between the *pedido* – which supposedly should be used only by one person, i.e., the king or landlord – and the other terminology used, perhaps it is possible establishing it by utilization. The first is a tax that should be intended and used by municipalities (counties); while the other taxes, the application of which were linked to the Crown, could be enacted at the regional or national levels (Gonçalves, 1964: 26–27). Another term used to designate extraordinary aid is *serviço* ("service"). However, in the selected sources, this word appears only once.[25]

About the *empréstimo*, it was a certain amount assigned to the monarch under the commitment to "return" it to the people afterwards, a fact that did not happen often, avoiding the essence of that mechanism (Gonçalves, 1964: 31–32). Comparatively, it was also defined as a "short-term credit operation" or a *préstamo* by the Castilians, or as a *donativo* (Ladero Quesada, 2009: 222). This financial instrument can also be analyzed through the parliamentary debates, where the rationale and approval had to be debated with people's representatives. On many occasions, kings, using the rhetorical tool of feigned humbleness, summoned the municipalities to the assemblies and addressed their endless economic difficulties. After a long rhetorical battle between representatives on both sides, what began as a modest plea for extra funds ended up as a *mútuo a fundo perdido*, that is, a non-repayable mutual. In other words, what was first requested as an *empréstimo* ended as a *pedido*, considering the fact that the amounts envisaged would not be returned in most cases. On the other hand, it also behaves as the former, due to the way it was requested and collected, as if it were a regular tax. In addition, it reveals the restricted power of municipal congressmen in the *Cortes*, despite the exercise of their role as a council, gathering on many occasions to address the kingdom's economic issues (Sousa, 1990: I, 182–183), and they yielded to the king's will, showing some degree of dependence, attesting to the strength and autonomy of political power.

In his reign, Afonso V would take particular advantage of these tactics, using as one of his usual negotiation tools the right to end the collection of *sisas*. Bearing in mind that sales taxes were supposed to be temporary, but ended up as permanent, he always promised to end them, in exchange for congressmen's goodwill to grant him extraordinary aids. Donations, the tutoring process of a young ruler and the need to please those who have helped to educate him, his descendants and friends may have opened the door to his excesses of granting endowments and privileges (Gomes, 2006: 56). Afonso became king in 1438, then only a six-year-old prince, and he was tutored by his mother, Queen Leonor of Aragon, until 1440, while she was regent and, after that, by his uncle, Infant Pedro, Duke of Coimbra, during his regency (1440–1448). Caught in the middle of noble intrigue for power between his uncle Pedro and his "half-uncle" Afonso, first Duke of Braganza (João I's bastard son), he was finally crowned in 1446, favoring the latter and fighting the former in a short-term civil war, ending at the battle in Alfarrobeira, in 1449 (Moreno, 1979: I, 426–428). Another idea that came against some scholars' harsh conclusions about the monarch is that the *Cortes* were essentially a time to dispatch the Crown's financial needs, leaving aside what could be some of the kingdom's most important administrative decisions, since the tendency of *the African* was to dispatch decisions without the presence of an assembly, following the king's personal character (Gomes, 2006: 69).

Despite the sovereign's individualist and centralist tendencies and considering that he could not appeal to new taxes without the consent of the *Cortes*, the assembly representatives were responsible for exposing the problems, analyzing the situation and the real needs, finding solutions and, finally, to grant (or not) the financial aid. The delegates, who were previously summoned, were not taken by surprise, since on many occasions the respective cities instructed them in advance about the procedures to be adopted according to the topics covered (Gonçalves, 1964: 45–46). Once the amount was determined, which was defined by a scale (half-*pedido*, one *pedido*, one and a half, two and so on), the total sum to be paid was divided among the municipalities, always having the *almoxarifado* as a main reference for both evaluation and money collection/reception (Gonçalves, 1964: 57–64). The *avaliadores* ("evaluators"), who were responsible for evaluating and researching the "contributors" assets, the *aquantiadores* or *contiadores* ("quantifiers"), that is, those who determined the amounts to be paid by each individual (on a scale of 0.5 to 3 pounds), regarding each person's properties (Gonçalves, 1964: 50–52), and the *sacadores* ("draftsmen"), directly in charge of money collection, were part of a heavy and complex structure that normally should only be assembled in extraordinary cases. Notwithstanding, the frequency of these extra allowances made them practically a permanent mechanism, especially after 1450. Not coincidentally, Parliament met twenty-four times in forty-three years of Afonso V's reign, an average of one meeting every two years (Sousa, 1990: I, 254–256), which gives us, at the same time, the institutional relevance of the *Cortes* and the measure of the kingdom's financial needs.

Due to the lack of surviving accounting books, lost in the destruction and fires that consumed the *Casa dos Contos* in the 1755 earthquake (Rau, 2009: 133–134; Pereira, 2003: 121), the option to obtain the necessary data and to carry out a study of this kind of income was also to analyze the acquittance letters' samples, granted by the king to local officials – that is, to the *almoxarifes* and also to the receivers, the agents responsible for receiving the money from tax leaseholders. In relation to extraordinary income voted in the assemblies, they were, as a rule, collected and verified in proper documents but could also be collected and reported together with ordinary income.[26] This particular source's example provides important information about the *pedido* of 1437, collected in that fiscal district during Duarte I's government in order to pool resources for the failed attempt to conquer Tangier. It is important to note here the lack of coherence and organization mentioned earlier, through the mixture of recipes attested by this source: specifically on this extraordinary aid, the responsible officer made a total of 24,738,049 pounds in revenue and 24,057,315 pounds in expenses. The residual value – 698,734 pounds – "transited" as part of following year's ordinary income. In addition, the *almoxarife* had been arrested due to the lack of money from extraordinary aids paid by the Jewish communes, being replaced by a temporary agent for two months. In the meantime, the debt was honored by his wife, and he would return to his post in the following year, facts which, on the other hand, showed the Crown's strict attention to fiscal affairs. Comparatively, the same year's ordinary income in the same locality was 19,454,330 pounds, about 21% less, although the extra collection was calculated in the proportion of 1.5 (one and a half *pedido*). If we convert it to a ratio of 1, that is, to a single one, we find a total of 16,038,210 pounds, minus 3,500,000 pounds but still very close to the values of a normal yield. In other words, the Royal Treasury could, as this case illustrates, double its revenues with extraordinary taxes. However, the values may vary according to the kingdom's region where the collection was made, not conferring to this case the assignment of the realm's *general rule*, which clearly it was not, as we can see in Table 4.1.

In another example,[27] it was reported an extraordinary collection, in 1446, of 106,654 reais for 1437's extraordinary collection which, when compared to the total regular income of the same year – 906,857 reais – is equivalent to 12% of that amount. However, it is important to point out that it had been collected only within local Jewish communes, and part of the payment had been made in kind – in this particular case, with 420 pieces of cloth from Castile.

However, as described earlier, this type of revenue was, as a rule, accounted for separately, in a document drafted specifically for this purpose, as an example

Table 4.1 Ordinary revenues versus extraordinary revenues in Portugal, c.1436–1449 (in pounds and reais brancos)

	Ordinary Revenues	*Extraordinary Revenues (Pedido)*
Lamego (1437)	19,454,330 pounds	16,038,210 pounds
Lamego (1441)	414,285 reais brancos	238,377 reais brancos
Guarda (1436)	33,660,636 pounds	3,732,890 pounds* (plus payment in kind – cloth)
Guarda (1449)	1,000,200 reais brancos	104,018 reais brancos
Guimarães (1445)	115,991 reais brancos	8,000 reais brancos

Sources: ANTT, *Chanc. D. Afonso V*, livs. 3, 5, 11, 18, 23, 25, 27 and 34; Leitura Nova, *Guadiana*, liv. 4.

of 1443 may indicate.[28] It reports the use of money for a specific purpose: the maintenance of walls and castles in the Alentejo or Entre-Tejo-e-Guadiana region.

Minting and war were important aspects of a kingdom's financial needs. In Portugal's case, extraordinary revenues could be a major boost in order to raise funds for costly enterprises. Two acquittance documents, of 1450 and 1453, illustrate this fact.[29] The first example concerns the amount collected in 1444 to help the Castilian king in war against the Infants of Aragon – 363,062 reais. The second example accounts for extraordinary aid for the same military campaigns – 163,252 reais in 1441 and 169,769 reais in 1444 – and was also collected to prevent currency devaluation, as well as a silver flow to other countries. The main question here that we would like to emphasize is: if small cities, like Moncorvo, could contribute with this amount, how much could the monarch obtain from the whole kingdom in every extraordinary collection throughout the country? Even with just some of the pieces, we can imagine this is likely the situation.

The selection of officials in charge of extraordinary rents, as well as those entrusted with lawsuits and issues related to this particular issue, were subjects in which representatives' towns and villages of origin refused to admit royal interference, although they were directly related to the privileges granted by the monarch. On some occasions, these officers were appointed by letter and were supposed to report to service (Gonçalves, 1964: 79) each time these extraordinary aids were collected. But the commandment was that those positions were occupied by different people, every time an extraordinary allowance was levied (Gonçalves, 1964: 80). On some occasions, the sovereign accepted some of the conditions established by the municipalities, meaning that cities should elect the officers (Gonçalves, 1964: 82–83). The monarch did not want to displease his subjects, nor did he want to create any resistance to the aids. Thus, the people could pay the contributions without any problems or complaints. In particular, the *avaliadores* and *sacadores* were appointed by popular election, even when the others were appointed by the king.

4.3. Expenditure

According to important scholars, expenditure is the starting point of late medieval and early modern finances. It must be considered, above all, from what the

State's primary obligations (Körner, 1995: 393) should be: to ensure obedience, obtaining the monopoly of force, neutralizing any possible focus of resistance and adopting what Max Weber called "legitimate violence". Moreover, to control and organize the economic dynamics, circulation of goods and services; provide the establishment of legal and material infrastructures to ensure production and trade; and finally, to play the central role of mediator in the cultural and spiritual life of its subjects, guarding and directing the best and most convenient way ideas and intellectual movements. Within these directives, however, separation and classification cause some difficulties, mainly because of the ambiguity with which many of them were described. Establishing categories was the first major challenge regarding the organization of this fundamental item of royal finances. In light of these precepts, and to reach a better understanding of this component, the categories are depicted and elucidated, as a fundamental step for analyzing the Portuguese Crown's ordinary expenditure:

1   **Personnel expenses/wages (Crown's officers)**: according to the most recent historiography, wages can be defined as scanty and deteriorating, in nominal terms, from the late fourteenth century until the early sixteenth century (Ferreira, 2007: 144). However, the point was to try to perceive this component in the documented description, as many times it was discriminated in conjunction with another type of payment, such as "provisions and clothing", "provisions, clothing and addition" or a surplus regarding some function previously carried out in extraordinary character, as in the case of João Gonçalves,[30] doorkeeper at the *almoxarifado* of Lamego, in 1435. Or as "provisions and clothing" only but followed by another kind of payment as a grace, for example, in a payment to Alvaro Gonçalves,[31] clerk of Setúbal's *almoxarifado* in 1439, which did not happen very often. Furthermore, it could be also described as "provisions, annuity and dwelling" or as "stipend and annuity". And even the "clothing" was mentioned in amounts, but could paid in kind, that is, with the clothes and/or fabrics themselves. Although it was mixed with other payments, this aspect of payment was defined as one of the components of ordinary spending.

2   **Tenças (pension; annuity)**: The *tença* – or *tenentia* – was a pension with which services rendered to the Crown were remunerated, attributed for the maintenance, more commonly to knights and noblemen who assisted the monarch in different situations – the *census pecuniarius vitalitius*, in the jurisconsults' common expression. It could be temporary or lifelong, thus opposing the *juro*, which was hereditary (Torres, 1985c: VI, 146). Annuities composed a large chunk of ordinary expenditure, automatically justifying their separation as a category on their own, to the point that the monarch was forced, on many occasions, to pay them with resources from extraordinary income. There were plenty of examples, as the acquittance letter to Vasco Afonso, king's esquire, responsible for collecting the *pedidos* in Torre de Moncorvo, between 1441 and 1448.[32] In 1441, annuities represented more than double what was spent on wages – 17,500 reais versus 8,245 reais,

respectively, which attests the importance of this component in the overall Crown's regular expenditure.

3   **Graces**: in its essence – *gratia* – it was defined as a recognition, gratitude, favor or benevolence,[33] close to *mercy*, although the distinction between the former and the latter within royal finances was very clear. They appear separately, with different values, in several occasions, in the expenses' list of the sources gathered. Within this context, the monarchical benevolence was extremely lavish, which led us to consider this element separately within the list of habitual expenditures. Examples were not hard to find. Based on the same extraordinary collection at Moncorvo in 1441, the graces constituted a total of 108,000 reais – more than ten times the amount paid in annuities – within a total of 163,251.5 reais, 66% of total expenditure. Another example was the acquittance to Garcia Fernandes, Infante Pedro's esquire, responsible for the collection of the *pedidos* in Abrantes, in the same year of 1441.[34] Only in graces, in that year, he paid 85,700 reais – more than seventeen times what was spent on wages in that year, for a total of 205,891.5 reais, or just over 41.5%. In any case, we do not intend to generalize these two cases because they were two peculiar *almoxarifados* with their own characteristics, so they probably do not reflect the general reality. Regardless of their particularities, those were still cases to be considered.

4   **Marriages**: the values referring to this segment of analysis vary greatly in the sources, which does not diminish its importance as a category of its own, nor in the characterization of the total spending directed to the nobility over the rest of the expenditure. Moreover, the pensions which the wealthy men, wealthy ladies, infants, knights, esquires or heirs annually received from the monasteries of which they had the patronage or any part of it, whether by foundation, purchase or inheritance (Serrão, 1984: 1, 517),[35] could also be included in the Crown's expenses, ordinary or extraordinary, as in the acquittance granted to João Cerveira,[36] Setúbal's *almoxarife* in 1449 and 1450, as well as in the letter given to Rui Lopes,[37] esquire of the royal household and responsible for the extraordinary collection – 4.5 *pedidos* – in Lamego between 1445 and 1449: 11,000 and 52,285 reais, respectively. Hence the reason why we choose this as one of the separate components.

5   **Mercies**: according to the traditional historiography, it has the same meaning of graces, benefits, *tenças*, donations and favors, but it is not like the categories previously established. Even in other Portuguese language dictionaries,[38] the meaning is still a "free gift" rather than a present offered as retribution (grace). However, this term is also defined as an "accounting or book entry".[39] Although closely related in fiscal terms, the effect produced is different because they constitute distinct payments in the expenditure list, regardless of whether they are ordinary or not, which has led us to separate them in a different group. With regard to their representativeness in the total amount, we limit ourselves to citing the end of the *Dictionary of History of Portugal* entry, when saying that "royal bounties often reached funds that significantly affected public revenues" (Torres, 1985a: IV, 276). Within the

initial conception of comparing the amounts spent on redistribution against the rest of the expenditure, this separation seems very important and needed.

6 **Dwellings**: this component would become fundamental in the duties' list and crucial in the royal accounts due to the disproportionate increase of nobility that surrounded Afonso V, which grew to the point of provoking endless grievances on the part of the provincial prosecutors in the *Cortes* gathered at Évora in 1481, and those of 1498 in Lisbon (Torres, 1985b: IV, 342). Although defined as an annuity (benefit, wage or pension) of variable value and enjoyed by noblemen whose names appeared in the royal house's books at the Royal Treasury's expense, they also constitute separate payments. Within the total, they represent the bulk of expenses reported by the sources, although more by the high quantity than by the individual value of installments. These are described in most cases as "dwelling and barley" or as "food, clothing and dwelling", an integral part of royal officials' wages, according to the example of the *annuity* and *dwelling* paid to Lamego's *almoxarife*, in 1437, worth 108,000 pounds for the whole year (9,000 pounds/month).[40] One of the Portuguese dictionaries affirmed that the term "differs from the *contia* and the *assentamento* ("settlement")".[41] For this reason, it was decided to separate it into its own category.

7 **Settlement (Assentamentos)**: as an agreement (or a sovereign's order) by which, mandatorily, the population concurred with some contribution, as for example cities' defense (Serrão, 1984: I, 234), as an extraordinary tax (*taille* or agreement with the city hall) the settlements would already have relevance for the municipal finances. However, the term also has the meaning of a mercy, paid in cash, to the noblemen who appeared in the King's books, when he grants them noble titles of Count, Marquis or Duke and, from that point onwards, they lose the dwellings.[42] Both are linked, but it was only possible to keep one of the housing aids. It would make sense, for the purposes of financial analysis, to unite them. Nevertheless the choice was to separate them in order to make the accounting as accurate as possible, along with the amount of benefits granted. In any case, it is important to note that this category could be responsible, in itself, for percentages that could exceed 82% of the total expenditure of an *almoxarifado*.[43]

8 **Duty Expenses/Provisions' acquisitions and others**: another important component of expenditure was the resources allocated to the provisions' acquirements, often directed toward to buying foodstuffs and equipment to be sent to African outposts.[44] In addition, as the category title itself states, here are described the expenses incurred by what was spent by officers to carry on their tasks, and shall not be mistaken, at any time, with the officers' *provision* previously described. Sometimes these expenses were quite reasonable, which attracted attention according to their description and led us to form a separate group from the others. In this category, it was also considered expenses with transference, i.e., renting mules for the transport of cash and goods, costs with paper, ink and books to make the accounting books, purchase of material (normally cloth) to make the bags to store objects or even

money that needed to be transported, expenses designated only as "small" and others with this profile.

9   **Others**: bearing in mind the amount of various costs that appeared listed in the sources, and which did not fit into any of the profiles defined by the categories listed earlier, we chose to separate them into another group. The main focus was not to open up the range of categories too much, which would make the analysis even more difficult. Although more generic and aware that these "others" or "miscellaneous" rubrics should be avoided whenever possible, we included in this category mixed and nondetailed expenditure, or in certain situations, alms to monasteries and religious orders and money for the orphans, for example.

Within the gathered set, the regular expenditure can be detailed, fundamentally, through the acquittances that dealt with the reigns of Afonso V and the first years of João II. From the perspective of source criticism, such meticulous descriptions can be interpreted as symptomatic of a Crown distressed by listing precisely what they're spending. With those costs properly measured and calculated and performing adequately in their accounts, in order to seek control of resources and not spending too much beyond their means, Portuguese kings tried to demonstrate their concern. This period, in particular, is relatively troubled, largely due to the very desire of Afonso V to follow in the footsteps of a dynasty which, for all intents and purposes, was still ephemeral. To summarize, the Avis dynasty since 1385, featured a king whose reign had been long but, for all effects, was a natural bastard son – João I – and who had been brought to the throne by an equivocal combination of social alliances and political accidents. He was followed by the brief reign of five years of his heir, Duarte I, outworn by the costs of the failed military campaign of Tangier in 1437. Ten years later, in 1448, the kingdom was threatened by a brief civil war between uncle and nephew (Infante Pedro and young prince Afonso, respectively). Within a dynasty affirmation process, the *African*[45] sought to consolidate it, to a great extent, through his monarchical project of income's direct redistribution or the nobility financial maintenance in exchange for political support and military service aimed at its preservation and stabilization.

During the reign of Manuel I (1495–1521), the acquittance letters did very little to explain the *almoxarifados'* expenses. This fact can also be understood to the other extreme, as a symptom of a period in which resources were abundant, still supported by the argument that little or nothing was found thereafter about the *pedidos* and *empréstimos*. The furthest record raised concerns with an acquittance to Álvaro Pires Machado, scribe in the province of *Trás-os-Montes* (Northeast).[46] In that source, he reported the accountability regarding the *pedidos* granted for the war against Castile in 1475, which does not detail general expenditure. The Fortunate[47] and his court experienced a new conjuncture of wealth, derived from overseas' commerce, which gave them resources, sumptuous constructions, sophistication, luxury and exoticism proportional to a king who had consolidated a true empire (Costa, 2005: 219). At its peak, in moments of abundance, expenses did not matter to a monarch and a kingdom in upward bias regarding other European courts (Costa, 2005: 204). Not by chance, this is also reflected in the absence of sources that were supposed to report extraordinary revenues. Of the 257 records collected between the beginning of his reign in 1495, and the first years of the reign of João III (1521–1557), only on two occasions were references to this type of expenditure found, which made no direct reference to his reign. There are many more records relating to overseas' trade. However, not being the focus of this study, we used a sample merely to establish a small comparison and to have a dimension of what would represent this new source of resources against the kingdom's ordinary revenues.

4.3.1. Ordinary expenditure

Analyzing the path of ordinary expenditure in the 1450s, we can see that it was normally, in a large number of cases, matched by regular revenues. However, it is important to remember the fundamental role of indirect taxes – *sisas* and *tithes* – expropriated from the councils and taken by the Crown. It seems clear that, without those concessions, those costs would hardly be covered.

Although many records show the values related to this component, there are not so many with detailed description within the categories stipulated earlier at the beginning of this section. In any case, these regular costs are duly identified in only four of the *almoxarifados*: Guarda, Lamego, Setúbal and Beja. Expenses were also meticulously identified in some of the components that constituted Lisbon's finances, notably those of the House of Supplication's chancery records and others related to the collection rights of *sisas* on colored cloths traded in the city. It is notorious the enormous expense's chunk essentially with three categories: annuities, graces and dwellings. The payment of those privileges to the nobility could mean more than 95% of total expenditure, as in the case of the Guarda's *almoxarifado* accounts[48] for 1436. There, Prince Henry the Navigator withdrew in that same year, 26,507,000 pounds – out of a total of 33,660,636.5 pounds collected by the *almoxarife* – even though it was used for the settlement of the city of Ceuta. Only this sum represents more than 78% of total revenues there in the respective period – more than 87% considering the expenditure. Yet in the same locality the following year, graces, on their own, were equivalent to approximately 55% of total expenses, another 18% in annuities and another 9% in dwellings. With these three components, 82% of the total expenditure is related to the redistribution policy. Less than 12% relate to the payment of wages, although it is important to note that many payments were combined, as described in the definitions presented at the beginning of this section. The remaining 6% relate to other expenses, purchases and miscellaneous expenditures.

Still in Guarda, in 1438, wage expenses jumped from 99,997 reais the previous year to 561,395.5 reais, an increase of more than 500%, as it can be seen in Table 4.2. Although this percentage value is impressive, it is also easily justifiable, with a number of "provision and wage" additions to people who were likely to participate in the ill-fated attempt to conquer Tangier, serving from Ceuta. Many

Table 4.2 Detailed expenditure at Guarda's fiscal branch (*almoxarifado*) (in approximate percentages of local total expenditure) in 1436, 1437, 1438 and 1449

YEAR	1436	1437	1438	1449
Personnel expenses/wages	3,7%	11,5%	65,5%	3,3%
Tenças	4,5%	18,6%	14,5%	28,2%
Graces	0,8%	54,9%	4%	1%
Marriages	–	–	–	–
Mercies	–	–	–	1,5%
Dwellings	1,8%	8,4%	–	0,8%*
Settlements	87,4%	–	–	–
Duty expenses/Provisions' acquisitions (in kind)	1,2%	1,3%	14,8%	64,6%
Others	0,6%	5,3%	1,2%	0,6%
TOTAL	100%	100%	100%	100%

* value concerning "dwellings and provisions" paid together, to Gonçalo Monteiro, respective *almoxarife*.

Sources: ANTT, *Chanc. D. Afonso V*, liv. 5, fl. 83v; liv. 11, fl. 47–47v and liv. 18, fl. 63–65.

of the payments were related to the "maintenance and wages of the time being in Ceuta", that is, people who served and, later received. Such as Álvaro de Barros, who received 300,000 reais "which took to Ceuta by order of the Lady Queen, my mother whose soul god would act to pay for provisions and stipends to some people who were there for our service".[49]

A decade later[50] the amount spent on wages in this *almoxarifado* was very small: 35,542 reais, or just over 3% of total expenditure – although the highest sum, in 1449 Guarda's accounting was assigned to Álvaro Fernandes, receiver of the Royal Treasury. He received the sum of 663,648 reais, approximately 64% of the total expenditure, to do some payments to the nobility: among those benefited by these resources were Duarte de Meneses, Diogo and Estêvão de Góis, and Vasco Fernandes Coutinho, first of the Counts of Marialva. One of the possible explanations for those payments could be the fact that they were partisans of the *African* in the battle of Alfarrobeira (Moreno, 1979: II, 792–795; 818–821; 874–881) that same year and, which shut down a civil war, with an enormous disruptive potential at an early stage. After the victory, they reaped the dividends of their political position. Another 303,869 *reais*, or approximately 28% were also related to annuities' payments (*tenças*) which, again, favored the same supporters, such as Duarte de Meneses, along with others such as João de Gouveia (Moreno, 1979: II, 825–827), Diogo Soares de Albergaria (Moreno, 1979: II, 687–690), Pero Lourenço de Almeida (Moreno, 1979: II, 708–710), among others. In addition to the two components – *tenças* and duty expenses/provisions' acquisitions – we then have the significant total of 92% of the expenditure of that fiscal year, directly or indirectly destined to the nobility, supporting the argumentation about the phenomenon of redistribution.

In Lamego, the situation was not much different, especially when the expenditure is observed in series between 1434 and 1441, as seen in Table 4.3.[51] In the first year, it is notorious the enormous amount reserved for the annual settlements'

Table 4.3 Detailed expenditure at Lamego's fiscal branch (*almoxarifado*) (in approximate percentages of local total expenditure), c. 1434–1441

YEAR	1434	1435	1436	1437	1438	1439	1440	1441
Personnel expenses/wages	0,9%	2,1%	1,96%	4,8%	2,9%	1,5%	0,7%	1,95%
Tenças	16,5%	13,1%	15,96%	11,1%	10,6%	44,9%	17%	11,7%
Graces	–	–	–	22,9%	12,7%	10,7%	4%	1,2%
Marriages	–	0,3%	–	–	–	–	–	–
Mercies	–	–	–	–	–	–	–	–
Dwellings	–	–	–	1,6%	1,7%	1%	46,5%	–
Settlements	82,4%	74,8%	81,9%	25,7%	–	23,2%	–	84,88%
Duty expenses/Provisions' acquisitions (in kind)	0,19%	0,1%	0,16%	33,88%	65,4%	3,9%	30,9%	0,2%
Others	0,01%	9,6%	0,02%	0,02%	6,7%	14,8%	0,9%	0,07%
TOTAL	100%	100%	100%	100%	100%	100%	100%	100%

Sources: ANTT, *Chanc. D. Afonso V*, liv. 27, fls. 116v and 133–136v.

payment to Prince Henry's household. His court was budgeted 13,862,600 pounds – out of a total of 14,518,000 pounds previously assigned. It represented 82% of 16,831,878 regarding that year's total expenditure planned, not unusual given the fact that he became Duke of Viseu[52] after the seizure of Ceuta in 1415. Furthermore, Lamego's *almoxarifado* was part of a tax jurisdiction that was inserted within his domains, although the regional supervisors (*Contadorias das Comarcas*) had not yet been created (Rau, 2009: 234–236).

In the following years, Prince Henry the Navigator withdrew generous sums from the treasury. In 1435 he received from that same *almoxarifado* 14,241,965 pounds, as part of his household annual settlement's sum; the following year, for the same reason, he received 13,387,202 pounds. In 1437, he took only 5,000,000 for the same reason, plus a "bonus" of 632,300 pounds as a mercy; in the next year, likely due to an exhausted treasury after the failed campaign of Tangier, no payment to Prince Henry appears but the sum of 1,085,000 pounds of the 4,000,000 assigned to him as a grace of that year. In 1439, the payments of his settlement amounted to 3,975,000 plus 700,000 per annuity, and a further 1,548,000 per royal decree – totaling 6,223,000 pounds. Finally, in 1440, there was no payment to the Prince. Regarding the *tenças* for the first year, it accounted for another 16% of this item, with special attention to the gratifications of 1,500,000 pounds attributed to Vasco Fernandes Coutinho (Moreno, 1979: II, 792–795), who received the same values in the following two years and other amounts for annuities and dwellings. Moreover, another 1,000,000 pounds to Diogo Gomes da Silva (Moreno, 1979: II, 949–951), who also received this same amount in the same years. Both would take Afonso V's party in the Battle of Alfarrobeira. Payments to officers would be less than 1%, and the residue would be distributed among alms and material expenses – such as the paper, parchments, cloth and rope to the bags in which the Queen's money was sent to village of Óbidos, and other small expenses.

Costs with officialdom and wage expenses also soared between 1434 and 1437. This item more than doubles between the first and second years, basically due to a single extraordinary payment to Vasco da Fonseca, judge of the *sisas* in Lamego, of 208,906 pounds, regarding his maintenance in 1434. Since then the judge's remuneration was shown in the following years, which is not the case in the expenditure description in the first year. In 1437, salary expenses took a giant leap to 940,778 pounds, which represents a significant increase over 400% in absolute values. On the other hand, it still represents only 5% of total expenditure.

In Setúbal's case, as seen in Table 4.4, the 1439 annual expenditure reported by João Cerveira,[53] receiver of the *almoxarifado*, did not give us sufficient data for a deeper analysis because the corresponding acquittance letter was incomplete. However, by means of another letter[54] granted to the same João Cerveira, royal household's esquire and also *almoxarife*, it was possible to perceive some situations for the following years of 1449 and 1450, although with a limited source sample. In the first year, the share related to the officials' remuneration concerns a little more than 1%. On the other hand, part of the settlement of Infanta Isabel, Afonso V's aunt, consumed 892,000 reais, more than 72% of that year's expenses.

Table 4.4 Detailed expenditure at Setúbal's fiscal branch (*almoxarifado*) (in approximate percentages of local total expenditure) in 1449 and 1450

YEAR	1449	1450
Personnel expenses/wages	1,2%	1,4%
Tenças	0,3%	1,5%
Graces	–	1,4%
Marriages	–	0,9%
Mercies	–	1,2%
Dwellings	–	16%
Settlements	72,6%	71,2%
Duty expenses/Provisions' acquisitions (in kind)	25,4%	5,75%
Others	0,5%	0,65%
TOTAL	100%	100%

Source: ANTT, *Chanc. D. Afonso V*, liv. 11, fl. 143v-144.

For Beja's case, it was possible to reconstitute a small sequence of data between 1439 and 1442 by means of three letters: the first one granted to Diogo Gonçalves Bocarro,[55] vassal, resident in town, and receiver of the respective *almoxarifado*, regarding the 1439 accounting. Furthermore, another one to João Rodrigues Costa,[56] concerning the accounts of 1440 and 1441, and the last one to Gonçalo Anes de Magalhães,[57] the royal household's esquire and also resident and receiver in town for 1442. Once again, the amount of payments attributed to the nobility, among *tenças*, graces, dwellings and settlements, is to be highlighted.

In the first year, officers' wages expenses totaled 1,642,194 pounds, which was equivalent to 4% of total expenditure. The larger portion was related to "miscellaneous" payments, with the purpose of fulfilling certain offices and services on behalf of the king, which accounted for 43%. Among these payments were, for example, wages paid to João Rodrigues Toscano and Rui Gomes da Silva, to perform reparations in some castles and in the houses within the castle of Campo Maior, respectively. There were also other payments, made to the own *almoxarife* João Rodrigues Costa, to spend some cash on the king's service. Also worth mentioning are the sums granted to Gonçalo Pacheco, treasurer of Ceuta's affairs in Lisbon, for two meat purchases valued at 3,000,500 and 3,500,000 pounds, respectively.

In addition, 8,915,554 pounds, or about 22%, were earmarked for other kinds of expenses, such as alms to the monasteries of St. Francis and St. Clara of Beja, valued at 10,000 pounds. Or the sum to the orphans of Beja and district, amounting to 6,615,553 pounds, paid in kind, money, silver and gold which had been taken to the army of Tangier. Added to this was the cash stipended to the royal household, as to Prince Henry, who received 353,500 pounds of 458,500 previously assigned to him that year. Moreover, other funds were allocated to Lopo Alvares de Moura (Sousa, 1747: XII, I, 461–462), son of Álvaro de Moura (Moreno, 1979: II, 895–896) – João I's esquire and member of the Royal council during the *African* government, with 472,626 pounds of part of payment of 525,000 pounds that were released there.

Finally, the remaining 31% were related to nobles' payments, standing out of the sum relative to the annuities, which benefited the Count of Arraiolos, Gomes Freire de Andrade, Mendo Afonso Cerveira, Duarte I's esquire and father of Duarte Cerveira (Moreno, 1979: II, 768–769), Afonso V's partisan in Alfarrobeira. Added to this is the remuneration to Prince João's annual settlement in two installments and Gonçalo Anes de Magalhães, Beja's *almoxarife*, previously mentioned, of 312,375 pounds received as part of the 450,000 released of half the money that had been awarded to him regarding his marriage.

The following year, wages constituted an even greater part of the whole, totaling 73,370 reais, or 7% of total expenditure. However, the percentage of costs related to payments granted to the nobility increased: the sum spent only in graces were 532,283 reais, plus 146,363 reais of *tenças*, another 7,000 reais assigned to a marriage, on top of 101,407 reais of dwellings and settlements, totaling at 787,053 reais, or 77% of that year's total expenditure. Only Prince João withdrew a generous sum, to which he had the right to his settlement and grace that year; his brother, Prince Henry the Navigator, received another considerable sum, as well as the Count of Arraiolos. Other expenses related to the offices and services performed on behalf of the king that year suffered a considerable reduction to 153,880.5 reais, 15% of the final amount. The remaining 1% refers to other expenses, mostly alms to the friars of S. Francisco and nuns of S. Clara of Beja. In 1441, expenditure with the offices slightly increased, to 9% of the total, while the expenses with services and services performed in the name of the king rose again to 49%, mainly due to a payment made to Fernão Gil, the monarch's treasurer, who received 363,050 reais, "for his office's costs" that year, which, compared to the amount dedicated to the nobles (between annuities, graces, dwellings and settlements) of 41%, totaling 356,827 reais, is quite significant. This decrease in payments is explained by the reduction in the *sisas* collection, which was the central pillar of the tax revenues. In fact, that was the central issue debated in the *Cortes* at Torres Vedras, in 1441, making it clear the need to improve its collection, thanks to concessions made in 1439 about specific items (Sousa, 1990: I, 360). Without that vital source of income, the redistribution policy would be at risk.

In the last year (1442), costs with officers' wages and provisions decreased to 6%, while payments to the nobility rose once again, reaching 78% of total expenditure, totaling 612,475.5 reais, among *tenças* (161.304), graces (20,900), marriages (7,460.5) and finally, dwellings and settlements (422,811), the largest share of this item. Repeatedly, substantial sums were referenced, such as 228,572 reais withdrawn by Prince João for his year's settlement. On top of that, the payment to Rui Gomes da Silva, a member of the Royal Council, who received 48,742 reais of dwellings owed to him and his sons, and Garcia Rodrigues de Sequeira, commander of the Order of Avis, for 54,571 reais of dwellings and other resources. Some "detached" expenses accounted for 15%, especially due to the payment made to Fernão Gil, the king's treasurer, in the amount of 114,091 reais. Other small costs and services executed in the king's name composed the remaining 1%, with a mere 1,928 reais, as observed in Table 4.5.

Table 4.5 Detailed expenditure at Beja's fiscal branch (*almoxarifado*) (in approximate percentages of local total expenditure), c.1439–1442

YEAR	1439	1440	1441	1442
Personnel expenses/wages	4%	7,25%	9,45%	6,1%
Tenças	17,7%	14,4%	9,8%	20,65%
Graces	7,2%	52,4%*	4,35%	2,7%
Marriages	0,8%	0,7%	–	0,95%
Mercies	0,4%	–	–	–
Dwellings	0,3%	0,4%	4,5%	13,8%
Settlements	4,8%	9,6%	22,5%	40,3%**
Duty expenses/Provisions' acquisitions (in kind)	43,1%	15,2%	49%	0,3%
Others	21,7%	0,05%	0,4%	15,2%
TOTAL	100%	100%	100%	100%

* Paid to Prince João, of "settlement and graces", paid together with no description/detail.
** Settlement paid to Prince João.

Sources: ANTT, *Chanc. D. Afonso V*, liv. 25, fl. 71–71v; liv. 27, fl. 65–65v; Leitura Nova, *Guadiana*, liv. 4, fl. 64–66v.

Regarding the cost of collecting *sisas* on colored cloths within the Lisbon tax area, they also offer a very small sample of three years in sequence: 1449–1451. The expenditure division observed is very uniform for almost all components, except for the first year, when the receiver of those taxes, João Afonso, receives 140,000 reais, "to apparel his body with gold cloth and silk".[58] If we combined this sum with the 1,322,972 received of his annual settlement, only these two combined would be enough to surpass the total revenues raised by that collection, of 1,405,714 reais. In addition, some expenditures on military and naval equipment were mentioned by two payments: one to João Sodré, *almoxarife* of Lisbon's warehouse, of 5,000 reais, concerning the bombards that were sent to Santarém by the king's order, and another one to Trisão Inglês ("English Tristan"), treasurer of Lisbon's shipyard, of 7,000 reais, related to the royal ballinger recently built there, of which he was in charge. Beyond that, little was spent with *tenças*, graces, weddings and mercies, just over 1%. Some general payments were made to Fernando da Guerra, archbishop of Braga, for his income from Torres Vedras, which totals 157,143 reais for each of the years in question. Furthermore, some payments were made to Queen Isabel: in the first year, 48,250 reais, for the governance of Master Martinho, her physicist; in the second year, 1,361,094 reais in payment of her annual settlement, apparel in cloth of gold and silk, through the incomes of Torres Vedras; in the third, she withdrew the considerable sum of 1,397,402 reais, for the same purposes. On top of that, the payments made in 1450 to Marco Lomellini, of 159,363 reais in silver, out of the 206,885 reais were assigned to him regarding the annual dwellings' payments; and in 1451, Lomellini with his Jewish partner, Judah Abravanel, received 183,900 reais part of the 200,000 for the same application.

With regard to what had been spent on the Office of the House of Supplication account,[59] we only have the expenditure details for 1452 and 1453 associated. In this sense, there was some difficulty in perceiving and separating some of the items mentioned in the sources. Expenditures totaled 1,051,415 reais for the two years of acquittance. Most were wages, of which we underlined the 910,069 reais for the receivers of the chancellery for their duty expenses, a figure that alone accounted for more than 86% of the amount not counting other remunerations. In addition, other amounts paid, totaling 74,826 reais, were paid to several people in the same years, taken as expenditure to the respective tax leaseholders and finally, three separate payments: one of 48,513 reais to Álvaro Fernandes de Monte Roio, noble of the royal household and Royal Treasury receiver, for general expenses of his office; another 1,000 reais, by grace attributed to Diogo Afonso, doorman of the chancery; and the last one to João Soveral, of 500 reais, as alms.

It was not possible to detail most of the expenditures. However, what immediately draws the attention were the high values spent on the nobility, making this component of royal spending virtually the center of royal spending, relatively to the control of state finances. Probably not all dwellings were listed, given that the means to meet those expenses of the royal entourage came from places and revenues of the most diverse and scattered throughout the kingdom.[60]

4.3.2. Extraordinary expenditure

With regard to extraordinary expenditure, it should first be pointed out that in order to describe this item of royal finances, we relied only on data from the source sample collected, from what was disbursed by the Crown compared to what was used by means of the fiscal instruments available to it, that is to say, the *pedidos* and the *empréstimos*, mainly concentrated in the reigns of Afonso V and João II. Here, we limited ourselves to observe and perceive the dynamics of what was possible to collect from the people and what those means were intended for. Apparently, at first, they served chiefly for war enterprises and marriages of princes and kings (Gonçalves, 1964: 130). Nevertheless, the sources gathered proved to be more than that. The distribution – or *redistribution* – of the income was fed back with part of these resources. The ordinary expense was also boosted with these earnings, in addition to paying war expenses, defense, maintenance of the existing equipment (walls, castles and others) or the acquisition of new warfare gear, in addition to financing of court marriages and, finally, the administration's part more directly linked to the monarch, the Royal Treasury, which concerned the king's household and its finances, an integral part of the *Contos* (Rau, 2009: 26–31).

It is possible to observe this phenomenon in Lamego by means of the accountability of the *pedido* collected to build the army for the siege of Tangier in 1437. Of the total raised by the extraordinary collection, the costs that actually concerned the people's preparation and of the garrisons for the campaign in question was 63% of total amount, which was normal and expected for this type of income. In other words, the court did not go to war spending from their own pockets.

The resources were withdrawn from those mechanisms and reallocated among the noblemen, and payments, as the one made to Fernão Coutinho, brother of Vasco Fernandes Coutinho, Count of Marialva, in the amount of 2,770,610 pounds, for the outfitting of thirty men of arms and forty-five men on foot to serve in the fleet that would assault that African outpost, was one item on this list of remunerations. On the other hand, payments regarding services on behalf of the monarch, as well as the operating costs of offices and functions constitute just over 28% of this component; of these, only the *pedido*'s receiver in Lisbon, João Esteves de Vila Nova, took out 6,293,000 pounds, "which the King ordered him to deliver to the expenses of his office", accounting for 92% of the total, in addition to another outstanding sum in his name, of 1,750,000 pounds, also for the same function exercised the previous year. A mere 0.5% was to pay graces in this particular case, and the remainder to salary payments – provisions and wages – mixed with benefits, such as the one paid to Vasco da Fonseca, footman of João I, in the value of 95,270 pounds, for his grace and his provisions, and of two men on foot to serve with him in the army of Tangier.

In another example, it is possible to verify the use of resources destined for a particular purpose, such as the service of the Jews and the tithes that were primarily directed toward to the maintenance of Ceuta and its blacksmiths. Of that collection done in 1437, whose accounts were provided by Afonso Cerveira,[61] receiver at the *almoxarifado* of Guarda, 33% of expenses were made up of payments that were made for the king's service. Except on two occasions, which was the compensation to João Esteves de Vila Nova to receive the tithes, in the amount of 19,736 reais, and another 330 reais concerning the money's transportation to Lisbon. The remaining 67% consists of remunerations to João de Queirós, of 43,300 reais and Luís Pires, Prince Pedro's esquire, of 21,648 reais, which we suspect were graces conceded as rewards for services to the monarch, an argument reinforced by another item paid to Gonçalo Vasques de Castelo Branco, in the amount of 6,000 reais of grace within that collection.

The kingdom defense structures' maintenance also appeared in the sources gathered, as in the case of an acquittance granted to Diogo Álvares,[62] esquire of Prince Diogo of Portugal, João I's grandson and realm's constable. He received the income destined to repair walls and castles in the Alentejo region, i.e., district of Entre-Tejo-e-Guadiana in 1442. The *Cortes* of Torres Vedras, in the previous year among the various subjects discussed, brought the fear of a possible Castilian invasion and, therefore, it was essential to ensure the border line's defense. It was urgent to obtain money from the people and, in order to avoid the cash drain (silver in particular) as well as its application in other situations. To this purpose, a *pedido* was drawn up and new legislation on the currency was issued, so as to avoid transactions with silver outside the royal exchanges and the consequent rise of its value beyond what was already practiced in other kingdoms (Sousa, 1990: I, 360). In this sense, he accounted for a total expense of approximately 121,938 reais, of which 60% was for repairs in all fortresses along the Castilian borderline – Mértola, Noudar, Mourão, Tercena, Alandroal, Elvas, Marvão and Castelo de Vide, among others, as well as to the purchase of military supplies and the *virotões* ("short arrows", projectiles for cross-bows), besides 30% reserved for wages and maintenance of the people involved. Furthermore, the other 10% were graces and other small expenses – rent of mules and messengers who had to receive the revenues in the hinterlands' localities, paper, parchments, paint, bags and others.

About the same *pedido*, another letter was issued to Garcia Fernandes,[63] Prince Pedro's esquire and receiver at the Abrantes' *almoxarifado*. The largest share of that expenditure was particularly related to "graces and supplies", more than 40% was spent in amounts attributed by the monarch without any sort of financial compensation, contrasting with pensions paid for services rendered. Along with this, some money to pay for foodstuffs' purchase, which constituted the other 59%, namely wheat and flour, delivered to one of Prince Pedro supplies' officer and other people in a sum of rations, in addition to provisions to the captain and people who were with him at the siege of Meira, and another part sent to Crato.

Another interesting feature is the presence of Moors as officers regarding the extraordinary collection within the *Algarve*, confirmed by a letter to Afonso Soeiro,[64] Prince Pedro's esquire. He was resident in Faro and receiver of the *pedidos* approved at the *Cortes* of Évora in 1442, facing the imminence of a conflict with Castile for the support given to Queen Leonor of Aragon to return to regency and her son's tutoring (Sousa, 1990: I, 362–363), future king Afonso V. That income was collected during the whole year, as well as the following year in Faro, Loulé, Silves and Tavira. Regarding the first, practically the total expenditure was represented by a payment to Gonçalo Papo, messenger of Prince João, in the amount of 60,400 reais. In the following year, this same expense is roughly divided into two payments: one to Gonçalo Esteves, withdrawer, resident in Tavira, in the amount of 20,382 reais. In short, the king was paying in kind the exchange deals made with Genoese merchants, goods bought with extraordinary revenues. The other payment went to Martim Pousado, Fernão Seixas' lieutenant and Faro's *almoxarife*, for the sum of 48,063 reais.

In Tavira, another *pedido* would still be taken, registered by a letter describing things destined for Ceuta,[65] in 1442. In that source, only a single grace was identified, in the amount of 1,000 *reais*, paid to João Garcia de Contreiras, royal household's knight, concerning some silver that had been bought. The purchase of that same silver generated most of that expenditure: 80,150 reais, being more than 80% of total. The residual consisted of small expenses (payments and supplies to the people who served in Ceuta) to the chief withdrawer of that *pedido*, Afonso Anes, and two others to Tomé Afonso, merchant, of 4,800 reais as part of a 20,800 reais payment that corresponded to 1,920 bushels of wheat given to the maintenance of those who were in that same African outpost, and to Tropel de Vivaldo, a Genoese merchant, of 6,000 reais related to a king's charter, who sent him to some places on his service.

Within this context, the acquittance attributed to Pedro Afonso Malheiro,[66] receiver of a *pedido* at Ponte de Lima's *almoxarifado*, with some funds related to Ceuta, supplies evidence of this and of more subsidies offered to the nobility. Moreover, other resources were already earmarked for military expenditures to prepare for a potential conflict with the Castilian kingdom. Of the total expenditure pointed out by this source, only 12% composed what had been spent with that African outpost; between purchases and duty expenses, another 12%; but the majority, 51%, was destined, in fact, for payments to the nobility who moved toward "the border of upper Minho river", for defense. The main receiver was the Duke of Braganza, for the sum of 200,000 reais. Moreover, some for the men of arms' maintenance sent to the northeastern border, plus another 20,000 reais for the expenditure he had made there. Also, another nobleman, Leonel de Lima, for 129,603 reais for his maintenance and his horses' that took him to his affairs within the embassy that went to Castile. Finally, the remaining 25% were made up of *tenças*, graces, mercies and dwellings. One of them, Sancho de Noronha, received 119,617 reais of his 1441 annual settlement that had remained to be paid. Moreover, Leonel de Lima was paid another 10,000 reais in graces. Rui Vaz Pereira, a royal household nobleman, received 20,000 reais of graces. Pedro Machado, esquire, also was paid 5,000 reais of grace, and Pedro Afonso, the *pedido*'s receiver, was given 2,000 reais regarding his task of collecting income.

In another acquittance issued to Rui Lopes,[67] royal household esquire and receiver of Lamego's *almoxarifado*, it was possible to observe the raise of endowments and warfare costs. Of the four *pedidos*' procedures between 1444 and 1449, the expenses involving marriages and the preparation for new military enterprises appeared in the foreground. That was mainly due to the Prince of Aragon's imminent victory over Juan II of Castile, and the need to help him (Sousa, 1990: I, 365–366), dealt with in the *Cortes* of Évora in 1444, besides the confirmation and betrothal of the *African* with Princess Isabel (Sousa, 1990: I, 367–371), daughter of the Regent, discussed in the following *Cortes* of Lisbon, in 1446, and again at Évora, in 1447. These two events took the first two extra collections, followed by the other two in addition to the tithes.

In this record, the great amount of benefits to the nobles is clear. Of the expenditure from the first collection, about 20% was destined to the payment of graces, including the individual payment to Prince Henry the Navigator, of 50,000 reais. From the other 30% of duty expenses and services rendered to the monarch, we highlight the remuneration to Fernão Gil, king's treasurer, and to his son, Álvaro Fernandes, regarding their positions, of 90,000 and 10,000 reais, respectively. Another 45% was related to other expenditure, such as the payment to Afonso Vaz, Prince Pedro's steward, of 104,000 reais. The remaining 5% consisted of payments for dwellings, wages and provisions made altogether. Related to the second collection, the same tendency remains. About 85% of expenditure was destined to "embedded" gratuities in the wages, as evidenced by the payments to Fernão Coutinho, a member of the Royal Council, of 225,400 reais, regarding wage, grace and maintenance for him and his people, when he went with Prince Pedro to the Castilian king's assistance.

Except for the small expenses, the remaining 15% consisted of more than one payment paid separately, with a single exception.[68] The third extraordinary collection, already destined to Afonso V's marriage, had as part of its costs one item that alone comprised 91% of that expenditure, destined to Diogo Afonso de Goião, resident in Santarém, in the amount of 508,795 reais, who were handed over to a series of officers. Finally, 77% of the final collection's expenses were spent on duty costs and items purchased, in which two items stand out: one to Fernão Gil, treasurer of the royal household, of 72,000 reais, and another to Leonardo Lomellini, of 170,500 reais, as part of the payment of certain golden and sirgo cloths imported from Italy.

In Torre de Moncorvo, another source illustrates the same redistributive procedure. In the acquittance given by Vasco Afonso,[69] royal household esquire and vassal resident in the same village and receiver in the respective *almoxarifado* regarding the *pedidos* collected between 1441 and 1448, which supposedly were relative to the preparations for kingdom's defense; 66% of that money was directed toward to the payment of graces. Furthermore, 92% of total was spent only on items intended for "redistribution". In the following collection of 1444, justified by the support to the Castilian king's aid, about 95% was destined for only two payments: Fernão Gil, royal treasurer, for 115,000 reais, with the justification not identified, and Afonso Vaz, Prince Pedro's steward, for another 40,000 reais, "for the maintenance of said Prince".

The marriage of Princess Joana, registered by the acquittance granted to João Lourenço da Seara,[70] royal household esquire and receiver at the *almoxarifado* of Lamego, follows the same line. Part of the *pedido* granted by the *Cortes* of Lisbon in 1455 (Sousa, 1990: I, 374–376), and still being charged in 1457, was responsible for an expense distributed as follows: approximately 50% for payments to Martim Zapata, identified only as treasurer, without further details, for a total of 101,893 reais; 17% related to the expenses with Queen Isabel; 13% for wages and provisions; another 13% to debt payments and embassies; and the remaining 7% at mercies and public officers' marriages. In any case, the phenomenon of *redistribution* was notorious, with payments made through the subterfuge of extraordinary revenues beyond the perception of the mechanisms involving the payments and the context in which each subsidy was raised with the people. The moments of greatest tension, the Avis' kings thirst for conquest, in particular that of Afonso V, maintained a state of "permanent" war, greatly burdening the treasury, which was fundamental to keep open a channel of dialogue with the peoples' representatives in the *Cortes*, in order to legitimize the use of this mechanism. This was fundamental to Portuguese finances and for the capture of wealth, on which all the political projects of the dynasty's maintenance would be based.

Notes

1 Beforehand, those taxes could be charged only on a particular product or kind, in a municipal or national context.
2 The same studies highlighted the near absence of extra charges to assist the Portuguese African outposts. See Faro (1965), Sousa (1990) and Henriques (2008).
3 ANTT, *Leitura Nova*, Além-Douro, liv. 3, fl. 285v-286.
4 ANTT, *Chanc. D. Afonso. V*, liv. 23, fl. 30.
5 The word *Foral* (*Fuero* in Spanish), which derives from the Latin word *forum*, designates a royal document which establishes a council or municipality, regulating its administration, borders and privileges.
6 ANTT, *Chanc. D. Afonso V*, liv. 18, fl. 63–65.

7 ANTT, *Chanc. D. Afonso V*, liv. 27, fl. 65–65v.
8 In 1435/1436, Duarte I (1433–1438) created a new currency: the *real*, with higher silver content in its composition, hence known as *reais brancos*. We used to convert the rate of 1 Real = 35 libras (pounds). To the use of those values and the monetary reform, see Barros (1945: III, 148–149); Duarte (2005). See also Marques (1996) and Ferreira (2007).
9 See Fernandes (2012).
10 See Saraiva (2003).
11 See Boissellier (2012).
12 ANTT, *Chanc. D. Afonso V*, liv. 23, fl. 30.
13 See Andrade (2005).
14 See Rau (1984).
15 See Silveira (2007).
16 See Oliveira (2008).
17 See Braga (1998) and Costa (2007).
18 It is estimated that 40% of lands and rights were under control of military orders at the end of the fourteenth century; of this total, approximately 25% belonged to the Order of Santiago. Fernandes (2002: 1, 72–73).
19 See Rodrigues (1998: 165–181).
20 ANTT, *Chanc. D. Afonso V*, liv. 34, fl. 162v. Published in Azevedo (1915: I, 412–416).
21 ANTT, Leitura Nova, *Além Douro*, liv. 4, fl. 104–104v.
22 ANTT, *Chanc. D. Afonso V*, liv. 27, fl. 133–136 v.
23 ANTT, Leitura Nova, *Estremadura*, liv. 4, fl. 281v-282.
24 ANTT, Leitura Nova, *Beira*, liv. 3, fl. 84–84v; ANTT, *Chanc. D. Manuel I*, liv. 5, fl. 9v; copied at Leitura Nova, *Estremadura*, liv. 13, fl. 197v. Published in Freire (1904: II, 360).
25 ANTT, *Chanc. D. Afonso V*, liv. 34, fl. 159v. Published in Azevedo (1915: I, 417–419).
26 ANTT, *Chanc. D. Afonso V*, liv. 27, fl. 133–136v.
27 ANTT, *Chanc. D. Afonso V*, liv. 5, fl. 83v. Published in Azevedo (1915: I, 331–339).
28 ANTT, *Chanc. D. Afonso V*, liv. 27, fl. 5v-6v.
29 ANTT, *Chanc. D. Afonso V*, liv. 34, fl. 68v-69. Published in Gonçalves (1964: 239–244): ANTT, *Chanc. D. Afonso V*, liv. 3, fl. 13v-15. Published in Gonçalves (1964: 246–257).
30 ANTT, *Chanc. D. Afonso V*, liv. 27, fl. 133–136v.
31 ANTT, *Chanc. D. Afonso V*, liv. 23, fl. 2–3; copied at Leitura Nova, *Guadiana*, liv. 6, fl. 122v.
32 ANTT, *Chanc. D. Afonso V*, liv. 3, fl. 13v-15. Published in Gonçalves (1964: 246–257).
33 Definition found in 2013/01/09 in the *Dicionário Houaiss da Língua Portuguesa*, online version [http://houaiss.uol.com.br].
34 ANTT, *Chanc. D. Afonso V*, liv. 27, fl. 129v-130v. Published in Gonçalves (1964: 228–232).
35 Serrão (1984: 1, 517).
36 ANTT, *Chanc. D. Afonso V*, liv. 11, fl. 143v-144.
37 ANTT, *Chanc. D. Afonso V*, liv. 34, fl. 68v-69. Published in Gonçalves (1964: 239–244).
38 Definition found in 2013/01/09, in Silva (1813).
39 Definition found in 2013/01/09 in the *Dicionário Houaiss da Língua Portuguesa*, online version [http://houaiss.uol.com.br].
40 ANTT, *Chanc. D. Afonso V*, liv. 27, fl. 133–136v.
41 Definition found in 2013/01/09, in Silva (1813).
42 Definition found in 2013/01/09, in Silva (1813).
43 ANTT, *Chanc. D. Afonso V*, liv. 27, fl. 133–136v.
44 For example, the acquittance granted to Martim Afonso, receiver of the Ceuta's goods at Beja's *almoxarifado* between 1451 and 1452, which account for many products accounted in kind, destined to supply that Portuguese in Africa. ANTT, *Chanc. D. Afonso V*, liv. 13, fl. 93v. Published in Azevedo (1915: I, 153–155).

45 Afonso V's epithet.
46 ANTT, *Chanc. D. João II*, liv. 19, fl. 91.
47 Manuel I's epithet.
48 ANTT, *Chanc. D. Afonso V*, liv. 18, fl. 63–65.
49 ANTT, *Chanc. D. Afonso V*, liv. 5, fl. 83v.
50 ANTT, *Chanc. D. Afonso V*, liv. 11, fl. 47–47v.
51 ANTT, *Chanc. D. Afonso V*, liv. 27, fl. 133–136 v.
52 For more about Henry the Navigator, see Costa (2009), Russell (2001) and Sousa (1991).
53 ANTT, *Chanc. D. Afonso V*, liv. 23, fl. 2–3; copied in Leitura Nova, *Guadiana*, liv. 6, fl. 122v.
54 ANTT, *Chanc. D. Afonso V*, liv. 11, fl. 143v-144.
55 ANTT, Leitura Nova, *Guadiana*, liv. 4, fl. 64–66v.
56 ANTT, *Chanc. D. Afonso V*, liv. 27, fl. 65–65v.
57 ANTT, *Chanc. D. Afonso V*, liv. 25, fl. 71–71v.
58 ANTT, *Chanc. D. Afonso V*, liv. 34, fl. 157v.
59 ANTT, *Chanc. D. Afonso V*, liv. 15, fl. 73v-74; copied in Leitura Nova, *Livro dos Extras*, fl. 84.
60 As in 1435 all the income assigned to Prince Henry's settlement came, almost totally, from Lamego's *almoxarifado*, the one to attend the Count of Arraiolos, in 1440, would come almost integrally from Beja's. ANTT, *Chanc. D. Afonso V*, liv. 27, fls. 65–65v e 133–136v.
61 ANTT, *Chanc. D. Afonso V*, liv. 5, fl. 83v. Published in Azevedo (1915: I, 331–339).
62 ANTT, *Chanc. D. Afonso V*, liv. 27, fl. 5v-6v.
63 ANTT, *Chanc. D. Afonso V*, liv. 27, fl. 129v-130v. Published in Gonçalves (1964: 228–232).
64 ANTT, *Chanc. D. Afonso V*, liv. 24, fl. 3–3v. Published in Gonçalves (1964: 233–235).
65 ANTT, *Chanc. D. Afonso V*, liv. 5, fl. 73v. Published in Azevedo (1915: I, 328–331).
66 ANTT, *Chanc. D. Afonso V*, liv. 34, fl. 159. Published in Azevedo (1915: I, 417–419).
67 ANTT, *Chanc. D. Afonso V*, liv. 34, fl. 68v-69. Published in Gonçalves (1964: 239–244).
68 Except for Diogo Soares de Albergaria, in the amount of 49,500 reais, for his wife's grace, dwelling and *tença*, and which partially covered what was owed to him.
69 ANTT, *Chanc. D. Afonso V*, liv. 3, fl. 13v-15. Published in Gonçalves (1964: 246–257).
70 ANTT, *Chanc. D. Afonso V*, liv. 36, fl. 123–123v. Published in Gonçalves (1964: 258–261).

Bibliography

Primary sources

ANTT, Chanc. D. Afonso V, liv. 3.
ANTT, Chanc. D. Afonso V, liv. 5.
ANTT, Chanc. D. Afonso V, liv. 11.
ANTT, Chanc. D. Afonso V, liv. 13.
ANTT, Chanc. D. Afonso V, liv. 15.
ANTT, Chanc. D. Afonso V, liv. 18.
ANTT, Chanc. D. Afonso V, liv. 23.
ANTT, Chanc. D. Afonso V, liv. 24.
ANTT, Chanc. D. Afonso V, liv. 25.
ANTT, Chanc. D. Afonso V, liv. 27.
ANTT, Chanc. D. Afonso V, liv. 34.
ANTT, Chanc. D. Afonso V, liv. 36.
ANTT, Chanc. D. João II, liv. 19.
ANTT, Chanc. D. Manuel I, liv. 5.
ANTT, Leitura Nova, Além Douro, liv. 3.

ANTT, Leitura Nova, Além Douro, liv. 4.
ANTT, Leitura Nova, Beira, liv. 3.
ANTT, Leitura Nova, Estremadura, liv. 4.
ANTT, Leitura Nova, Estremadura, liv. 13.
ANTT, Leitura Nova, Guadiana, liv. 4.
ANTT, Leitura Nova, Guadiana, liv. 6.
ANTT, Leitura Nova, Livro dos Extras.

Secondary sources, royal chronicles and dictionaries

Azevedo, P. de. (1915–1934). *Documentos das chancelarias reais anteriores a 1531 relativos a Marrocos*, 2 vols. Lisbon: Academia das Sciências de Lisboa.

Dicionário Houaiss da Língua Portuguesa, Online version [http://houaiss.uol.com.br/].

Faro, J. (1965). *Receitas e despesas da Fazenda Real de 1384 a 1481: subsídios documentais*. Lisbon: Instituto Nacional de Estatística.

Fernandes, R. (2012). *Descrição do terreno ao redor de Lamego duas léguas [1531–1532]*. Edição, estudo introdutório e Apêndice documental de Amândio Jorge Morais Barros. Casal de Cambra: Edições Caleidoscópio.

Freire, A. B. (1904). Livro das Tenças del Rei, in *Archivo Historico Portuguez*. Lisbon: Of. Typographica-Calçada do Cabra, 81–157; 201–227.

Freire, A. B. (1903–1916). Cartas de Quitação del rei D. Manuel, in *Archivo Historico Portuguez*, 11 vols. Lisbon: Of. Typographica-Calçada do Cabra.

Freire, A. B. (1908). Outro capítulo das finanças manuelinas, os Cadernos dos Assentamentos, in *Archivo Historico Portuguez*. Lisbon: Of. Typographica-Calçada do Cabra, 233–240; 443–444.

Lopes, F. (1945). *Crónica de D. João I*. Edição prefaciada por António Sérgio. Porto: Livraria Editora Civilização.

Serrão, J. (1984–1985). *Dicionário de História de Portugal*, 6 vols. Porto: Livraria Figueirinhas.

Silva, A. M. (1813). *Diccionario da lingua portugueza – recompilado dos vocabularis impressos ate agora, e nesta segunda edição novamente emendado e muito acrescentado, por Antonio de Moraes Silva*. Lisbon: Typographia Lacerdina. [Available Online in the Brazilian Studies' Digital Library, at the University of São Paulo (Brasiliana USP): www.brasiliana.usp.br/dicionario].

Sousa, D. A. C. de. (1735–1749). *Historia genealogica da Casa Real Portugueza: desde a sua origem até o presente, com as Familias illustres, que procedem dos Reys, e dos Serenissimos Duques de Bragança*, 13 vols. Lisbon: Academia Real.

Torres, R. A. (1985a). "Mercê", in *Dicionário de História de Portugal*. Porto: Livraria Figueirinhas, 4, 276.

Torres, R. A. (1985b). "Moradia", in *Dicionário de História de Portugal*. Porto: Livraria Figueirinhas, 4, 342.

Torres, R. A. (1985c). "Tença", in *Dicionário de História de Portugal*. Porto: Livraria Figueirinhas, 6, 146.

Studies

Andrade, A. A. (2005). A estratégia régia em relação aos portos marítimos no Portugal medieval: o caso da fachada atlântica, in *Ciudades y Villas Portuárias del Atlântico en la Edad Media*. Najera. Encuentros internacionales del Medievo: 27–30 de julio 2004, Logroño: Instituto de Estúdios Riojanos, 57–89.

Andrade, A. A., & Silveira, A. C. (2007). Les aires portuaires de la péninsule de Setubal à la fin du Moyen Âge, in *Ports et littoraux de l'Europe atlantique. Transformations naturelles et aménagements humains (XIVe-XVIe siècles)*, sous la direction de Michel Bochaca and Jean-Luc Sarrazin. Rennes: Presses Universitaires de Rennes, 147–165.

Barros, H. da G. (1945). *História da Administração Pública em Portugal nos Séculos XII a XV: 2ª edição dirigida por Torquato de Sousa Soares*, 11 vols. Lisbon: Livraria Sá da Costa Editora.

Boissellier, S. (2012). *La Construction Administrative d'un Royaume: Registres de Bénéfices Ecclésiastiques Portugais (XIII-XIVe Siècles)*. Lisbon: UCP-CEHR.

Bonney, R. (1995). Revenues, in R. Bonney (ed.), *Economic Systems and State Finance*. Oxford: Oxford University Press, 423–505.

Braga, I. M. R. M. D. (1998). A produção artesanal, in A. H. de O. Marques (dir.), de J. J. A. Dias (coord.), *Nova História de Portugal – vol. V: do Renascimento a crise dinástica*. Lisbon: Ed. Presença, 182–194.

Braga, P. D. (1998). *Setúbal medieval: séculos XIII a XV*. Apresentação de A. H. de Oliveira Marques. Setúbal: Câmara Municipal de Setúbal.

Costa, J. P. O. e. (2005). *D. Manuel I: um príncipe do Renascimento*. Mem Martins: Círculo de Leitores.

Costa, J. P. O. e. (2009). *Henrique, o Infante*. Lisbon: Esfera dos Livros.

Costa, M. L. F. (2007). A construção naval, in J. Mattoso (dir.), de J. R. Magalhães (coord.), *História de Portugal – vol. V – No Alvorecer da Modernidade (1480–1620)*. Mem Martins: Círculo de Leitores, 314–332.

Duarte, L. M. (2005). *D. Duarte: requiem por um rei triste*. Mem-Martins: Círculo de Leitores.

Duarte, L. M. (2006). A memória contra a História: as sisas medievais portuguesas, in D. Menjot & M. Sánchez Martínez (dir.), *Fiscalidad de Estado y fiscalidad municipal en los reinos hispánicos medievales: estudios dirigidos por Denis Menjot y Manuel Sánchez Martínez*. Madrid: Casa de Velázquez, 433–445.

Fernandes, M. C. R. de S. (2002). *A Ordem Militar de Santiago no séc. XIV*. M. A. dissertation. Porto: Faculty of Arts.

Ferreira, S. C. (2007). *Preços e Salários em Portugal na Baixa Idade Média*. M. A. Thesis. Porto: Faculty of Arts.

Gelabert González, J. E. (1995). The Fiscal Burden, in R. Bonney (ed.), *Economic Systems and State Finance*. Oxford: Oxford University Press, 539–576.

Gomes, S. A. (2006). *D. Afonso V: o Africano*. Mem Martins: Círculo de Leitores.

Gonçalves, I. (1964). *Pedidos e empréstimos públicos em Portugal durante a Idade Média*. Lisbon: Cadernos de Ciência e Técnica Fiscal: Centro de estudos fiscais da direcção-geral das contribuições e impostos – Ministério das Finanças.

Gonçalves, I. (1987). As finanças municipais do Porto na segunda metade do século XV. Porto: Câmara Municipal do Porto, 1987.

Henriques, A. M. B. de M. de C. (2008). *State Finance, War and Redistribution in Portugal (1249–1527)*. Ph.D. Thesis. Department of History, University of York.

Körner, M. (1995). Expenditure, in R. Bonney (ed.), *Economic Systems and State Finance*. Oxford: Oxford University Press, 393–422.

Ladero Quesada, M. A. (2009). *La Hacienda Real de Castilla (1369–1504): estúdios y documentos*. Madrid: Real Academia de la Historia.

Ladero Quesada, M. A. (2011). *Fiscalidad y Poder Real en Castilla (1252–1369)*, 2nd ed. Madrid: Real Academia de la Historia.

Magalhães, J. R. (2012). Breve Panorama da História Económica em Portugal (1860–2004), in J. R. Magalhães, *No Portugal Moderno: Espaços, tratos e dinheiros – Miúnças 3*. Coimbra: Coimbra University Press.

Marques, A. H. de O., & Serrão, J. (dir.). (1987). *Nova História de Portugal, vol. IV – Portugal na crise dos séculos XIV e XV*. Lisbon: Ed. Presença.

Marques, A. H. de O., & Dias, J. J. A. (1998). As Finanças e a Moeda, in A. H. de O. Marques (dir.), de J. J. A. Dias (coord.), *Nova História de Portugal, vol. V – Portugal do renascimento à crise dinástica*. Lisbon: Ed. Presença, 249–276.

Marques, M. G. (1996). *História da Moeda Medieval Portuguesa*. Sintra: Instituto de Sintra.

Mattoso, J. (2006). Dois séculos de vicissitudes políticas, in J. Mattoso (dir.), *História de Portugal, vol. III: A Monarquia Feudal*. Mem Martins: Circulo de Leitores, 20–171.

Merêa, P. (2006). Organização Social e Administração Pública, in P. Merêa, *Estudos de História de Portugal*. Lisbon: INCM, 129–231.

Moreno, H. B. (1979–1980). *A Batalha de Alfarrobeira. Antecedentes e significado histórico*, 2 vols. Coimbra: Imprensa da Universidade.

Oliveira, J. A. (2008). *Na Península de Setúbal, em finais da Idade Média: organização do espaço, aproveitamento dos recursos e exercício do poder*. Ph.D. Thesis. Lisbon: Nova University of Lisbon.

Pereira, J. C. (2003). *Portugal na Era de Quinhentos: estudos varios*. Cascais: Patrimonia.

Rau, V. (1984). As Marinhas de Setúbal e de Alcácer do Sal, in *Estudos sobre a História do Sal Português*. Lisbon: Presença, 66–88.

Rau, V. (2009). *A Casa dos Contos: os três mais antigos regimentos dos contos*. Lisbon: Imprensa Nacional-Casa da Moeda [re-edition of 1951 and 1959 original prints].

Rodrigues, A. M. S. A. (1998). A produção agro-pecuária, in A. H. de O. Marques (dir.), de J. J. A. Dias (coord.), *Nova História de Portugal, vol. V – Portugal do renascimento à crise dinástica*. Lisbon: Ed. Presença, 165–181.

Rodrigues, T. F. (1982). Para a História da Administração da Fazenda Real no Reinado de D. Afonso V (1438–1453), in *Homenagem a A. H. de Oliveira Marques*. Lisbon: Editorial Estampa, Separata de Estudos de História de Portugal, vol. I (sécs. X–XV), 273–289.

Russell, P. (2001). *Prince Henry 'The Navigator': A Life*. New Haven: Yale University Press.

Saraiva, A. M. de S. (2003). *A Sé de Lamego na primeira metade do séc. XIV (1296–1349)*. Leiria: Edições Magno.

Schulze, W. (1995). The Emergence and Consolidation of the 'Tax State'. I – The Sixteenth Century, in R. Bonney (ed.), *Economic Systems and State Finance*. Oxford: Oxford University Press, 261–279.

Serrão, J. V. (dir.). (1980). *História de Portugal – vol. II – Formação do Estado Moderno (1415–1495)*, 2nd ed. Lisbon: Editorial Verbo.

Silveira, A. C. (2007). O espaço peri-urbano de Setúbal na Baixa Idade Média: produções e estruturas produtivas, in B. Arizaga Bolumburu & J. Solórzano Telechea (eds.), *La Ciudad Medieval y su influencia territorial* – Nájera, Encuentros internacionales del Medievo, Nájera, 26–29 de julio 2006. Logroño: Instituto de Estudios Riojanos, 161–180.

Sousa, A. de. (1990). *As cortes medievais portuguesas: 1385–1490*, 2 vols. Porto: INIC.

Sousa, A. de. (2006). 1325–1480, in J. Mattoso (dir.), *História de Portugal – vol. IV: A Monarquia Feudal*. Mem Martins: Circulo de Leitores, 8–89.

Sousa, J. S. de. (1991). *A Casa Senhorial do infante D. Henrique*. Lisbon: Livros Horizonte.

5 The geography of early modern Portuguese fiscal dynamics

5.1. Kingdom's zones with higher contribution capacities

Following the indications given by a relevant secondary source, within the *Sumário das rendas do Rey do anno de 1473* (Faro, 1965: 55–117) – i.e., a survey of the realm's set of revenues – we were able to have an initial estimate of which *almoxarifados* would be more profitable, excluding Lisbon's case that deserves a separate analysis, due to its clear and evident difference of scale in relation to the rest of the kingdom. When producing a ranking of the kingdom's tax units and their respective revenues, we note some interesting points, as we can observe in Table 5.1.

Contradicting what was supposed to be a manifest condition, namely that seaports and frontier zones with Castile would be the places where the revenue would most likely abound more evidently, Santarém appears as the unit with the highest revenue collection totals among all. The sources alone do not provide enough information to explain this fact. However, the difference between the first and the Estremoz's *almoxarifado*, a place of passage and which can be a trace to this argument, is "relatively" small, amounting to 141,000 reais. Comparatively, this value is almost as much as the collection in Loulé, but it should be emphasized that, in many cases, this inequality factor may come from values that transited from previous accounts. In a sense, they are "leftovers" from the accounts of previous years, which feed and artificially increase the following year's income, a quite common situation in the royal accounts' procedures, already demonstrated and solidly present in the source documentation.

As a "photograph" regarding a particular moment of Portugal's revenues, these numbers can be interpreted within some limitations, but still very useful to raise some questions and comparisons. On the other hand, Santarém's formula for reaching this level of income cannot be found in land taxes, which did not generate income greater than 37,000 in 1500 (Viana, 2000: 556–558). Considering the 1473 values as standard, it would be an insignificant amount of the total – just over 1%, and only the *sisas* collected on wine sales of that county would not worth less than 100,000 reais,[1] which, nevertheless, represented less than 5% of the values found. Nor would urban houses' rents be the main factor, as they were

Table 5.1 Kingdom's fiscal branches (*almoxarifados*) and its respective revenues in 1473 (in reais brancos)

Almoxarifados/Cities	Revenues
Santarém	2,240,000
Estremoz	2,099,000
Setúbal	2,057,000
Beja	2,000,000
Évora	1,799,000
Porto	1,795,000
Guarda	1,545,000
Guimarães	1,500,000
Coimbra	1,489,500
Portalegre	1,123,000
Silves	821,000
Aveiro	777,000
Ponte de Lima	766,000
Leiria	740,000
Torre de Moncorvo	664,000
Óbidos	650,000
Faro	475,000
Vila Real	463,000
Viseu	460,000
Abrantes	457,500
Lamego	410,000
Sintra	380,500
Lagos	359,000
Alenquer	355,000
Loulé	160,000

Source: Faro, Jorge (1965). *Receitas e despesas da Fazenda Real de 1384 a 1481: subsídios documentais.* Lisbon: INE, 82–85.

even less significant (Viana, 2000: 564) than other properties' rents. However, its productive fabric was quite diverse, with the treatment and use of leather and skins, metals, armory and the kingdom's main rope manufacturer.[2] In this sense, granting the rights of indirect tax collection (*sisas* and tithes) collected by private investors – that is, the *almoxarifado*'s income leasing – should be, as in the other cases, the main source of revenues, although we do not have documentation proving this by this particular period, but for some years further ahead. In 1497, only this component (the leasing) was worth 2,200,000 *reais* – approximately 92% of the total delivered.[3]

The possibility of profit regarding the Castilian cloth's trade, combined with the income resulting from the taxing of commodities entering the Portuguese ports, attracted the attention of people who had the capital to invest in the tax farming. In this sense, the case studies that follow here, Estremoz and Setúbal, illustrate this situation well. For the former, we know the income's values from 1495[4] onwards. However, the sources give us the certainty of renting the income collection of the respective *almoxarifado* only after 1511.[5] Although tax-farmers were not identified, we can deduce by analyzing the source that the leasing refers to values ranging from 67 to 95% of the total delivered per year to the *almoxarife*. Furthermore, the rights on cloths' trade, chickens' due[6] and some other duties from the same year or from previous years, which may have been levied on the same tenant, were supplemented by other rents. In the latter case, it is already known that there were leaseholders of each tax for the respective *almoxarifado* since 1439:[7] of the eighteen earnings listed, only two clearly state that there were no tenants for that year, one does not identify it, and another does not give any indication in this regard. All others were duly passed on to their interested parties. Already in the sixteenth century, between 1521 and 1524,[8] Setúbal's case suggested impressive leasing percentages within the total amount collected, comprising between 97 and 98% of the total.

With regard to the Alentejo cases, Beja had the tax leasing, presence, and identification of tenants already indicated in the letters as early as 1440.[9] Of the sixteen sources of income identified for that particular year, in five situations there were no interested investors, representing more than 30%: the general *sisas*, the *sisas* on cloth and wines in Beja within its perimeter; the general *sisas* of Torrão; the general *sisas* of Alvalade; the general *sisas* of Santiago do Cacém, Sines and Colos, together; the general *sisas* of Messejana, Aljustrel, Panóias and Casével, together, and the fishing *tithes* of Odemira. On this date, approximately 70% of the total delivered to the *almoxarife* was related to rents leased to third parties. By the 1490s, this policy continued in practice,[10] however without being able to identify leaseholders and percentages within the total amount collected. In the next century, in 1506,[11] tax farming represented 93.5% of the total received by the main officer that year; in 1508,[12] rising to 95%; and in 1509 and 1510, it comprised respectively 97.2 and 98% of the total.[13] By means of this sampling, we also noticed a trend toward a gradual increase in leasing compared to the totals collected each year, at least in this particular case.

In Evora, the trend was probably similar, although it is only possible to assume the existence of tax leasing, based on the sources collected, from 1497 onwards.[14] Regarding this case, in one of the letters we have the indication of a particular tax being levied, the *rendas rameiras*, a term which appears in chapters 67 and 68 within the treasurer's internal regiment of 1516, to designate a sort of an auction. It says:

> the accountant shall put the said incomes into public auction, and there shall be a deposit covering the sum of which each one has demanded in the Bureau; officers will receive and collect them within the determined time limits, without having to send them to the Treasurer's office.
>
> (Carneiro, 1818: 115–116)

characterizing the public sale to which the taxes were placed. Here in this case, 97.7% of the total value was gathered by the *almoxarife*; later, we have another indication of this practice in 1519,[15] when the *almoxarifado*'s leasing made up 97.2% of the total revenues collected, now by a different official.

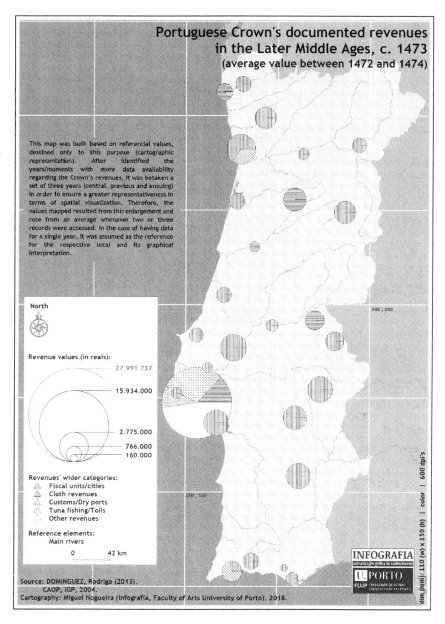

Portuguese Crown's documented revenues in the Later Middle Ages, c. 1473
(average value between 1472 and 1474)

This map was built based on referential values, destined only to this purpose (cartographic representation). After identified the years/moments with more data availability regarding the Crown's revenues, it was betaken a set of three years (central, previous and ensuing) in order to ensure a greater representativeness in terms of spatial visualization. Therefore, the values mapped resulted from this enlargement and rose from an average whenever two or three records were accessed. In the case of having data for a single year, it was assumed as the reference for the respective local and its graphical interpretation.

North

Revenue values (in reais):
27.991.737
15.934.000
2.775.000
766.000
160.000

Revenues' wider categories:
Fiscal units/cities
Cloth revenues
Customs/Dry ports
Tuna fishing/Tolls
Other revenues

Reference elements:
Main rivers

0   42 km

Source: DOMINGUEZ, Rodrigo (2013).
CAOP, IGP, 2004.
Cartography: Miguel Nogueira (Infografia, Faculty of Arts University of Porto), 2018.

INFOGRAFIA
comunicação gráfica do conhecimento
U.PORTO
FLUP FACULDADE DE LETRAS
UNIVERSIDADE DO PORTO

dim. (mm): 110 (w) x 150 (h) | color | 600 dpi's

Map 5.1 Portuguese Crown's documented revenues in the later Middle Ages, c.1473 (average value between 1472 and 1474)

Unexpectedly, Porto was not in the top five of revenue collection. Of course, in order to put these findings in perspective, we have to acknowledge that in our case we are not counting the customs receipts or the royalties on the Castilian cloths that would enter there. In any case, it is surprising, from a certain point of view, that the *almoxarifado* of a city such as Porto, with a great commercial and maritime movement, did not reach this level with the collection of tax revenues that implies integration of the state finances. Regarding the city's finances during the 1450s, it has already been well explored based on the local documentation (Gonçalves, 1987: 8) referring to the *Livros dos bens do Concelho* (municipal properties' books). It should be noted that these resources did not mix with those that the local fiscal unit would collect for the Crown, except for the rights to the *sisas'* income and other levies, which were an extraordinary municipal resource, taken from the city hall by João I (Gonçalves, 1987: 49), although with the people's consent, in the midst of the interregnum crisis.

Hence, within the compiled set of sources, the first indication of the auctioning in that locality dates back to 1499.[16] That year, the *almoxarifado*'s leasing was granted for 1,934,000 reais, or 59.6% of the total value received and mentioned in the respective acquittance letter, of 3,243,570 reais. However, it is worth clarifying here that the same source included the customs office, which formed a portion of one of the years regarding the auctioning of that unit. The whole lease, for the years 1498, 1499 and 1500, had been agreed to comprise the value of 4,400,000 reais, for the three years combined. However, in this source, the official reported only one installment, which amounted to 1,309,570 reais, the other 40.4% of the total amount mentioned by the document. Subsequently, for the year 1507,[17] we can find another reference that mentioned values much lower than the previous ones, but similarly "mixed" with other revenues. It is known that these collections were also leased, but the combination of rents among other *almoxarifados* beyond Porto, makes a more detailed analysis impossible, so that we are not sure how much that year's lease is worth.

Lastly, a final indication[18] from 1519 and 1520 allows us to clarify the situation: in the first year, out of a total of 7,288,000 reais received, approximately 39.1% related to the *almoxarifado* leasing (2,851,534) and another 35.9% (2,618,566) corresponded to the customs', also leased. In addition, this included 23.8% of the duties on the cloths collected there (1,730,463), also rented to investors (0.95% or 70,005 reais), as well as notaries' pensions in that city (0.25% or 18,000 reais). In the following year, the values of the *sisas*, houses' rent and pensions were maintained, increasing only the percentage and the amounts collected with the transfer of the *almoxarifados'* revenues, and a small reduction in percentage terms but an increase in values for customs. Of the total for that year – 7,828,023 reais – 43.2%, or 3,380,907 reais, related to the former and 33.5%, or 2,628,748 reais, referred to the latter.

The city of Guarda, a military and commercial reference point at the Portuguese-Castilian border, about 100 kilometers south of Douro River's main track, offers us an exceptional case to analyze more carefully due to the very reasonable amount of data available for that *almoxarifado*, particularly for Manuel I's reign.

We were able to get a reasonable series of income data, lacking the collections' values only in eight of the twenty-six years of his governance. Comparatively, for the fifteenth century, we can find only five income records for the whole forty-eight years of Afonso V's reign, another four appointments for the reign of João II and the remaining twenty-two records were related to the following period of rule. The earliest reference to leasing taxes in Guarda dates back to 1436: a set of ninety duties – ranging from *sisas* on cloth and wine, to taxes on the Jewish community, *sisas* collected at local fairs on cloths and Jews, the *reguengos* and tolls, composed this complete set.[19] Excluding the revenues directly channeled to the monarch, such as the notaries' taxes and others that already had a previously defined destination, such as the Jews' contributions that were assigned to Ceuta's blacksmiths, all others were leased to investors and yielded 32,173,502 pounds, or 95.5% of the total collected that year – 33,660,637 pounds or approximately 961,732 reais – by the respective *almoxarifado*.[20]

After this, we only found another mention of tax leasing in that locality in 1496 and 1497, without any further details.[21] Only the full lease amounts are known – 2,633,333 reais and 2,790,000 reais, respectively – but it is not possible to calculate the percentage value because the document describes revenues for years other than these. Later, for the years 1503 and 1504, it is possible to get the relative shares again:[22] for the first year, approximately 69.3 per cent of income was related to tax leasing; and in the following year, this figure dropped to 65.4% of total. In the years 1510 and 1511, these numbers corresponded to 96.3 and 96.4%, respectively, of the totals collected in those years, in that order.[23] Ten years later, in 1520, this figure declined very slightly,[24] to approximately 95.1% of the total collected. In any case, the tax collection evolutionary curve relative to that locality is very revealing,[25] reaching the 8,347,784 reais in 1522. Lamego, in the upper Douro valley, also recorded an exponential growth regarding its collection: from 414,285 reais collected in 1441, it amounted to an astonishing 4,445,010 reais in 1521, registering a growth over ten times[26] the initial sum.

In Guimarães, at Northwest Portugal, the values of taxes and royal rights are known for 1445 – 115,991 reais – but the sources do not clarify whether they were leased or not.[27] After that, we examined two references: an indication for revenues in 1473 and, further, only twenty-three years later we have the total collected by that *almoxarifado*. It is worth noting the exponential growth of revenues· in that locality, in 1496 amounting to 1,313,229 reais, although we do not have any more specific indications on the leasing procedures.[28] The first indication appears in 1505, but without further details: it gives us the impression that the auction values related to the total referred, by the terminology used in the documentation, that is to say, "by which the said *almoxarifado* was farmed".[29] In the following decade, the growth in values continued at a vigorous pace: the totals received by the *almoxarife* were 1,914,586 reais in 1516, and 2,326,366 reais for the following two years,[30] which also indicated a growth pattern. And finally, for 1521 and 1522, it is known that the leasing was responsible for approximately 87.4% of the total collected in both years.[31] It must be emphasized here that we have been working with nominal values, and a new study would be needed in order to find out whether or not there were financial losses in this space of time, calculating inflation and currency debasement impacts.

The case of Coimbra is one of those that we can only perceive in the last years of the fifteenth century. Between 1473 and 1498, the first references in the set of sources at our disposal focus on the auctioning of that fiscal unit, implies a substantial growth pattern,[32] in nominal values, superior to 38%. In the same year of 1498, as in the case of Guimarães, there was another indication about the respective *almoxarifado*'s income, which matched the acquittance letter's total value. Later on, in 1517, we have another clue to the leasing of almost all of those revenues,[33] with the exception of the 1% destined for the "meritorious works" (Sousa, 1783: I, 122–123), and money channeled to charity and assistance, prescribed by the official's regiment, edited during the Manueline governance. Finally, as early as 1521, the revenues of that unit had already more than doubled,[34] soaring from 2,059,452 reais collected in 1498, to 4,152,131 reais.

In any case, this may indicate some questions to be pondered: would this rise in the amounts collected, regardless of the *almoxarifado* or tax, be indicative of a greater interest of investors in those localities, in certain occasions? Would higher collections mean more tax-farmers who were willing to get involved in this business? Was there a "market" for auctioning and leasing? Given the existence of the branches and public sale sessions, we think that this is a hypothesis not to be discarded, but it needs further research whether it can be confirmed or not. In any case, we do not know for sure if there were more people bidding and paying more for the leasing, in order to make sure that the business could be profitable, or because the Crown sought to increase its revenues, aiming at a compensation for monetary losses. Regarding the previous case of Coimbra, in certain years, like 1500 and 1501, the sums did not behave in a constant way,[35] that is, they were much lower. Those losses in the collection, both there and in other places, were also quite similar to the absence of tenants in other places or regions, as we shall see in detail later. It seems that these factors were intertwined. The investor had to do his "feasibility study" to look for signals and indications of good yields: if, for example, he decided to invest in the collection of *sisas* on wines in a certain place, a few months earlier he sought to collect information about that year's harvest, whether it would be good or not, if there would be more or less wine. If he decided to lease the *sisas* on meat, he could verify the conditions of the herd, if there were many cattle, whether it was a dry year or not, what would be the potential supply of the product compared to its demand. In short, he would look for elements that would help him make a better decision.

In global terms, no other kingdom's province had grown in fiscal terms as much as the Algarve region, which made a quantitative and qualitative leap in this period, and this development can be observed in many ways. The same summary of 1473 mentioned Faro's incomes (without local customs), the Kingdom of Algarve's customs – whose collection should be centralized, and whose center was in Faro – in Silves, Loulé, and Lagos. However, in the late fifteenth and early sixteenth centuries, records indicate, in addition to what already existed, another *almoxarifado* and customs in Tavira and Vila Nova de Portimão, two other customs – in

Faro and Lagos – as well as another cloths' *almoxarifado*, responsible for taxing all the textiles entering through the Algarve region. Regarding the tax revenues, Loulé had a notable increase, practically doubling its income between 1473 and 1518, making it a total of 318,150 reais in the last year,[36] although this number was small compared to other *almoxarifados* in the same period. For example, the revenues in Lagos grew almost 500% in thirty-nine years, from 359,000 reais to 1,741,300 reais in 1512.[37] In addition to the fiscal units, the *almadravas* factory (concerning the tuna fishery and trade) showed very promising signs of a vigorous fishing industry[38] in the context of the entire state's finances (Magalhães, 1988: 195), representing almost 1.5% of the total state revenues in 1588 and reaching its peak at the end of the sixteenth century (Magalhães, 1988: 196).

The area of *Trás-os-Montes* (Northeast Portugal), represented by the *almoxarifados* of Vila Real and Torre de Moncorvo, also displayed a very significant increase in their collections:[39] both grew more than 600%, reaching, in the former case, the total of 3,124,521 in 1521, of which 97.9% was leased, while the latter one, in the same year, amounted to 4,047,899 reais, of which 97.8% was equivalent to leased revenues. This growth may be related, to a great extent, to the mining activity, which was strong in the whole region but especially in the second location, mainly the iron ore extraction (Duarte, 1995: 102–103). In Entre-Douro-e-Minho province, Ponte de Lima also followed this trend: from the small collection of 48,970 reais in 1445,[40] it soared to 766,000 reais recorded in the 1473 *Summary*, reaching the sum of 2,585,600 reais in 1517,[41] indicating an exponential growth pattern.

5.2. Scale differences: Lisbon and the kingdom

Lisbon, as the kingdom's economic center, kept an immeasurable distance from the other Portuguese cities and towns (Pereira, 2003: 179–186). This gap was reflected in the state's fiscal revenue collection comparatively with other local fiscal branches' total revenues, as seen on Table 5.2. Some scholars have already mentioned that the great international trade was centralized there, as well as the presence of the great Jewish merchants (Tavares, 1982: 285). The royal charters granted to those merchants allowed them to export and import goods by sea in the name of Christians. Moreover, with or without these charters, the merchants had to pay royalties owed to the king, in addition to being able to exchange money abroad. Along with the acquittances that account for royal rights and tax-farmed profits, many of them acted in partnerships with Italian businessmen. All these functions served to draw a unique panorama of what is also the Crown's central point in fiscal terms.

There was therefore a clear distinction, in comparative terms, between Lisbon and the rest of the kingdom, which began with the sources of taxation. The very production of the acquittance letters and their contents are indicative of this disparity, reflecting a more complex fiscal organization. As we look at the set of sources collected, we can observe these factors clearly: while Guarda's *almoxarife* gives an account of what was amassed in 1436, referring to all types of rents

Table 5.2 Lisbon's revenues versus rest of the kingdom (in reais brancos)

Year	Lisbon revenue	Value	Almoxarifado	Value
1447	Sisa on colored cloth	1,371,429	Santarém	568,800
1449	Sisa on colored cloth	1,405,714	Guarda	996,700
1449	Aver-do-Peso	1,152,029	Setúbal	1,233,851
1449	Sisa on wine	409,337	Óbidos	93,000
1496	Aver-do-Peso	1,650,500	Guimarães	1,313,229
1497	Sisa da marçaria (wood)	1,430,323	Vila Real	882,417
1498	Sisa on regular cloth	2,986,828	Coimbra	2,059,452
1498	Sisa on wheat	1,231,846	Lamego	1,000,000
1499	Portagem (toll)	1,925,000	Porto	1,934,000
1500	Sisa on regular cloth	3,000,000	Évora	2,207,000
1502	Sisa on regular cloth	4,000,000	Beja	3,570,000
1512	Sisa on fruit	1,021,000	Faro	707,000
1513	Sisa on regular cloth	5,319,330	Estremoz	3,892,819
1520	Sisa on wheat	1,666,500	Tavira	1,668,520
1521	Paço da madeira (wood)	2,482,277	Lagos	1,491,471

Sources: ANTT, *Chanc. Afonso V*, liv. 11, fls. 47–47v and 143v–144; liv. 34, fl. 157v; Leitura Nova, *Além Douro*, liv. 1, fls. 138v-139 and 236v; *Estremadura*, liv. 8, fl. 250–250v; *Guadiana*, liv. 7, fl. 169–169v; FREIRE, Anselmo Braamcamp. "Cartas de quitação del Rei D. Manuel", in *Archivo Historico Portuguez*, vol. II, n° 7, 1904, 352; vol. II, n° 10, 1904, 422; vol. III, 1905, 393, 394, 479 and 480; vol. IV, 1906, 74 and 237; vol. V, 1907, 73, 74, 75, 79, 80 and 235; vol. VIII, 1910, 392–393; vol. IX, 1914, 433, 434, 436 and 456.

and sales taxes collected therein,[42] in Lisbon there was a specific receiver exclusively assigned to collect the profits on the colored cloths' sales taxes[43] (*sisas*). While the *almoxarife* of Setúbal accounts for all that has been collected,[44] namely all the tithes and taxes received, in Lisbon the *aver-do-peso* ("commodities sold by weight") office had a prominent *almoxarife* and *recebedor* ("receiver"), and his income appears mentioned in a document produced solely for this purpose,[45] although without more details, with the respective tax-farmers. Even with regard to the sources' description of the extraordinary revenue, we can perceive this difference: while the values of the 1437's *pedido* for the Tangier's Navy were brought together with the other regular revenues in the account rendering of Lamego's *almoxarifado*, in the case of Lisbon we did not find this occurrence. In short, critical review of the sources allows us to examine this from an administrative and fiscal perspective.

On the other hand, we have previously noted the acquittance letters produced only for this purpose (extraordinary revenues) in Lisbon, in conjunction with the letters and rights of indulgence granted by Pope Nicholas V,[46] for the years 1452 and 1453, "for the repair, conservation and defense of our city of Ceuta". It should be noted that an overall study of the ecclesiastical taxation in Portugal in the later Middle Ages is yet to be done, as well as a work on the Church's contribution to the Portuguese state taxation. In any case, even as we acknowledge the importance of ecclesiastical income, here we focused on the state finances and royal revenues.

Lisbon, as a reality apart from the rest of the Crown's fiscal local branches, had consequently a much broader range of revenues available, widely varied, whose values were much higher comparatively than in the rest of the country. In many cases, a single source of income could be equal or superior to an overall revenue pool of an *almoxarifado*'s. The revenues collected there were mainly in the form of sales taxes (*sisas*) on standard and colored cloths, wines, meat, manufactured goods, bread, wheat, fruit, real estate, fish, wood and the *aver-do-peso*. Furthermore, taxes on currency and minting rose, since the state was one of the currency's search agents, "influencing the levels of monetary issuance when emitting commodity currency" (Sousa, 2003: 771). Also, the same occurred with the House of Supplication chancellery (court fees), the customs, the warehouses,[47] the *Paço da Madeira* (office destined to the control of wood traffic and other goods), the imposition on the salt and the toll rights. The chancellery records that were collected noted the existence of a respective *almoxarifado* or receiver for each of these particular revenues, which contributed to the differentiated perception of Lisbon's fiscal dimension (Henriques, 2008: 142).

Based on some of the figures obtained through these sources, it is possible to make some comparisons between Lisbon's revenues and the totals collected in the *almoxarifados* throughout the kingdom, for the years in which the sources allow us to do so. The discrepancy between the Crown's income in other fiscal units and the taxes collected in the capital (Oliveira, 1804: 113–119) becomes quite apparent through this comparison.

Another significant difference can be detected when we compare the mainland's revenues with the overseas' earnings from the same type of source. For instance, the treaty of Guinea,[48] between October 1486 and August 1488, generated the impressive sum of 95,306,252 reais, especially when we realize that Lisbon's customs,[49] the most important source of income for the entire Portuguese State, in 1488 and 1489 yielded 11,098,039 reais. Later on, for the same deal between 1494 and 1497, the revenues that were reported amounted to 221,367,997 reais for the respective three years, combined, corresponding with the taking care of treasures and the dealings.[50] Moreover, the pepper monopoly[51] between 1506 and 1507 accounted for the enormous sum of 119,079,028 reais. It should be noted here that we are talking about the monopoly of only one specific product, in a particular year, among the infinity of items that came from the conquered outposts, in particular from India. How much would the Crown benefit from other commodities, such as cloves, anise, saffron, among many others, in different localities, in other years? Furthermore, from other commodities coming from early-stage Colonial Brazil? Here we have only a few small pieces of the puzzle for a deeper understanding of how these new revenues would be fundamental within the Portuguese fiscal context, and how they radically altered it.

An important indication of improvement in the kingdom's financial conditions can be found in João II's answer to the Catholic kings' aid request for the War of Granada, within the *reconquista* scope, in Spanish territory. The Portuguese monarch had granted economic support through what appears to be a controlled situation, since "the realm's needs and ours are so many that our treasury regarding the

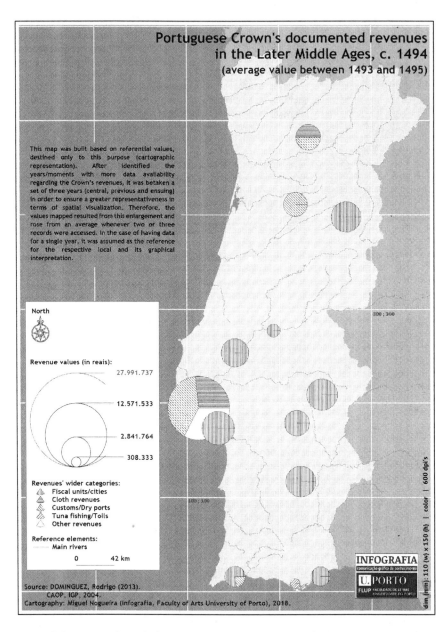

Map 5.2 Portuguese Crown's documented revenues in the later Middle Ages, c.1494 (average value between 1493 and 1495)

Guinean money is enough" and, given the urgency and necessity of the neighboring kings,

> we send forth from whence some money might be taken from us, and from other necessities it was ordained, and we believe that we may be able to do it elsewhere, that it is not so much as we rejoice according to our will.

(Chaves, 1983: 302)

Such was the financial stability that it was possible for the *Perfect Prince* to honor his commitments when he collected the churches' silverware to pay for the war with Castile, which, at the beginning of his reign, would not yet have been paid (Marques, 1989: 212). We do not know if they were totally compensated but, at least partially, we can say yes, given the two acquittance letters[52] of 1502 and 1512, reporting all that he had received and spent for the same purpose, which contains in the sums of 11,669,882.5 and 1,546,302.5 reais, respectively, considerable money from the *Casa da Mina*, paid by its treasurer and foreman, Fernão Lourenço.

These new income sources would be essential in order to fill in the blanks that Portugal's fiscal system was not able to fulfill by itself. The collection structure, its dynamics, and management within the country focused exclusively on redistribution, and in many situations it was not able to meet the kingdom's needs, as well as to sufficiently cover the state's organization expenditure itself. Or, even to face extraordinary situations for which there were already exceptional aid collections assigned. For example, the noblemen housing payments[53] in 1495 were done, partially, with 1,000,000 reais from the *Casa da Mina*. The rest came from the Madeira Island's sugar profits.

Even diplomatic and military missions could be funded with overseas' profits, such as the sending of two ambassadors to England[54] between 1493 and 1494. Most of that money came from the *Casa da Mina*, about 190,000 reais, representing about 75% of the total amount destined for that mission. In fact, the embassies and military companies, as previously mentioned in this study and properly treated by Iria Gonçalves,[55] were mainly supported by extraordinary revenues; that is, the *pedidos* and *empréstimos* voted by the people's representatives at the *Cortes*. The same source would provide further means, about 150,000 of the 327,680 reais to the Entre-Douro-e-Minho fortresses' maintenance,[56] demonstrating the power and multiple uses of Mina's resources for various purposes in different locations.

The *Mina* also started serving other commitments, as well as Ceuta and the Indies would also contribute to the kingdom's administrative apparatus expenditure within Portugal's mainland.[57] Some of the Algarve's *almoxarifados* in 1511, 1512 and 1513, reported that they had received, "for expenses of the mentioned office, in the mentioned years", the amount of 1,990,000 reais: some from Ceuta (1,811,731 reais) and some from India (74,000 reais), resulting in 95% of the total coming from outside the kingdom, thus not from the income collected in that jurisdiction. We do not see how it would be possible for Ceuta to chip in, given the various accounts of the difficulties facing the maintenance of that outpost (Zurara,

1978: 117–119). We think that it may be possible to explain this situation with the idea that revenues that were already destined to Ceuta may have been diverted from their main purpose.

From what we have just discussed, the potentiality of extraordinary resources coming from the new outposts occupied by Portugal, both in Africa and the Indies, and the clear and notorious preponderance of Lisbon in fiscal terms, particularly when compared with the other cities of the kingdom, is quite evident. Time would accentuate this difference even more. Father Nicolau de Oliveira, in his chronicle of early seventeenth century, exalted the city with the typical exaggeration of these sources' rhetoric exercise, as the "chief and head of the kingdom, and more populous than all of Europe (if it does not seem to someone who I say very much in saying that all the world)" (Oliveira, 1804: 112), in which the revenues were so many that "only in a tide I saw here in Lixboa to go fishing for sardines, one hundred and twelve boats", whose tithing would render to D. Teodósio II, then Duke of Braganza, about "twenty-two thousand and five hundred cruzados". It seems to us that their exaltation, as well as the disparity described *vis-a-vis* the rest of the country, was not at all rhetorical, since their origins were well grounded in the phenomenon of hierarchical inequality of the values demonstrated here.

5.3. Most important types of revenues in each location

There is no universal formula for taxation that fits as a model locally, and even more difficult in broader terms, for kingdoms. However, we have tried to identify some patterns and dynamics regarding tax collection in various regions with the available data. Within the numbers we have found, it is perfectly plausible to identify trends.

From the sources gathered, we find that the ordinary revenues were completely detailed for three different places, which represents a sample in each region: Guarda (Northeast), Setúbal (Atlantic shoreline, south of Lisbon) and Beja (Spanish border, southern hinterlands).[58] As for the first city's case, the revenue collection was founded on one particular tax, with three central variations or pillars: the *sisas* gathered from all kinds (also known as "general"), the wine selling, and the colored cloths sold. In the list of identified items, we verified that a same tenant could lease the collection of different types of *sisas* in the same area, or even those of other localities. Many of them were registered together, as "wines and general *sisas*", or "cloth, wines and general *sisas*" or as "cloths, Jews and general *sisas*". These – denominated by us as 'mixed', for the purpose of separating into categories – were also connected to the taxes on normal cloths and on fairs' transactions and sales (see Figure 5.1).

Another important aspect to emphasize refers to the joint ventures made to invest in tax farming. Despite the difficulty and the high sums required, some levies did not have investors; conversely, for the same reason, there were few cases of direct taxes, rents and royal rights collected, and even their percentage value, within the total, was relatively small. Most of these revenues, clearly, arose from the general *sisas*. Analogously to the tenants, regarding this case study, there was

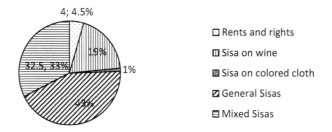

Figure 5.1 Guarda's revenues (in approximate percentages of total local) in 1436

a considerable number of Jewish investors, but most of them were Christian, in part contradicting the logic of massive Jewish involvement in financial activities. The sample is not big enough to draw any definitive conclusions, but this strategic presence in the border areas was indicative (Tavares, 1982: 43).

Within what we recognize as ordinary revenues, in general terms, the overall *almoxarifado*'s collection depended to a large extent on the tax leasing. In the most remote, or probably less profitable or more difficult areas to collect, there was a conspicuous absence of tenants. In such cases, their revenues were normally collected by the *almoxarife* himself, another official or a local resident designated for that task.[59]

In Setúbal, meat, cloths, wine and bread were the only commodities cited separately in the tax description, and this occurred only for the village of Setúbal, i.e., excluding the surroundings, which already shows the difference between the "head" of jurisdiction and the rest of other towns that composes the *almoxarifado*'s range of influence. Here we can observe that almost 100% of the taxes were leased and the respective leaseholders all listed. In addition, another issue raised in this particular case: the *sisas* were only identified by the locality, without mentioning its type. It is not known whether the mention referred to a tax on a specific commodity or just the general ones. In the previous case, at Guarda, there was a difference in designation. Some were just designated as "general *sisas*", while for other localities the mentions were in *sisas*, which makes us think that they may have been all kinds of sales taxes collected in that place. Nevertheless, concerning the values collected, we can draw attention to the sums raised in villages such as Alcácer do Sal, Almada, Sesimbra and Palmela within the total set of the respective *almoxarifado* (see Figure 5.2).

In this situation, the *sisas*' and tithes' lease collection vis-à-vis only the Ribeira de Setúbal (city area close to the port) exhibited some peculiarities, also given the amount collected which, originally, was contracted for more than the double than the estimated value at the auction. There, as in Guarda, the Jewish community also appeared as investors, alone or in partnerships. In addition, relatively to the investment power necessary for this type of initiative, merchants also appeared in the list of identified tenants, proving their potential for investment, capital, and

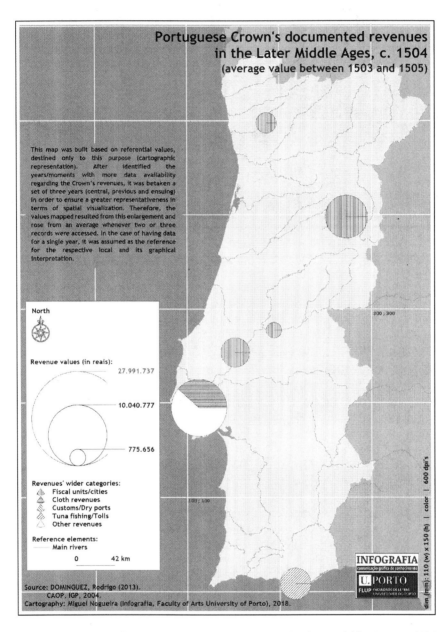

Portuguese Crown's documented revenues in the Later Middle Ages, c. 1504
(average value between 1503 and 1505)

This map was built based on referential values, destined only to this purpose (cartographic representation). After identified the years/moments with more data availability regarding the Crown's revenues, it was betaken a set of three years (central, previous and ensuing) in order to ensure a greater representativeness in terms of spatial visualization. Therefore, the values mapped resulted from this enlargement and rose from an average whenever two or three records were accessed. In the case of having data for a single year, it was assumed as the reference for the respective local and its graphical interpretation.

North

Revenue values (in reais):
27.991.737
10.040.777
775.656

Revenues' wider categories:
Fiscal units/cities
Cloth revenues
Customs/Dry ports
Tuna fishing/Tolls
Other revenues

Reference elements:
Main rivers

0   42 km

Source: DOMINGUEZ, Rodrigo (2013).
CAOP, IGP, 2004.
Cartography: Miguel Nogueira (Infografia, Faculty of Arts University of Porto), 2018.

INFOGRAFIA
comunicação gráfica de conhecimento
U.PORTO
FLUP FACULDADE DE LETRAS
UNIVERSIDADE DO PORTO

dim. (mm): 110 (w) x 150 (h) | color | 600 dpi's

Map 5.3 Portuguese Crown's documented revenues in the later Middle Ages, c.1504
(average value between 1503 and 1505)

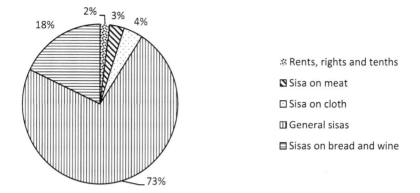

Figure 5.2 Setúbal's revenues (in approximate percentages of total local) in 1439

the activity's diversification (Dominguez, 2009: 110–113). Rents and royal rights occupied a very small part of the total, which proves, in terms of revenues, the trend of a transformation since the late fourteenth century. This change reflected, bottom line, one of the main aspects related to the transition from a domain state to a tax state, that is, when the private revenues of the monarch are now surpassed by the public revenues derived from a general system of tax collection (Ormrod, 1995: 123).

Regarding the third case, at Beja (see Figure 5.3), from the outset, the values, while much smaller, were accounted for in a different currency (white reais) rather than in *libras*. Unlike what is demonstrated in the sources concerning Guarda, but in line with what happened in Setúbal, we cannot distinguish whether the *sisas* described and listed were for general purposes or whether the amounts mentioned referred to all kinds of sales taxes. It is also important to note that, unlike the other two previous situations, in this case there was no distinction or predominance of any particular kind of tribute. There were none in particular that stood out.

We noticed, however, that many of the localities listed within Beja's fiscal records did not have tax-farmers, unlike in the other two previous cases, which had almost 100% of taxes leased. It is not entirely surprising that this was the case for the Entre-Tejo-e-Guadiana district, which encompassed the present territories of Alentejo and Algarve; namely, the entire southern half of Portugal. Long distances between the villages and counties, as well as the amplitude of the *almoxarifado*'s fiscal jurisdictions, would probably not have provided the most profitable conditions for the potential tax farming investors. On the other hand, some important revenues, such as Beja's *sisas* on cloths, wines and the general ones were not leased, as in Santiago do Cacém and Sines, both important ports on the Portuguese Southern Atlantic coast. For other small villages in the hinterlands, such as Alvalade or Aljustrel, it is feasible that they did not inspire particular interest in financial terms due to the excessive cost and labor in collecting them and little income justifying them.

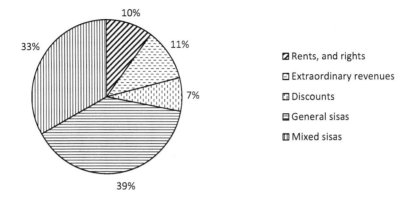

Figure 5.3 Beja's revenues (in approximate percentages of total local) in 1440

In this particular *almoxarifado*, the "discounts" granted by the monarch should be highlighted. Virtually all the acquittances had a reduction or mercy, normally granted to the *almoxarife*, receiver or tenant, indicating that the monarch had been informed about the difficulties in raising the amounts previously stipulated in the contracts signed by the tenants. In many cases, values were not achieved, regardless of the motivations. However, a poor prior assessment of the risks involved was liable to punishment, even though it might directly have involved the main local officer, i.e., the *almoxarife*. There the reduction was granted for noble and exceptional motives at the same time: for alms, simple reductions or even lower profitability, forcing the king to lease a combination of taxes from several villages to the same tenants. In the latter case, the leaseholders never paid the total, no property was found to cover the losses and the tenants fled to Castile. In the second case, it involved a Jewish investor with a partial payment and his Christian associate paid half of his share, while the Jewish investor paid on his and his guarantors' behalf, who fled to Castile as well. Regularly, a substantial share of those leases were not delivered to the Crown. However, this should have been carried forward as part of the following year's revenues, but in practice this was not what happened; the debt accumulated with that of the following year, and the amount was normally granted as mercy to the *almoxarife*, not incurring any kind of penalty.

Another relevant aspect of Beja's case was the report of regular revenues combined with extraordinary revenues, which in this case made up to 11% of the total collected. This was an unusual procedure for this situation, since this type of income was usually reported in their own documents. That amount was due to four *pedidos* charged on the Jewish commune of Beja and three applications targeting the Moorish communes of Beja and Moura, totaling the sum of 130,844 reais. These seven requests were not reported in the previous table because they were not regular collections, although this expedient – the *pedidos* to Moors and

Jews – was something fairly frequent, arising in times of great economic difficulties, military campaigns' costs, nobles' marriages, defense of the kingdom etc. Usually, they also occupied a more onerous character for the Jewish population rather than for the Muslims or Christians (Tavares, 1982: 159–160). In this particular situation, the money collected was used to finance the Navy to succor Ceuta in 1440. For the Muslim communities, it was an affront to pay for an army[60] that was going to help the Christians control Ceuta.

5.4. Credit and taxation: concentration of interests

Border towns like Guarda, and large ports such as Lisbon, under normal circumstances, tended to be the centers that aroused greater interest among the potential leaseholders. The Jewish community, composed by some great businessmen of the time, obviously preferred to invest in areas with large commercial flows and big urban centers (Tavares, 1982: 44–45). In many cases, they did it in association with Italian merchants, who were strong financial partners able to boost the profits and expand business across the Mediterranean and Atlantic. Tax leasing was probably a key business branch, which would provide them with liquidity and streamline capital flow. As a result, they would greatly expand their ability to offer credit, which will be detailed later. This type of initiative was not unique in the peninsula, since other communities, for example in the Kingdom of Valencia, already proceeded this way by diversifying and generating capital for multiple businesses (García Marsilla, 2002: 97).

In Portugal, some evidence of this diversification was found, as well as the partnerships between the locals and Italians, through the examination of some of the acquittance letters between the 1440s and 1460s, concerning different businesses: the *aver-do-peso*, colored cloths, the court's chancery, payments on noblemen's housing and the "English Quarter". These sources provided some clues regarding a possible concentration of interests in certain segments. Within the investment plans to be analyzed, the deal[61] typically concerned the leasing of sales taxes on commodities sold by weight, between 1444 and 1449 (see Table 5.3); the analysis revealed some interesting features. In these years, however, only figures relating to the totals received in each year and the respective tenants were identified. It is interesting to look at the evolution of this revenue in the period.

It should be noted that the amounts received in the first two years were clearly well below the stipulated. Consequently, the tenants had to bear the losses. However, the evolution of the amount received between the second and third years was of particular interest, since it rose by more than 4,800%. In addition, it is also worth mentioning the change and variation of the tenants' associations from year to year. Moreover, there were Christian tenants in the first year of the five-year leases, many with heavy losses. Later, after registering a very strong increase in the values collected in 1446, there were noblemen and ecclesiastical investors, evidently attracted by the excellent perspectives of profit that were to come. This profit continued to grow the following year, and it was under the control of the Jewish tenants subsequently.

Table 5.3 Revenues of *aver-do-peso* in Lisbon (in reais brancos)

YEAR	1444	1445	1446	1447	1448
TOTAL RECEIVED/ COLLECTED	34,634	21,143	1,031,439	1,042,857	1,081,066
TOTAL LEASED IN CONTRACT	888,571.5	977,143	1,031,439	1,042,857	1,080,000
TENANTS	Nuno Fernandes, João Afonso, David Gabay, Jacob Colodro and their partners	Salomon Latam, David Naomias, David Gabay and their partners	David Gabay, Moussem Beacar and their partners	Álvaro Gonçalves (Lisbon archbishop's servant), Pero Anes (Prince Fernando's servant) and their partners	Abraham Zarco, Abraham Faião the old, Master Nacim Crispim, David Naomias, Farão "rich man" and their partners

Source: ANTT, Leitura Nova, *Estremadura*, liv. 8, fl. 237–237v.

Regarding the tax farming business of the *sisas* on colored cloths in Lisbon (see Table 5.4), the sources gathered[62] between 1449 and 1454 allowed us to reconstruct a similar picture of revenues for that period. Right off the bat, there was an increase in the values received, with a strong rise between the first and second year; further down, another relevant rise between the sixth and seventh, and then a fall and a stabilization. In addition, on the tenants' list, the was a predominance of the Jewish community, some of them merchants, and some already involved with the *aver-do-peso* tax leasing, and others with similar last names, who appeared here in conjunction with different investments. This also reflects the difference between the contracts and the collection (as seen in Figure 5.4), as well as a possible diversification of activities within the same families of wealthy traders and men of successful businesses, managers of the destinies of Lisbon's community and influential in the county's organization (Tavares, 1982: 131–134).

Within a framework of a possible investment diversification, the leasing of noblemen's housing subsidies' payments was what seemed to attract greater interest, given the amounts involved. In this situation, the leaseholders received from the monarch the permission to make the respective payments and were in charge of raising the necessary amounts to make the respective payments. The resources were released by the king, and the tenants sought them out where they existed. With this, it is even possible to verify the existence of other leaseholders from other tax collections.[63] Through examination of the sources, it was possible to extract a set of relevant information in this sense (see Table 5.5).

Table 5.4 Revenues of sales taxes (*sisa*) on colored cloth in Lisbon (in reais brancos)

YEAR	TOTAL RECEIVED/ COLLECTED	TOTAL LEASED IN CONTRACT	TENANTS
1446	774,879	1,371,429	Judas Alho, Levi and their partners
1447	1,371,429	1,371,429	Nacim Faião, David Negro "the young" and their partners
1448	1,372,610	1,371,429	Guedelha Negro, Jacob Faião, Jacob Colodro and their partners
1449	1,405,714		Abraham Zarco, Master David and Albotene (all Jewish residents in Lisbon), and their partners
1450	1,542,857*	1,542,857*	David Negro "the young" and Abraham Zarco, Jewish merchants, residents in Lisbon, and their partners
1451	1,628,571*	1,628,571*	Salomon Faião and their partners
1452	2,174,926.5	2,314,286	Guedelha Vivas and their partners
1453	1,805,714	1,805,714	David Negro, David Gabay and Judas Albotene, Jewish merchants, residents in Lisbon, and their partners
1454	1,814,406	1,937,143	Isaac Amado and his partners

* The values of 1450 and 1451 are indexed in libras (54,000,000 and 57,000,000, respectively). Converted in reais brancos, following the rate of 1 real to 35 libras, we reach the presented values.

Source: ANTT, *Chanc. Afonso V*, liv. 3, fl. 29–29v and liv. 34, fl. 157v; Leitura Nova, *Estremadura*, liv. 4, fl. 288–288v and liv. 8, fl. 250–250v.

The central aspect here is the Italian investors' strong presence, with the participation of the Lomellini, whose presence in Portugal is already known and well-studied,[64] featuring the brothers Leonardo and Marco as partners in this company between 1447 and 1449. The second also appears in partnership with the same Jewish leaseholder, in 1450 and 1451, in the expenditure list of a different acquittance, i.e., he received money from another tax collection for the colored cloth's *sisas* in Lisbon, "from which the rent is deducted for the dwellings' payments of the residents of our household, to whom they had the incumbency to pay".[65] This highlights also that only in the second year there was an unfavorable difference to be covered by the dealers. For the other three years, there were very reasonable positive balances, which may also be part of the deal, thus these excesses would revert partially or fully to the investors, although there was no mention of this in the source. What is certain is that businessmen did not invest with low gain prospects, even when negotiating deals bestowed directly by the monarch, so that the royal interest was not disrespected and, at the same time, could have an outcome normally favorable to interested investors (Tavares, 1982: 279–280).

In another letter, another important Jewish businessman, Guedelha Palaçano, together with some partners, received the total value of 18,484,235 reais between 1475 and 1479 "from the time that he had the dwellings' deal with his partners,

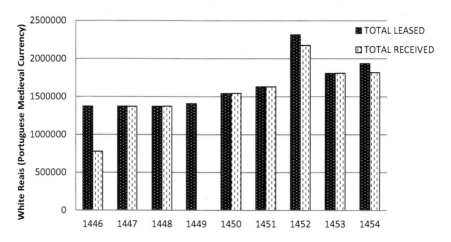

Figure 5.4 Total leased versus total received regarding the sales taxes (*sisa*) on colored cloth in Lisbon (in reais brancos/white reais – Portuguese Medieval Currency)

Table 5.5 Revenues of royal dwellings' payments, c.1446–1449 (in reais brancos)

YEAR	TOTAL GATHERED	TOTAL SPENT	PREMIUM	PARTNERS
1446	1,948,748	1,945,902	30,000	Judah Abravanel and João Dias Beleágua (esquire, Lisbon's resident, and Prince Pedro's servant)
1447	2,418,902	2,788,382	42,000	Judah Abravanel and Leonardo Lomelim (Italian, merchant based in Lisbon)
1448	2,584,493	2,280,310	42,000	Judah Abravanel and Leonardo Lomelim (Italian, merchant based in Lisbon)
1449	3,564,204	3,501,754	54,000	Judah Abravanel and Marco Lomelim (Italian, merchant based in Lisbon)

Source: ANTT, *Chanc. D. Afonso V*, liv. 3, fl. 86v-87; copied at Leitura Nova, *Livro dos Extras*, fl. 149v-150.

when was prince our King João, whom God almighty had". It should be noted that thirty years earlier the total value for a similar deal, although shorter, was 10,516,348 reais. There was, therefore, a variation of more than 75% of the funds earmarked for that purpose, which naturally explained the attraction of interested parties.

The Chancellery of the House of Supplication also offered reasonable possibilities of gain. As the highest instance of justice for superior appeals, the House judged only certain crimes. Chaired by a *regedor* ("chief justice") and divided in two sections, it evaluated demands, decided pardons or sentences' commutations and considered petitions from lower instances. Its tasks included the deliberation of cases of gold, silver and currency exports, setting of the clerk remuneration and also stipulating rates of emoluments,[66] which could be quite seductive. One of the acquittance letters of 1455[67] accounted for all that was received and spent in 1452 and 1453 by a group of Jewish tenants. For those years, the investors' treatment totaled 36,000,000 libras equivalent to 1,028,571 reais – 18,000,000 libras per year. In this particular case, the business proved profitable for the Crown, albeit modestly, due to the low values of the arbitration processes submitted in the years in question.

Finally, the business of the English Quarter[68] can also be examined via Juda Abravanel's diversified business roll. Another letter from 1467[69] confirmed his investments in Flanders: the lease of this activity for three years was worth 3,000 crowns, yielding 504,000 reais, which was paid to Vicente Gil, a powerful merchant. That sum was quite high, especially considering the fact that he appeared to have been the sole investor.

From the sources gathered, we can ascertain that there was enough evidence not only of the varied range of commercial and financial options available to Jewish and Italian (and Portuguese, of course) investors but also the concentration of interests in certain branches of taxation and finances. Apparently, it was worth investing not only in business and good relations with the monarch but also from the strategic point of view of liquidity and easy access to money, wherever and whatever it was needed for.

It is also clear that, in order to carry out major initiatives, such as war, it was fundamental that a kingdom had to be in a situation, if not economically privileged but at least unhindered, with favorable conditions for obtaining credit from strong economic groups. Regardless of the kingdom or monarch, the more distinct the conditions were, the greater and more equipped an army that could be in its service. However, the difficulty in managing military expenditure only with regular resources was quite evident. The use of the *empréstimo* and other extraordinary sources, as well as the use of the new "monetary technologies" – namely, using bills of exchange instead of carrying large cash-filled trunks or the artifice of public debt to generate a faster cash flow – was a necessity common to all western medieval kingdoms (Chevalier, 2002: I, 50–52).

War changed the nature of revenues in a profound way within the context of Portuguese royal finances. This effect was fundamentally carried out by the *sisas*' profile revolution, becoming a permanent income, which allowed them to "escape the effects of the devaluation and currency *breaks* that had plagued the monarchs of the past, and at the same time connected their wealth with the economic dynamics of the kingdom" (Henriques, 2008: 180–181). Credit, either on a small or large scale, had a preponderant role with regard to the advance of money in moments of urgent need. It could be translated into requests to individuals with greater possibilities, even foreigners and rivals from opposite sides in the same conflict (Chevalier, 2002: I, 53–57). Or in public interventions, in the case

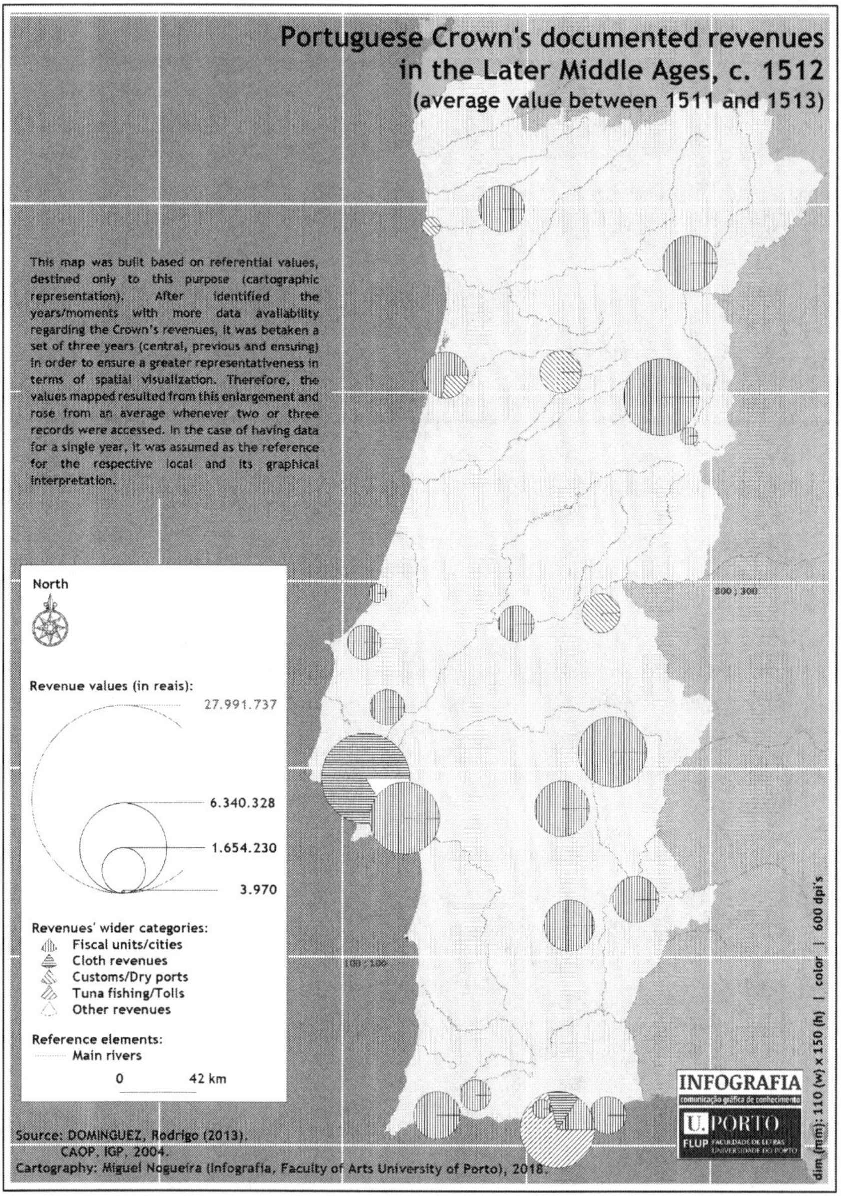
Portuguese Crown's documented revenues
in the Later Middle Ages, c. 1512
(average value between 1511 and 1513)
This map was built based on referential values, destined only to this purpose (cartographic representation). After identified the years/moments with more data availability regarding the Crown's revenues, it was betaken a set of three years (central, previous and ensuing) in order to ensure a greater representativeness in terms of spatial visualization. Therefore, the values mapped resulted from this enlargement and rose from an average whenever two or three records were accessed. In the case of having data for a single year, it was assumed as the reference for the respective local and its graphical interpretation.
North
Revenue values (in reais):
27.991.737
6.340.328
1.654.230
3.970
Revenues' wider categories:
Fiscal units/cities
Cloth revenues
Customs/Dry ports
Tuna fishing/Tolls
Other revenues
Reference elements:
Main rivers
0
42 km
300 ; 300
100 ; 100
INFOGRAFIA
U. PORTO
FLUP
dim (mm): 110 (w) x 150 (h) | color | 600 dpi's
Source: DOMINGUEZ, Rodrigo (2013).
CAOP, IGP, 2004.
Cartography: Miguel Nogueira (Infografia, Faculty of Arts University of Porto), 2018.

Map 5.4 Portuguese Crown's documented revenues in the later Middle Ages, c.1512 (average value between 1511 and 1513)

of seeking credit through the issuance of debt securities (Menjot, 2008: 705). What was particularly important pertained to the process streamlining, so that the resources arrived faster into the state coffers. On the other hand, this form of financing would charge its price in the medium term, when the kingdom opted to follow the path of debt consolidation. The *Padrões de Juro* ("Portuguese debt securities"), in their first issuances during in the sixteenth century, would suffer disproportionately due to the higher interest rates charged (Ferreira, 1985: IV, 512–513; Magalhães, 2012b: 87–100). In one of those situations, related to the issue of credit diligence in other markets, in 1458, Diogo Dias de Abreu, knight of the Portuguese royal household, was sent to Barcelona to obtain money in the respective *taulas de canvi* ("exchange currency bureau") for the purchase of gunpowder and other things for Afonso V.[70] Those products were loaded on a caravel, which was shipwrecked on the way, but some of the cargo was still saved. In another source, the king's chaplain and Canon of Coimbra, Vasco Peres, reported that he received money from the same *taulas* in Barcelona, mentioning the same Diogo Dias.[71] Nevertheless, the letter did not clarify if it was the same money.

In the case of military enterprises, the same investors' group that were interested in the auction processes of the *sisas* and other taxes, as well as the royalties' payments, was also financially involved with the Crown. On several occasions, they would help the monarchs in times of emergency to obtain money, mostly for that purpose. As much as the *pedidos* and the *empréstimos* served in this regard, the financial boost provided by this network of Jewish merchants and investors was quite reasonable as they also advanced substantial sums of credit. In the case of preparations for the war with Castile in 1478, the same Guedelha Palaçano who assisted the monarch with more than 1,000,000 reais in cash and cloth (Tavares, 1982: 132) was also the same one that leased payments of the duties detailed previously. Others, in partnership with Porto merchants, engaged in the business concerning the exchange and fiscal resources received for the Navy against the Turks.[72] Money, which was redirected for the seizure of Alcácer Ceguer, "whom the said master sent to the bank of Cosmo de Medici or other banks where he was well paid". Merchants acting as "ambassadors" put forth their good image as successful businessmen who abide by their commitments, serving as a bridge between the monarch that was not always reliable and international financial institutions.

The hiatus between the ordinary and extraordinary tax collection and the effective money delivery to the royal treasury, which was as a problem to be overcome, was also the source of another phenomenon: the emergence of usurers and loan sharks among the Crown officers. In addition, there were examples of people within the administration who became leaseholders of some duties and taxes, probably obtaining precious "inside information" in the process. As an example, the case of Gonçalo Anes is symptomatic, *almoxarife* at the city of Guarda,[73] as previously mentioned. When presenting the account of his own collection in 1436, he pointed out himself as the tenant of the *sisas* on cloths sold at the fair of S. Bartholomew, in Trancoso, in that year, amounting to 430,220 libras, as well as the collector of the *sisas* on the Jewish merchants of the same fair, for

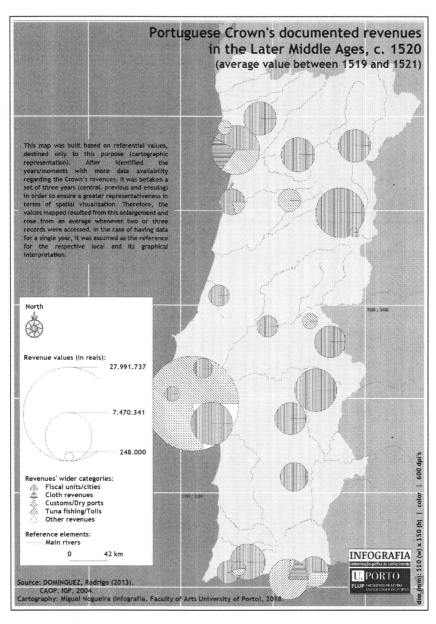

Map 5.5 Portuguese Crown's documented revenues in the later Middle Ages, c.1520 (average value between 1519 and 1521)

whose rights there was no investor that year. In another case, Fernão Cardoso, receiver of the *almoxarifado* in Torre de Moncorvo[74] and dry ports of *Trás-os-Montes*, while accounting for the money he received and spent between 1455 and 1456, and the *pedido* collected for Infanta Joana's marriage, mentioned the former *almoxarife*, João Esteves, who had loaned the king 20,000 reais for his sister's wedding. Altogether, a major part of the sources indicated the renting of revenues but, particularly regarding the acquittances granted since the reign of Manuel I, the tenants were not identified, making it impossible to disclose more examples. Nevertheless, in Algarve, some situations were revealed, such as the case of João Cordovil,[75] a tenant and at the same time a receiver in Lagos between 1506 and 1507, and Pero Machado,[76] leaseholder and receiver of the Silves' *almoxarifado* in 1513. From the present day perspective this perhaps would have constituted a huge conflict of interests, but at that time, if it did not constitute the perfect scenario for the monarch, at least it did not cause any astonishment or lead to more habitual and practical issues in terms of supervision. In Portugal, this practice was common, confirmed by the amount of legislation against usury or "onzena", for which examples go back to the reign of Dinis I (1279–1325) and were also very alive in the Afonsine Ordinations, the compilation of laws gathered under Afonso V (1438–1481), and also in the Manueline Ordinations[77] under Manuel I (1495–1521).

Notes

1 ANTT, *Chanc. D. Manuel I*, liv. 31, fl. 107; copied at Leitura Nova, *Estremadura*, liv. 1, fl. 223. Published in Marques (1988: III, 486–487).
2 Viana (2000: 577). See also Beirante (1980, 1981).
3 ANTT, *Chanc. D. Manuel I*, liv. 28, fl. 5v; copied at Leitura Nova, *Estremadura*, liv. 2, fl. 54v. Published in Freire (1905: III, 387–388).
4 ANTT, *Chanc. D. Manuel I*, liv. 31, fl. 99; copied at Leitura Nova, *Guadiana*, liv. 1, fl. 80. Published in Freire (1904: II, 80).
5 ANTT, Leitura Nova, *Guadiana*, liv. 7, fl. 185 v-186.
6 Known in Portuguese as the *foro das galinhas*, we believe it was a levy regarding poultry (bird breeding) within Royal lands.
7 ANTT, *Chanc. D. Afonso V*, liv. 23, fl. 2–3; copied at Leitura Nova, *Guadiana*, liv. 6, fl. 122v.
8 ANTT, *Chanc. D. João III*, liv. 13 de doações, fl. 26v. Published in Freire (1914: IX, 435).
9 ANTT, *Chanc. D. Afonso V*, liv. 27, fl. 65–65v.
10 ANTT, *Chanc. D. Manuel I*, liv. 16, fl. 77; copied at Leitura Nova, *Guadiana*, liv. 5, fl. 100. Published in Freire (1905: III, 389).
11 ANTT, *Chanc. D. Manuel I*, liv. 7, fl. 38v; copied at Leitura Nova, *Guadiana*, liv. 7, fl. 158. Published in Freire (1907: V, 323).
12 ANTT, Leitura Nova, *Guadiana*, liv. 7, fl. 136v-137.
13 ANTT, *Chanc. D. Manuel I*, liv. 42, fl. 12; copied at Leitura Nova, *Místicos*, liv. 5, fl. 136. Published in Freire (1905: III, 388).
14 ANTT, *Chanc. D. Manuel I*, liv. 31, fl. 8v; copied at Leitura Nova, *Guadiana*, liv. 1, fl. 73. Published in Freire (1906: IV, 74).
15 ANTT, *Chanc. D. João III*, liv. 1 de doações, fl. 50. Published in Freire (1910: VIII, 399).
16 ANTT, *Chanc. D. Manuel I*, liv. 6, fl. 27v; copied at Leitura Nova, *Alem Douro*, liv. 3, fl. 197v. Published in Freire (1907: V, 73).

17 ANTT, *Chanc. D. João III*, liv. 13 de doações, fl. 15v. Published in Freire (1914: IX, 434).
18 ANTT, *Chanc. D. João III*, liv. 1 de doações, fl. 116v. Published in Freire (1910: VIII, 407).
19 ANTT, *Chanc. D. Afonso V*, liv. 18, fl. 63–65.
20 Conversion rate: 1 Real = 35 libras (pounds).
21 ANTT, *Chanc. D. Manuel I*, liv. 17, fl. 4; copied at Leitura Nova, *Beira*, liv. 2, fl. 152. Published in Freire (1903: I, 247).
22 ANTT, Leitura Nova, *Beira*, liv. 3, fl. 84–84v.
23 ANTT, Leitura Nova, *Beira*, liv. 3, fl. 92.
24 ANTT, *Chanc. D. João III*, liv. 1 de doações, fl. 9. Published in Freire (1910: VIII, 393).
25 ANTT, *Chanc. D. João III*, liv. 45 de doações, fl. 125v. Published in Freire (1914: IX, 464).
26 ANTT, *Chanc. D. Afonso V*, liv. 27, fl. 116v.
27 ANTT, *Chanc. D. Afonso V*, liv. 34, fl. 162v. Published in Azevedo (1915: I, 412–416).
28 ANTT, Leitura Nova, *Além Douro*, liv. 1, fl. 236v.
29 ANTT, *Chanc. D. Manuel I*, liv. 36, fl. 28v; copied at Leitura Nova, *Além Douro*, liv. 5, fl. 5v. Published in Freire (1904: II, 235).
30 ANTT, *Chanc. D. Manuel I*, liv. 38, fl. 123v; copied at Leitura Nova, *Além Douro*, liv. 5, fl. 34v. Published in Freire (1904: II, 36).
31 ANTT, *Chanc. D. João III*, liv. 12 de doações, fl. 56. Published in Freire (1914: IX, 443–444).
32 ANTT, *Chanc. D. Manuel I*, liv. 17, fl. 34v; copied at Leitura Nova, *Estremadura*, liv. 2, fl. 104v. Published in Freire (1907: V, 79).
33 ANTT, Leitura Nova, *Estremadura*, liv. 12, fl. 35v. Published in Freire (1907: V, 473).
34 ANTT, *Chanc. D. João III*, liv. 12 de doações, fl. 6v. Published in Freire (1914: IX, 439).
35 ANTT, *Chanc. D. Manuel I*, liv. 7, fl. 9; copied at Leitura Nova, *Estremadura*, liv. 12, fl. 2. Published in Freire (1904: II, 427).
36 ANTT, Leitura Nova, *Guadiana*, liv.7, fl. 191. Published in Freire (1906: IV, 476).
37 ANTT, Leitura Nova, *Guadiana*, liv. 7, fl. 169–169v.
38 Cunha (1972: 18–20). See also Magalhães (1988, 2012a: 64).
39 ANTT, *Chanc. D. João III*, liv. 1 de doações, fl. 29. Published in Freire (1910: VIII, 395).
40 ANTT, *Chanc. D. Afonso V*, liv. 34, fl. 162v. Published in Azevedo (1915: I, 412–416).
41 ANTT, *Chanc. D. Manuel I*, liv. 38, fl. 121v; copied at Leitura Nova, *Além Douro*, liv. 5, fl. 36v. Published in Freire (1906: IV, 446).
42 ANTT, *Chanc. D. Afonso V*, liv. 18, fl. 63–65.
43 ANTT, Leitura Nova, *Estremadura*, liv. 4, fl. 288–288v.
44 ANTT, *Chanc. D. Afonso V*, liv. 11, fl. 143v-144.
45 ANTT, Leitura Nova, *Estremadura*, liv. 8, fl. 237–237v.
46 ANTT, Leitura Nova, *Livro dos Extras*, fl. 89–91.
47 According to the *Sumário das rendas do Rey do anno de 1473*, the warehouse and the *almoxarifado* of Lisbon were different branches, mainly because they are listed in the budget receiving different sums: 180,000 *reais* and 4,700,000 *reais*, respectively. See Faro (1965: 82–83).
48 ANTT, *Chanc. D. Manuel I*, liv. 17, fl. 20; copied at Leitura Nova, *Estremadura*, liv. 2, fl. 97v. Published in Freire (1906: IV, 284–285).
49 ANTT, *Chanc. D. Manuel I*, liv. 34, fl. 79v; copied at Leitura Nova, *Estremadura*, liv. 2, fl. 4v. Published in Freire (1903: I, 94).
50 ANTT, *Chanc. D. Manuel I*, liv. 17, fl. 20; copied at Leitura Nova, *Estremadura*, liv. 2, fl. 98. Published in Freire (1906: IV, 285–286).
51 ANTT, Leitura Nova, *Guadiana*, liv. 7, fl. 158v-159v.
52 ANTT, *Chanc. D. Manuel I*, liv. 6, fl. 39; copied at Leitura Nova, *Livro dos Extras*, liv. 6, fl. 26. Published in Freire (1903: I, 243–244); ANTT, *Chanc. D. Manuel I*, liv. 7, fl. 32; copied at Leitura Nova, *Místicos*, liv. 6, fl. 112v. Published in Freire (1903: I, 244).
53 ANTT, Leitura Nova, *Livro dos Extras*, fl. 163v-164.
54 ANTT, *Chanc. D. Manuel I*, liv. 28, fl. 51v; copied at Leitura Nova, *Estremadura*, liv. 2, fl. 60. Published in Freire (1904: II, 235–236).

55 Gonçalves (1964: 40–41).
56 ANTT, Leitura Nova, *Além Douro*, liv. 1, fl. 26–26v.
57 ANTT, Leitura Nova, *Guadiana*, liv. 7, fl. 174–174v.
58 ANTT, *Chanc. D. Afonso V*, liv. 23, fl. 2–3; copied at Leitura Nova, *Guadiana*, liv. 6, fl. 122v; ANTT, *Chanc. D. Afonso V*, liv. 27, fl. 65–65v.
59 As an example, the sales taxes charged on Jewish merchants (*sisa judenga*) at St. Bartholomew fair, in the village of Trancoso, in 1436, were not leased, and it was collected by the local *almoxarife*, Gonçalo Anes.
60 *Monumenta Henricina* (1965: VII, 176).
61 ANTT, Leitura Nova, *Estremadura*, liv. 8, fl. 237–237v.
62 ANTT, Leitura Nova, *Estremadura*, liv. 8, fl. 250–250v; *Chanc. D. Afonso V*, liv. 34, fl. 157v; *Chanc. D. Afonso V*, liv. 3, fl. 29–29v; and Leitura Nova, *Estremadura*, liv. 4, fl. 288–288v.
63 ANTT, *Chanc. D. Afonso V*, liv. 3, fl. 86v–87; copied at Leitura Nova, *Livro dos Extras*, fl. 149v-150; ANTT, Leitura Nova, *Livro dos Extras*, fl. 172v-173; ANTT, Leitura Nova, *Livro dos Extras*, fl. 163v-164.
64 See Rau (1968).
65 ANTT, *Chanc. D. Afonso V*, liv. 3, fl. 29–29v.
66 Regarding the House of Supplication, see Costa (1996: 71–102).
67 ANTT, *Chanc. D. Afonso V*, liv. 15, fl. 73v-74; copied at Leitura Nova, *Livro dos Extras*, fl. 84.
68 We do believe, with not much certainty, that this *quarto dos ingleses* was a tax charged on the goods and transactions made by English merchants at the Portuguese factory in Flanders.
69 ANTT, Leitura Nova, *Estremadura*, liv. 4, fl. 217v-218. Published in Tavares (1982: 288–289).
70 ANTT, *Chanc. D. Afonso V*, liv. 36, fl. 223.
71 ANTT, *Chanc. D. Afonso V*, liv. 36, fl. 155–155v.
72 ANTT, Leitura Nova, *Além Douro*, liv. 3, fl. 285v-286.
73 ANTT, *Chanc. D. Afonso V*, liv. 18, fl. 63–65.
74 ANTT, Leitura Nova, *Além Douro*, liv. 4, fl. 104–104v.
75 ANTT, Leitura Nova, *Guadiana*, liv. 7, fl. 145–146.
76 ANTT, *Chanc. D. Manuel I*, liv. 15, fl. 63; copied at Leitura Nova, *Místicos*, liv. 5, fl. 139v. Published in Freire (1905: III, 475–476).
77 *Ordenações Afonsinas* (1984: II, 303; 521–525); (1984: IV, 93–99); *Ordenações Manuelinas* (1984: II, 148–150).

Bibliography

Primary sources

ANTT, Chanc. D. Afonso V, liv. 3.
ANTT, Chanc. D. Afonso V, liv. 11.
ANTT, Chanc. D. Afonso V, liv. 15.
ANTT, Chanc. D. Afonso V, liv. 18.
ANTT, Chanc. D. Afonso V, liv. 23.
ANTT, Chanc. D. Afonso V, liv. 27.
ANTT, Chanc. D. Afonso V, liv. 34.
ANTT, Chanc. D. Afonso V, liv. 36.
ANTT, Chanc. D. Manuel I, liv. 6.
ANTT, Chanc. D. Manuel I, liv. 7.
ANTT, Chanc. D. Manuel I, liv. 15.
ANTT, Chanc. D. Manuel I, liv. 16.

ANTT, Chanc. D. Manuel I, liv. 17.
ANTT, Chanc. D. Manuel I, liv. 28.
ANTT, Chanc. D. Manuel I, liv. 31.
ANTT, Chanc. D. Manuel I, liv. 34.
ANTT, Chanc. D. Manuel I, liv. 36.
ANTT, Chanc. D. Manuel I, liv. 38.
ANTT, Chanc. D. Manuel I, liv. 42.
ANTT, Chanc. D. João III, liv. 1 de doações.
ANTT, Chanc. D. João III, liv. 12 de doações.
ANTT, Chanc. D. João III, liv. 13 de doações.
ANTT, Chanc. D. João III, liv. 45 de doações.
ANTT, Leitura Nova, Além Douro, liv. 1.
ANTT, Leitura Nova, Além Douro, liv. 3.
ANTT, Leitura Nova, Além Douro, liv. 4.
ANTT, Leitura Nova, Além Douro, liv. 5.
ANTT, Leitura Nova, Beira, liv. 2.
ANTT, Leitura Nova, Beira, liv. 3.
ANTT, Leitura Nova, Estremadura, liv. 1.
ANTT, Leitura Nova, Estremadura, liv. 2.
ANTT, Leitura Nova, Estremadura, liv. 4.
ANTT, Leitura Nova, Estremadura, liv. 8.
ANTT, Leitura Nova, Estremadura, liv. 12.
ANTT, Leitura Nova, Guadiana, liv. 1.
ANTT, Leitura Nova, Guadiana, liv. 5.
ANTT, Leitura Nova, Guadiana, liv. 6.
ANTT, Leitura Nova, Guadiana, liv. 7.
ANTT, Leitura Nova, Livro dos Extras.
ANTT, Leitura Nova, Místicos, liv. 5.
ANTT, Leitura Nova, Místicos, liv. 6.

Secondary sources, royal chronicles and dictionaries

Azevedo, P. de. (1915–1934). *Documentos das chancelarias reais anteriores a 1531 relativos a Marrocos*, 2 vols. Lisbon: Academia das Sciências de Lisboa.

Carneiro, M. B. (1818). *Resumo chronologico das leis mais uteis no foro e uso da vida civil publicadas até o presente anno*, vol. I. Lisbon: Impressão Régia.

Chaves, A. L. de. (1983). *Livro de Apontamentos (1438–1489)*. Códice 443 da Colecção Pombalina da BNL, introdução e transcrição de Anastásia Mestrinho Salgado e Abílio José Salgado. Lisbon: Imprensa Nacional – Casa da Moeda.

Faro, J. (1965). *Receitas e despesas da Fazenda Real de 1384 a 1481: subsídios documentais*. Lisbon: Instituto Nacional de Estatística.

Ferreira, M. E. (1985). Padrões de Juro, in Dicionário de História de Portugal. Porto: Livraria Figueirinhas, 4, 512–513.

Freire, A. B. (1903–1916). "Cartas de Quitação del rei D. Manuel", in *Archivo Historico Portuguez*, 11 vols. Lisbon: Of. Typographica-Calçada do Cabra.

Marques, J. M. da S. (1988). *Descobrimentos Portugueses: documentos para a sua História*, 5 vols, 2nd ed. Lisbon: INIC.

Monumenta Henricina, 15 vols. Comissão Executiva do V Centenário da Morte do Infante D. Henrique. Coimbra: Graf. Atlântida, 1960–1974.

Oliveira, F. N. de. (1804). Livro das Grandezas de Lisboa. Lisbon: Impressão Régia, 1804.

Ordenações Afonsinas. (1984). Edição fac-similada da edição feita na Real imprensa da Universidade de Coimbra, no ano de 1792, 5 vols. Lisbon: Fundação Calouste Gulbenkian.

Ordenações Manuelinas. (1984). Edição fac-similada da edição feita na Real imprensa da Universidade de Coimbra, no ano de 1797, Prefácio de Mário Júlio de Almeida Costa, 5 vols. Lisbon: Fundação Calouste Gulbenkian.

Serrão, J. (1984–1985). *Dicionário de História de Portugal*, 6 vols. Porto: Livraria Figueirinhas.

Sousa, J. R. M. de C. C. e. (1783–1791). *Systema, ou Collecção dos Regimentos Reaes*, 6 vols. Lisbon: Oficina de Francisco Borges de Sousa.

Zurara, G. E. de. (1978). *Crónica de D. Duarte de Menezes: edição diplomática de Larry King*. Lisbon: Universidade Nova de Lisboa – Faculdade de Ciências Sociais e Humanas.

Studies

Beirante, M. A. (1980). *Santarém Medieval*. Lisbon: FCSH.

Beirante, M. A. (1981). *Santarém Quinhentista*. Lisbon: Livaria Portugal.

Chevalier, B. (2002). Le financement de la première guerre d'Italie, in P. Contamine, J. Kerhervé, & A. Rigaudière (dir.), *L'impôt au Moyen Âge: l'impôt public et le prélèvement seigneurial, fin XIIe – début XVie siècle*. Actes du colloque tenu à Bercy les 14, 15 et 16 juin 2000. Paris: Comité pour L'Histoire Économique et Financière de la France, I, 41–66.

Costa, Pre. A. J. da. (1996). A Chancelaria Real Portuguesa e os seus registos, de 1217 a 1438, Revista da Faculdade de Letras: História, série II, 13, 71–101.

Cunha, R. B. da S. (1972). *Subsídios para a conservação do peixe em Portugal dos séculos XII ao XVI*. Coimbra: Coimbra Editora.

Dominguez, R. da C. (2009). *Mercadores e banqueiros: Sociedade e Economia no Portugal dos séculos XIV e XV*. Brasília: Hinterlândia Editorial.

Duarte, L. M. (1995). A actividade mineira em Portugal durante a Idade Média, Revista da Faculdade de Letras: História, série II, 12, 75–112.

García Marsilla, J. V. (2002). *Vivir a Crédito en la Valencia Medieval: de los orígenes del sistema censal al endeudamiento del municipio*. València: Universitat de València.

Gonçalves, I. (1964). *Pedidos e empréstimos públicos em Portugal durante a Idade Média*. Lisbon: Cadernos de Ciência e Técnica Fiscal: Centro de estudos fiscais da direcção-geral das contribuições e impostos – Ministério das Finanças.

Gonçalves, I. (1987). As finanças municipais do Porto na segunda metade do século XV. Porto: Câmara Municipal do Porto, 1987.

Henriques, A. M. B. de M. de C. (2008). *State Finance, War and Redistribution in Portugal (1249–1527)*. Ph.D. Thesis. Department of History, University of York.

Magalhães, J. R. (1988). *O Algarve Económico (1600–1773)*. Lisbon: Editorial Estampa.

Magalhães, J. R. (2012a). Panorama social e económico do Algarve na época de D. Jerónimo Osório, in *O Algarve na época moderna: miúnças 2*. Coimbra: Coimbra University Press, 55–68.

Magalhães, J. R. (2012b). Padrões de juro, património e vínculos no século XVI, in *No Portugal Moderno: Espaços, tratos e dinheiros – Miúnças 3*. Coimbra: Coimbra University Press, 87–100.

Marques, J. (1989). O Príncipe D. João II e a recolha das pratas das igrejas para custear a guerra com Castela, *Actas do Congresso Internacional Bartolomeu Dias e a sua época, vol. I*. Porto: Universidade do Porto – Comissão nacional para as comemorações dos descobrimentos portugueses, 201–219.

Menjot, D. (2008). Les enjeux de la fiscalité directe dans les systèmes financiers et fiscaux des villes castillanes aux XIVᵉ et XVᵉ siècles", in *Actas La fiscalità nell'economia europea (sec. XIII-XVIII)*, 39th Settimana di Studi dell'istituto "Francesco Datini" di Prato a cura di Simonetta Cavaciocchi. Firenze: Firenze University Press, 699–729.

Ormrod, W. M. (1995). The West European Monarchies in the Later Middle Ages, in R. Bonney (ed.), *Economic Systems and State Finance*. Oxford: Oxford University Press, 123–160.

Pereira, J. C. (2003). *Portugal na Era de Quinhentos: estudos varios*. Cascais: Patrimonia.

Rau, V. (1968). Uma família de mercadores italianos em Portugal no século XV: os Lomellini, in *Estudos de História: mercadores, mercadorias, pensamento económico*, vol. 1. Lisbon: Editorial Verbo, 13–57.

Sousa, R. M. de. (2003). Moeda e Estado: políticas monetárias e determinantes da procura (1688–1797), Análise Social, XXXVIII, 168, 771–792.

Tavares, M. J. P. F. (1982). *Os Judeus em Portugal no Século XV*, 1st ed. Lisbon: Nova University of Lisbon.

Viana, M. (2000). A propriedade do concelho de Santarém em 1500, Arquipélago: História, 2nd, IV/2, 551–584.

6 Administrative and fiscal structures in Western European context

Taxation should not be seen merely as an instrument to cover public expenditure. As an institution, it has a broader meaning, within the context of economic development. It indicates a greater desire on the part of the State, as a regulator of a society and provider of its infrastructures, to increase its sources of income and because of this, to control popular demands, through the political and economic arrangements with privileged social groups, as well as to exert greater tax pressure on taxpayers. However, the choice of those who could be taxed or not, that is, the arrangements and paths of wealth redistribution, the taxation setting levels and the economic/social dynamics that were established around the fiscal regime is of the utmost importance for the genesis of fiscal administrative structures. Moreover, that scenario was also fundamental for the tax system's success, as well as for the relationship between the population and the ruling urban elites (Menjot, 2008: 700). From whom would the money be collected? Were any groups more taxable than others? Who pays more and who pays less? Usually the vast majority of the inhabitants were taxable. However, exceptions were frequent, and the amount of privileges legally granted by the king strongly encouraged clientelism and, as a side effect, often put royal finances in dire straits (Menjot, 2008: 721).

In order to compensate for this, the administrative and fiscal structure was designed and built from the perspective of revenues, its dynamism and growth. But much more important, however, was the decision not simply to collect but actually to account for revenues and, to a lesser extent, for expenditure. In other words, to make state officials responsible for the money collected and dispensed in the name of the monarch (Ormrod & Barta, 1995: 63). This state was, simultaneously, taking the first steps toward enhanced and better integrated financial control mechanisms. Improvements were very much needed, and new structures (or policies) were essential to better meet the needs of a realm whose economic activity had already developed in different directions. The Portuguese economy's structure, as well as the fiscal demands and institutions were not the same as those in the twelfth and thirteenth centuries. Besides, the fundamental reason for the development of a more advanced fiscal system and institutions in this or any other era was clearly financial need: revenue growth usually reflects an equal or proportional – and even higher – increase in expenditure (Ormrod & Barta, 1995: 72).

In any case, there are a number of complex factors to be taken into account, both for the construction and to a system reformation, which were largely overshadowed by political issues. Hence the most recent analysis strongly suggests that the fundamental reason for the divergence regarding the development of administrative and fiscal structures that appeared post-1200 lies in the nature of tenurial relationship between the ruler and his closest major subjects. In Europe, where feudalism flourished naturally in the institutional ruins of the Roman Empire, the aristocracy retained a high degree of autonomy, even when confronted with the most ambitious centralizing tendencies. On the other hand, in realms where this feudal system was introduced as the substrate of political organization, the monarchy was able to transcend lords' private rights, maintaining the collection of older tributes and, at the same time, developing the collection of new ones (Ormrod & Barta, 1995: 72–73). The perspective presented to us by the Bonney-Ormrod model, with respect to the strategies of state organization, suggests that Portugal was a singular case as it demonstrates a mixture of these two issues, that is, a kingdom in which the nobility resisted, as long as it could, to a slower centralization process under Afonso V's reign. Nevertheless, the process was resumed and boosted by his successor, gaining a new impetus with Manuel I, who wisely maintained the nobility's privileges, prominent positions within the administrative apparatus, rents and land rights. Thus, he was also able to maintain the Portuguese monarchy's capacity to develop new methods of sales taxes collection, concentrating on consumption, following the trend of other Western European kingdoms but without giving up the previous taxes already existed since the *reconquista* times. As to this continuity of structures/systems, it can be seen in two ways: by their productivity and/or ability to satisfy the monarch's needs, or as their inflexibility and maintenance were convenient to political figures subordinate to the king and desirous of avoiding more effective control on the part of the state (Ormrod & Barta, 1995: 79).

When observing the Portuguese kingdom's administrative financial operation and then of the empire, it is possible to identify a series of changes, fundamentally carried out by a process of broadening horizons, in several different contexts. Those conditioning elements were brought, first, by the *reconquista*, second, following that period, by the process of institutional consolidation, the occupation, settlement and development of agricultural and commercial activities, afterwards, the fourteenth-century crises and wars, both internal and external, both offensive and defensive, within the House of Burgundy and the rise of the House of Avis and, finally, by the oceanic expansion, by the discovery and annexation of new lands, by the control of maritime routes and by the maintenance of new commercial outposts. Other studies have already and properly highlighted the rise and evolution of new structures, without necessarily or completely destroying the older ones. Moreover, this new hybrid system, partially running alongside and partially following it, would operate in very distinct conditions and environments, and in different institutional frameworks (Pedreira, 2010: 55).

In this chapter, the composition of this administrative structure will be analyzed, with particular attention paid to the branches that controlled and coordinated the fiscal elements, trying to perceive what was changing and what was maintained over time, and whether this was due to political interests and economic reasons, or for technical reasons, in an attempt to maintain or improve, consciously or otherwise, the system.

6.1 Building the cornerstones

Bearing in mind the most recent developments within the Portuguese historiographical debate on royal finances, we must first consider "the creation of the state and the phenomenon of centralization" (Barata & Henriques, 2012: 277) – the second in particular – as starting points for discussion. In this context, the first question that arises is the emerging need, alongside with the concept of kingdom, to create an apparatus, with defined functions, i.e.,

> a set of employees and services that, together with the monarch, assures the administration and the answer to the facts and petitions that are presented to the Court, translated in the making of the respective letters, justice and grace or finances.
>
> (Homem, 1990: 25–26)

Chronologically, the royal house would develop the first structure created with the intention of exercising financial control – designated as *ovençais del-rei* ("the king's rights collection office") – within the framework of a feudal monarchy in Portugal, defined by some scholars as a political power that did not make a clear distinction between public and private (Mattoso, 2006: 287). This bureau would lodge all those who were involved in some way with the king's house and the governance of its finances (Barros, 1945: III, 202–204), among them a series of officers, all coordinated by the *Porteiro-Mor* ("main doorman"), a position that would remain until the end of Dinis I's reign (Homem, 1990: 121) in 1325. Between the reign of his father, Afonso III (1248–1279) and his, important fiscal changes would occur in the national panorama.

The flourishing of cities, by means of commercial activities and economic growth, as well as the increase of production and its means, drew the Crown's attention to this urban wealth. As part of this process, the king himself would become a property owner in several municipalities. The city's fiscal potential awakened the interests of a monarchy eager to increase its revenues. It was necessary, therefore, to create a framework to collect and manage the rents, to which the monarch was entitled. This collection, according to some scholars, was divided in two levels: locally, executed by the *mordomo* (from the Latin *maior domus*; "chamberlain"), and regionally, executed by the *almoxarifes*. Some rent collections started to be gathered in cash,[1] and the very phenomenon of leasing the tax collections, that is, tax farming became a widely used expedient at that time (Mattoso, 2006: 289–290). This can be considered as marking the transition from *feudal* monarchy to a *state* monarchy, although several feudal characteristics remained until the end of the fourteenth century, especially in terms of state organization (Mattoso, 2006: 292–293). The idea of centralization is based precisely on this gradual process of limiting the power of lordships and councils, and the corresponding concentration of prerogatives of the monarchy in this historical course (Mattoso, 2006: 297–298). This story goes hand in hand with the debate over the ownership of fiscal rights in localities and, especially, in the cities, and the agents who symbolized this process were the doormen, bailiffs and *almoxarifes* (Mattoso, 2006: 304), the monarch's direct representatives with regard to the care of his resources.

To some scholars, "the attribution of tax collection to the *almoxarifes* within well-defined districts, with their fields of action and jurisdiction sharply increased, is one of the outstanding administrative innovations regarding the whole process" (Henriques, 2008: 131). On the other hand, for others, this turning point lies in the introduction of the *Vedores da Fazenda* ("top fiscal officers") in 1370, during Fernando I's reign, recently discussed in other works.[2] However, technically, the point of view celebrated within early-twentieth-century Portuguese historiography (Merêa, 2006: 173), namely that the *Ouvidor da portaria* ("ombudsman regarding the doormen officials") was the immediate predecessor of the *Vedores* from the point of view of financial administration, which was based on a scarce documentary base since it dealt with references taken only from legislative sources (Homem, 1990: 122). According to a different group, the *Vedores* were fundamental elements of a process of an ongoing specialization (Homem, 1990: 123–124). As to its origin, according to the most recent historiographical work,

> it must be recovered in the king's income management in Lisbon, more specifically within his House, and his institution reveals the importance of this process from the point of view of the adoption, on a national scale, of an originally municipal and urban model of supervision, as well as the good acceptance and large-scale use of royal rent leasing.
>
> (Henriques, 2008: 139–140)

Within this set up, just below the *Vedores*, an audit mechanism was inserted. The *Casa dos Contos*, whose creation dates back to 1290, originally came from the group of clerics that controlled the books of *almoxarifes'* scribes in each locality, and which were regularly reported – the *Livro dos Contos*. Those were records of a series of payments and allowed effective control of debtors within the city of Lisbon (Henriques, 2008: 137–138). Even in the earliest days of its existence, the *Contos* effectively exercised control over royal finances, a scenario that would begin to change by the 1350s. As time passed by, the *Casa dos Contos*, initially an auditing body, became the central body of control, a fundamental pillar of the structure, thanks to the growth and complexity of the taxation mechanism. The staff's expansion, both in the fiscal apparatus – with accountants, withdrawers and receivers regarding the collection of ordinary revenues, and evaluators, quantifiers and collectors, with regard to *pedidos* and *empréstimos* – and in legal practices, led to this internal transformation, in view of the fact that these structures were directly intertwined.

With Pedro I (1357–1367), a new wave of renewal within the fiscal apparatus was felt, not only due to the enlargement of the administrative system itself, but especially because of the replacement of older officers with newer ones, with new functions, most significantly after the *Cortes* of 1361, at Elvas (Homem, 1978: 66–67). Following this line of thought, we also should not forget the *Ouvidores da Portaria* (sort of Ombudsmen of the Ordinance), whose existence was demystified by some scholars (Homem, 1990: 125), and distinguished as *Ouvidores dos feitos de el-Rei* ("ombudsmen of the King's deeds"), as well as the *sisas'* judges, the judges of the King's deeds and the *corregedores* ("supervisors") of each region, invested by Afonso IV (1325–1357) with controlling power regarding municipal income during a time of the growth in the municipal mercantile elites (Coelho, 1988: 41–42). About this point there was a doubt about the figure of the accountant, already existing, and of his acquaintance with the *Contos'* clerks (Gomes, 2006: 123). Mainly because, on the other hand, it is believed that there was a representative officer of the *Contos* in each *almoxarifado* designated by the central structure to audit *in loco* the accounting in each unit. This function would be assigned, at the beginning, to the *Contos'* own scribe, who acted as the counters of the regional accounting branches' most reliable officer, elaborating and recording the documentation to be examined, compiled and later stored in Lisbon (Rau, 2009: 276–277). A few examples can be listed, such as the acquittance given to João Lourenço da Seara,[3] receiver of the *pedidos* taken at Lamego, in 1441. In the expenditure list described in this source, although with a series of incomplete information, there was a payment recorded to Pedro Afonso, "scrivener of the *Contos* in the aforesaid comarca (region) which the mentioned lord Infante Henry ordered to give as a grace", in the amount of 2,000 reais. Another source[4] also gives an account of a Pedro Afonso, possibly the same one, as "scrivener of the *Contos* at the *almoxarifados* of Viseu and Lamego". Another officer, Gonçalo Anes de Magalhães, receiver of Beja's *almoxarifado*, presented his accounting regarding the 1442 tax collection, "which was acknowledged, through our order, by Estevão Martins, our *Contos'* clerk in the said *almoxarifado*".[5] That these present officers would therefore be the link between the central body (the *Contos'* Lisbon Central Office) and the local bodies, i.e., the *almoxarifados* and the *Contadores das Comarcas* ("districts' counters"), can be seen as a very plausible hypothesis.

In João II's reign, the clerks would play a fundamental role as a direct link to the central office, and this can be observed through the details provided by some sources. One example is the acquittance given to Álvaro Pires Machado,[6] "scribe of our *Contos* in the district of Trás-os-Montes", regarding 424,487 reais he had received and expended from the extraordinary revenues, the *pedidos*, granted to fund the war with Castile in 1475. With that officer's oversight, it was possible to check whether the king's demands were actually fulfilled or not, by checking the books of the *Contos'* clerks against those of the *almoxarifado*'s scribes. It is observed in an acquittance given to João Dias,[7] who received some money to be spent in the kings' service, for the remodeling of the palaces of Santarém, according to the books of Fernão Martins, "clerk of the *almoxarifado* which was in charge of this expenditure, and whose revenues were commissioned in the years of 1482 and 1483, in which the said money was received". This books' cross referencing became, then, a key point to avoid fraud and misappropriation of funds destined to objectives previously defined, or in regular tax collections and even for extraordinary aids.

However, even in the same period, the district's counter, who stands above the clerk in terms of hierarchy, apparently assumed responsibility for exercising this function. It is noteworthy that their responsibilities would only be clarified by the Regulation of districts' counters, within the main *Regimento e ordenações da fazenda* ("Regiment and Ordinances of the Finances"), issued in 1516 (Carneiro, 1818: I, 112–136). At any rate, it seems that, in fact, from then on this would be the link between "local and central administration, through the different reigns, in some cases identified as the "king's accountant" or "our bookkeeper/auditor". As a few examples during João II's governance, an acquittance was granted to Álvaro da Guarda,[8] king's buyer, for everything he received and spent between 1485 and 1488, and for which he gave his account to "João Freire, accountant of our house", and that same officer (João Freire) would check the accounting of Fernão Lopes, Guarda's *almoxarife* regarding his duty in 1485, 1486 and 1487.[9] Another officer, Tristão Ferreira,[10] *almoxarife* at Abrantes, had his accounts, "taken by João Matella, our accountant in the counters of Santarem". In the following reign, it is possible to observe the permanence of this official as an instance of convergence between local and central taxation, using king's trustworthy men (nobles) in key-positions, as it can be seen in a few examples, such as the acquittance granted to André Gago,[11] receiver at the *almoxarifado* of Setubal, regarding his service between 1494 and 1496. The officer who checked his accounting was Alvaro Calado, "knight of our house and our accountant in Setubal". Such evidence clarifies the detail in the first *regimento* which requires the *counters* coming to the court (Rau, 2009: 204–205) every three years, so that they could render their accounts to the *Vedor da Fazenda* (top fiscal officers). Given this guideline, it is clear that they were located in each of the regional subdivisions. This whole process can be seen from the perspective of a monarchy within a process of centralization, which, by passing on the supervision tasks to the higher levels of bureaucracy and bringing them closer to the king, allowed for a closer watch on the local authorities regarding royal taxation.

But, in the end, what does all this mean?

It remains the case that the Portuguese fiscal mechanism is far too elaborate to interpret fully. The conflation/distinction between the public finances and the king's private treasury is a subject of much controversy, although some scholars report that until João I's reign there were well-defined assignments, performed, in practice, by the central accountants (tax auditors) in Lisbon (Rau, 2009: 33–38; Barros, 1945: III, 204–208). Their task consisted of checking the accounting books of each *almoxarifado*. But in this same reign, tax collection became more fragmented: accountants were then controlled by the *Vedores da Fazenda*, effective controllers of royal revenues, a superior instance placed between the accountants and the king. In addition, there were a number of other positions operating under different rules and procedures (Gomes, 2006: 121), impracticable from the point of view of conflicting interests, which hampered communication between the many different layers of tax collection and supervision, in the name of a presumed more efficient presence of political power in the kingdom's most remote areas. A confusing fiscal bureaucracy is the mother of inefficiency, and this usually means losing money. Instead of going into the royal coffers, royal resources ended up, frequently, in the pockets of collectors, accountants, notaries, tenants and transporters at each collection level (Duarte, 2006: 437–438). With tasks and functions clearly distributed and determined, the authority of tax collectors was supposed to be strengthened.

Beyond that, Lisbon, as a city, had its own fiscal and economic bureaucracy gravitating around the *Casa dos Contos*, the central fiscal bureau (Godinho, 2009: 136). When Dinis I (1279–1325) created it, this administrative organization centralized the tax collection of the whole kingdom in a time which the spoils of *reconquista* formed the bulk of royal revenues. Later, with the creation of the *Contadorias dos Almoxarifados* ("fiscal audit units") during Afonso V's reign, the tax collection should have become, at least theoretically, more decentralized. Each accountant was responsible for supervising the tax collection in his region and would respond directly to the *Contador-mor* ("Chief Accountant"), who was also under the supervision of the *Vedores da Fazenda*, already mentioned. Lisbon had two instances of control: one to supervise the royal house accounts, known as *Contos do Rei e Casa* ("king's and royal household central financial bureau"), and another, known as *Contos de Lisboa* (Lisbon's *Contos*), which centralized the collection of revenues from the *almoxarifados* in each region. Lisbon also had its *taracenas* ("shipyards"), a minting house, the king's treasury, the public works' *almoxarifado*, the royal armory's warehouses and other economic governance divisions. In Porto, there was also, besides the customs and the *almoxarifado*, a minting house, *taracenas* and the royal warehouses (Gomes, 2006: 122–124).

Afonso V was behind many of the changes in the kingdom's tax organization. On one hand, some historians assert that public finances developed consistently, and the Portuguese State exhibited a remarkable level of bureaucratic culture (Gomes, 2006: 124–125). On the other hand, the linkages between the central government and the various layers of local administration did not work well enough, less in the sense of communication between headquarters and the regions, widely known as costly and generating parallel powers, and more in the sense of being a heavy machine, tangled and difficult to navigate, with an evident excess of personnel unnecessary for the proper functioning of the royal fiscal apparatus. The complaints of people in parliamentary debates, expounding on the excessive number of positions, their prodigal gifts and typical aristocratic insubordination are symptomatic of this phenomenon.[12]

In any case, we believe that the interpretations developed by previous historians are far too simplistic, given the complexity of the structures, which had several points of contact between them, and one of the elements that has not yet been duly depicted is the very disposition of the district's accountants and the *almoxarifado*'s catenation, according to its upper control unit, the *Vedores da Fazenda*.

6.2 A flawed foundation

When studying the finances of France's first war with Italy, some historians (Chevalier, 2002: I, 44–45) depicted an excessive amount spent on the conflict and its political and financial consequences: an uncontrolled "floating debt", the participation of merchants in funding, either by collection of fees on business and goods or through direct loans and various budgetary problems. But beyond that, it demonstrates how complex it is to expand collection whenever the bases on which the tax system is founded are already flawed, that is, when the vices that were created within the structure were inescapable, given the deep roots of certain practices that ultimately confused private interest with the community's welfare.

Within the idea of conflict between public and private, it is relevant to make a careful observation regarding some of the aspects that integrated the Portuguese fiscal foundations. At the outset, one point that can be stressed is the functions' accumulation. The very creation of the *almoxarifados* and the investiture of their officers, the *almoxarifes* themselves suggests an imperfection within the structure. As pointed out by other scholars, the origins of this position, which date back to the twelfth and thirteenth centuries, were identified with "an operation essentially focused on the revenues' advancement regarding rights' collection in the southern kingdom's municipalities" (Henriques, 2008: 117–118). In fact, following this argument, the *almoxarifados* would theoretically be closer to the duties of the *almojarife mayor* in Castile, which acted as the king's main financial agent by "providing financial liquidity by advancing taxation profits" (Ladero Quesada, 1997: 52). In this sense, he would behave more as an operator rather than a manager, a fact that does raise many concerns and doubts.

In any case, the *almoxarifado* office is seen as a parallel to the original Muslim *al-musharif*, who was supposed to go after royal gains, "competing" with other urban authorities. Not being a municipal official, the Portuguese *almoxarife* was subject to higher judging instances and, "while working for his own gain, he proceeded as the king's delegate to the municipalities, that is, as a tenant, he was first zealous for his own interests" (Henriques, 2008: 131). From this particular standpoint, the comparison with the Mozarabic official is more accurate. It is not by chance that many of these royal officials appeared in the sources gathered as tenants and *almoxarifados'* receivers, or even as tenants and *almoxarifes*, as previously seen. Furthermore, the legislation on *onzena* ("usury") is quite significant in both law compilations, the Afonsine and Manueline Ordinances. There was no way to consider this situation as conflicting, given the precedent created by the structure and attribution of functions already enshrined in customary practices. Moreover, this office accumulation had no legal limitation within legislation. And despite the ban to fiscal officials to lend money, many of them were tax farmers at the same time.

From the standpoint of practicality, this form of stewardship was extremely convenient to the monarch. By delegating a number of positions and services to the same person, and usually a member of his entourage, the monarch knew that he will have to control a single individual, and the fault, from the judgment of state management, was exactly there. By not focusing on the institution's organizational form, this privileged the relationship with individuals and left aside the development of an apparatus that would need clearer processes to function better or that, at least, would require a more incisive presence of the auditing bodies. However, the tendency was for a simple expansion of the administrative and fiscal apparatus, regardless of efficiency or problems to be circumvented, that is, the royal bureaucracy was developed, but it followed the old practice of assigning multiple functions to the same official, whether close to the monarch or not. Even beyond the question of the *almoxarifes'*, according to some scholars' indications, the upper management of "public services" was mixed with the king's/royal household private services, and the separation of the two only occurred gradually, accompanied by the increasing importance of literacy in governance.

However, the occupation of key ministries continued to be "under the exclusive control of the nobility" (Merêa, 2006: 172). In addition, the phenomenon of public-private disentangling and the growth of the public sphere would only occur later in parallel with the growth of modern armies. This occurred especially in the 1550s, with the bureaucratic reorganization into modern states, which would also take place under the influence of the Roman Law (Schulze, 1995: 268), although in Portugal it was already visible in the beginning of the thirteenth century. Finally, the picture that was portrayed is a structural development, but still with the same problems of the individualized and particular treatment of the kingdom's financial issues. Here we have the point of contact for another of the financial organization's root problems: the centralization/growth dichotomy of the fiscal machine.

And why a dichotomy? The Portuguese monarchy's centralization process, which has already been analyzed by other scholars,[13] stood in opposition to the need to extend administration, including fiscal affairs, which clearly followed the decentralization idea, for which the evidence was the attribution of tax authorities' positions to new *almoxarifes* and the creation of new offices, not only as a reward for services rendered by court nobles but also in an attempt to improve collection efficiency and increase revenues. Moreover, this sixteenth-century expansion of the fiscal machine generally reflected the kingdom's economic growth but more specifically that of a few particular regions. The dry ports[14] and income generated by the passage of goods and products through the Castilian borderline needed more active fiscal checkpoints, attracting the Crown's attention: in the Northeast, more precisely in Trás-os-Montes, at Freixo de Espada-a-Cinta[15] and Bemposta (Machado, 1998: 283), opened by Afonso V and closed by João II; within Beira's district, at Sabugal (Moreno, 1993: 345–358), Penamacor[16] and Castelo Branco;[17] in Entre-Tejo-e-Guadiana, at Serpa, Moura, Mourão, Elvas, Mértola, Campo Maior and Olivença; finally, in Algarve, at Alcoutim and Castro Marim. By sea, Porto's regional accounting branch had taken over Vila do Conde's customs;[18] Guimarães' branch had the Viana do Castelo's customs.[19] Also at the Estremadura region, it was created Aveiro's customs.[20] Within Setúbal's jurisdiction came a new customs process in Sesimbra. The Sines' customs were associated with Beja. But what is really noteworthy was the fiscal system's growth in Algarve, a result of revenue growth boosted by trade and fishing activities.[21] Originally, this accounting area had, in the 1450s, five *almoxarifados*: Tavira, Faro, Loulé, Silves and Lagos, one general customs for the whole region, toll rights and the Almadrava's factory. In the following century, customs' activities were decentralized, and four new branches were created in that region, in addition to the main one: Tavira, Faro, Lagos and Portimão. Two other warehouses were added to the others, in Portimão and Aljezur, and the cloths' dues that enter through south came to be collected independently. By the 1450s, it is possible to reconstruct, to a large extent, the network of the state's fiscal units, as the sources allow us. On the other hand, for the following century, fiscal units are revealed in smaller places, such as Sabugal and Alfaiates,[22] within Guarda's fiscal custody. Also, bear in mind the case of Pederneira,[23] an integral part of Leiria's accounting, or Moura,[24] within Beja's accountancy, and in some cases not even justifying the installation of a warehouse, such as Nisa,[25] within Évora's accounting district. Although, no previous references to these cases were found in the surviving sources, this does not necessarily mean that they did not exist before.

Following some scholars' indications, the expansion of the *almoxarifados*' model nationwide allowed the Crown to achieve three objectives with a single action, i.e.,

> the convergence of different revenues and rights within a single territorial unit under an officer that could concentrate, allocate, and transfer those resources; the production of expendable earnings, which the system based on the landowner model did not allow; and the permanent presence of a clerk in all transactions carried out by the *almoxarife*, making it possible for the king to "systematically audit" his men.
>
> (Henriques, 2008: 141)

However, this same context produced two important side effects for the functioning of the royal finances. First, the revenues' stagnation, which in times of peace and monetary stability was not particularly a problem, and could even be, on one hand, "a positive thing from the standpoint of revenues' predictability and accounting" (Henriques, 2008: 141). On the other hand, it could be highly detrimental in times of war and inflation, leading the Crown to bail itself out from extraordinary revenue streams, more or less frequently, depending on the severity of the situation.

Second, it produced other means of cheating the tax system by the same *almoxarifes*, detected in the *Cortes*' complaints on several occasions, whether due to abuses,[26] the functions' accumulation that gave rise to a series of conflicts of interest or for other reasons. These issues were probably responsible for the institution of the district's counters in Afonso V's reign who clearly intended to curb such situations. However, this same initiative was itself challenged by the same parliamentary assemblies held at Lisbon in 1459. But the demands for its abolition and for its functions to be attached to ordinary judges (Sousa, 1990: II, 361) were ignored. Furthermore, the monarch equally disregarded the proposals for the clerks' removal, the rendering of accounts by the *almoxarifes*' at the end of each year to the central accountants at Lisbon's *Contos*, and the request for the closure of the *Vedores*, keeping only one and working at the king's court (Sousa, 1990: II, 364). Nothing was more natural, since most of these positions were occupied by court noblemen, whether they were the royal household's *fidalgos*, knights or esquires, united mainly through their political and power relations with the sovereign.

Last, another important point to emphasize within the perspective of a weakened structure in its bases is the abuse committed by fiscal agents. Those were, to a large extent, directly related to the thread established at the beginning of this chapter, i.e., the confusion between private interests and the so-called *common good* that was often overlooked, especially when we visited the *Cortes*' records, which was the main stage for the prosecutors' complaints. They protested against the excesses committed by the royal tax officers, by the judicial agents who associate themselves with these particular tasks, such as the *corregedores das comarcas* ("districts' corregidors") (Homem, 1990: 114–119), the *sisas*' judges (Barros, 1945: IX, 446–447) and the judges of the king's deeds (Homem, 1990: 136–138) and the other protagonists involved in the tax collection process, such as tenants, leaseholders, executors and others. However, we believe that a good starting point for the discussion is the very royal attitude toward the subject of the *sisas*. What do we mean by this? First place, we previously emphasized the municipal/council aspect of this tribute, in essence, serving fundamentally and exclusively local common interests, boosting the collection for repairs to walls, castles and the performance of public works in general, focusing the local community. The allocation of this resource was affected as soon as it was granted to João I. back in the crisis of 1383–1385. After the wars with Castile, its restoration was constantly demanded by the peoples' representatives in parliament, until the *sisas* were seized and incorporated into the central finances. The absorption of this tax was not justified for the war alone but for the support of the state, an argument also invoked by João II and finalized by Manuel I (Cruz, 2001: 128–131). The final message that is conveyed here is that the local population's interests and welfare was a secondary consideration next to the monarch's need to raise revenue. The provision of the state was not something "visible" to the population. Rather regularly used infrastructure that had a positive impact on citizens' daily lives, such as bridges, streets, roads, and other works, was neglected and the problems arising from this lack of infrastructure would continue. And the people were aggravated in the name of *tenças*, graces, marriages, dwellings and settlements (Cruz, 2001: 127–128). The king's individual and private interest, and his state's, prevailed over the *public* interest.

It was also observed that the exactions committed by the royal officialdom, which always acted in the monarch's name but which prevaricated and exercised a power that, in practice, had serious implications to its functioning. There were many denunciations that have come to us through the lines of Gama Barros in his *History of Public Administration* and Armindo de Sousa in the *Portuguese Medieval Cortes*, both true sources of information about this subject. The *sisas*' judges, who judged the suits concerning that tribute, were not at all well regarded.

On the contrary, they were much questioned by the population (Barros, 1945: IX, 447–448), who saw a series of issues in their appointments. Judges were appointed for this function in agreement with the tax-farmers themselves, who put as a condition in their lease contracts, that they were to elect the judges who would judge their lawsuits. Beyond that, the excessive remuneration paid to other royal officers and these, not satisfied, still exercise the function of inquirers within the kingdom's various localities, usurping the rights of those who already had a royal charter for its exercise, causing glaring errors in the inspection and, by consequence, in the tax system. This complaint was evasively answered by Afonso V in the *Cortes* of Santarém, in 1468 (Sousa, 1990: II, 381). Still in relation to the judges, more apparent irregularities were reported at the 1455 assembly in Lisbon. There, prosecutors saw their request partially conceded by the monarch, who gave an account of the request so that the *sisas'* judges could not be royal officials, such as accountants, *almoxarifes* and clerks, who might be at risk of making partial judgements, always favorable to the monarch, who paid their wages and other remunerations as tithes and graces (Sousa, 1990: II, 352). Another complaint mentioned the multiplicity and consequent excess of private judges who, according to the prosecutors in 1459, numbered more than twenty, with many clerks and officers (Barros, 1945: IX, 450). Furthermore, at the assembly of 1468, in Santarém, the *sisas'* judges were demanded by the municipal prosecutors, asking that they (*sisas'* judges) should not possess their own seals and that they could not make inquiries of the facts that were judged.

The leaseholders themselves, who were not part of the officialdom but were embedded in the tax system, in a way, by association, also committed excesses in the exercise of their authority, if we can believe the various complaints of prosecutors on multiple occasions. At the parliamentary assembly of Santarém, in 1451, the representatives submitted to the monarch a resolution not to be sued for debts contracted prior to the leases, and requested that judges could be able to compel those still unclaimed to pay their debts incurred before starting new leases, and the payment could be made with the incomes' profits they collect. Not enough, that the goods of the leaseholders and his guarantors to be demanded, a request which the King promptly rejected (Sousa, 1990: II, 345). In the *Cortes* of Lisbon in 1459, the representatives demanded that the leaseholders of the tithes on cloth who came from Castile should not take the cloths that they received from their clients for the making of their garments and which were not demanded by the garments brought dressed from the neighboring kingdom (Sousa, 1990: II, 361). Add to this the privilege enjoyed by the collectors of public revenues, who could not be sued either by creditors in tax disputes. Not even when accused in criminal matters, except before the district's counters and the *Vedor da Fazenda* (Barros, 1945: IX, 451), a prerogative that would be questioned again at the assemblies of 1481–1482 in Évora-Viana do Castelo. There, prosecutors asked the tenants to be tried by ordinary judges when their crimes and debts predated the lease. Then this request was finally accepted by the King (Sousa, 1990: II, 448).

Apart from the mentioned excesses, there are also examples of frauds and associations to circumvent existing legislation and procedures, as in the case of adjustments,[27] recorded in complaints at the *Cortes* of 1439, in Lisbon (Sousa, 1990: II, 327). The leaseholders and Crown's officials, even when the rents were not leased, charged the countrymen and farmers, and were also accused of having received the covenants and *sisas* in the clerk's absence and did not register them intentionally, so they could receive it twice (Barros, 1945: IX, 468–469). Another issue claimed by the people at the *Cortes* of 1455, in Lisbon, was the delivery, by the clerks, of the *sisas'* books to strangers, who altered them by removing the debtors' names. That complaint was dealt with by the king, who forbade such practice, but this same measure was subsequently revoked, as Prince Fernando considered that the collection had decreased due to such prohibition (Barros, 1945: IX, 472). Several complaints against abuses committed by the *siseiros* ("*sisas'* leaseholders") range from the deliberate absence of the *siseiro* in a place or village, to offenses to women, even to locking the debtors in their houses (Barros, 1945: IX, 477–48). At the *Cortes* of Guarda in 1465, the municipal representatives intervened to prevent improper collusion between the tenants of *sisas* on meat and the butchers, in order to avoid a price rise caused by a deliberate attempt to raise the tax collection, a request granted partially (Sousa, 1990: II, 375), and which was again scrutinized in the following meetings of Santarém in 1468, and answered again in the same way (Sousa, 1990: II, 377). At this same meeting, the prosecutors further requested that the king should not permit the *siseiros* to act in bad faith, by demanding from the people "aids" under coercion, i.e., under the threat of malicious citations, and that the aforementioned should be condemned only through evidence and oath (Sousa, 1990: II, 379). Yet at the *Cortes* of 1472–1473 in Coimbra-Évora, leaseholders and clerks were sued by prosecutors for abuses committed against weavers by seizing their looms (Sousa, 1990: II, 420). In the following assembly in 1475, again in Évora, the people's representatives asked the king to determine what the judges should do when royal tenants were convicted in both instances, i.e., the *Casa do Cível* e *Suplicação*, that is, whether judges could chose to execute if the counters (district accountants) prevented it.

6.3 A dilemma: to lease or to manage directly?

Before any decision about the initiative of collecting taxes, to modify them, to create new ones or even to extinguish others, one of the great dilemmas faced by the monarch, in fiscal terms, is first whether he should take control of both its gathering and the theoretical/legal instruments that supports it. If the choice is taken, it is necessary to create and organize a collection instrument which is capable of ensuring the efficient operation of this apparatus to ensure certain levels of profitability as required by the Crown. A second alternative is to transfer this office to third parties under the condition of the advance payment of a fixed amount, previously evaluated and fixed, to obtain this concession for a defined period.

Scholars on the subject of taxation have argued, for some time, that the goal of increasing revenue among Western European kingdoms during the Middle Ages was left to the option of a fragmented revenue collection, i.e., tax farming. This meant, in practical terms, that it was necessary that there should be a reasonable number of people with the capacity to invest and, potentially, this activity should be profitable. Specific attractive yields awarded at the best possible price, and, most important, perhaps, the small risk of insolvency from the leaseholders, since each collection unit was supposed to have and establish its own guarantees. On the other hand, there are two strategic points that argue against this alternative: different leasing rates, from one region to another, referring to the same tax, or even different rates between urban and rural regions, regarding the same tax, which hinders accounting which would perhaps have been more optimized if it were a single value. Finally, there was the issue of various collection rates for different leasing contracts, so that unifying them meant creating more confusion in something already quite complex (Bonney, 1995: 439).

Another variation described by the same experts is in the direction of a "hybrid administration", i.e., the state controlled the direct taxes' collection, which could mainly feed the King's personal treasury, while indirect taxation was in the hands of interested and potential leaseholders. This has been highlighted, mostly, regarding the Italian city-states, as well as in France, in the times of absolute monarchies (Bonney, 1995: 440). In Genoa, until 1326, the decision on the collection or lease of direct taxation was annual. Years later, in 1340, the municipality approved a law that established the leasing of all the collection of those fees (Bonney, 1995: 441). There was not, according to historians today, a determining factor for this choice to be made. There were a number of interrelated issues that needed to be considered before the final decision: what was the economic situation regarding the state in each case, whether there was a crisis or pressure for an immediate increase in revenues, a careful assessment, followed by a comparison of the number of employees (potential or invested) versus the number of tax farmers, potential or already listed. Other unattainable issues were very relevant, such as the level of compliance with tax obligations, and last, its fiscal nature/culture, i.e., how the foundations for taxation were established in that place and what were its characteristics (Bonney, 1995: 440–441). There was also a great difficulty, on the part of monarchs, to objectively see their own collection structures as a revenue raising mechanism whose main purpose was maximum efficiency rather than a source of patronage or political favor, constituting a major obstacle to their growth. On the other hand, a problem that directly arose from this situation was the confusion between the collection and credit structures, as leaseholders could be potential sources of loans, in the absence of appropriate banking structures (Bonney, 1995: 442).

When we observe the constitution and development of the Portuguese fiscal machine during the early modern times and the situations described, we see some similarities, in which some of these points previously observed serve as a guide to perceive the options taken by the Crown. There was a clear option for leasing, but it could be changed according to the economic context and levels of political pressure exerted by the people's representatives. An example of this situation can be seen at the *Cortes* of 1459 in Lisbon, when the monarch denied the prosecutors' demand requesting that the correctional chanceries could not be rented (Sousa, 1990: II, 368). The same request was submitted at the Guarda's assembly of 1465, in a different way, i.e., the representatives demanded that the king should take measures he understands best to avoid the abuses committed by those chancelleries' leaseholders, and finally, not only was the request granted, but the monarch opted for the abolition of this type of leasing (Sousa, 1990: II, 373).

There were, within the kingdom, a number of people willing and able to invest in tax farming, whether they were foreigners or not. What is clear, given what has already been discussed previously is that, following the supply and demand model, there was a capital offer and, more importantly, there was the main public requirement from the interested parties that was established by the contracts and could vary, depending on the region and level of profitability/investment. Moreover, regarding the Portuguese case, the premise that the Jews formed the major/dominant investors can no longer be supported, as an absolute truth or as only "market" players, although they did compose the main investors' group. It should also be highlighted that further studies of genealogy involving tax farmers would be helpful. There were, however, extremely attractive revenues, particularly in Lisbon and some other border areas, which have been duly demonstrated before, and often leased at derisory prices, in which is notorious the monarch's eagerness to get rid of the responsibility for collecting those taxes. As for the risks involved, in some situations, we can argue that they were, in practice, very few. Not by chance, it is noticeable that there were a large number of people interested in collecting rents at the largest city and head of the realm, whether it be taxes from customs, toll charges or indirect taxation. Or even in border regions, at strategic products' crossing points and, therefore, places where tax collection would be more profitable and guaranteed, except for some unexpected and abnormal situation. Looking at the revenues' evolution, either in nominal values or not, in places such as Guarda or in Estremoz, at the border area, it is quite clear there were tax farming tendencies in these localities.

As for the negative aspects, the kingdom did not suffer from any of the difficulties listed previously: there was no variation in rates, from region to region, being uniformly levied. In this case, the process of strengthening central power seems to have positively "contaminated" taxation (Bonney, 1995: 438–439). From this point of view, Portugal had a uniform fiscal format. To some extent, someone can question the fact that the kingdom has problems regarding the measurement units nationally used. The difficulty in implementing the weight and volume capacity measurement laws at various times (Mattoso, 2001: 904–905), as well as the attempt to reform the standards in 1455, by Afonso V, gives an idea of some confusion within the country (Viana, 2011: 280–281). As a result, it is possible to try to understand the reasons behind more or less tax revenues in certain regions of the kingdom, as well as some difficulty of goods' distribution and circulation, due to the excessive variety of weights, measures and currency in circulation (Barros, 1945: X, 97–101) but, anyway, this did not cause a direct but an indirect interference in the tax collection. Even the issue of difference in tax leasing contracts does not apply to the Portuguese case, since there was no change in rates to be levied, but rather on the nominal values of each leasing, which could grow as time, inflation and demands of interested parties allowed.

Bearing in mind what concerns a "mixed" management of both direct and indirect taxes, similar to what was happening in some regions of France until the mid-seventeenth century, it seems to us that the Portuguese Crown, to a large extent, developed alongside this fiscal trend. When looking at the acquittance letters gathered for this study, a clear difference between the values collected regarding the two types of collection is noticeable. The overwhelming majority of the tax collection, as previously mentioned, refers to *sisas* and other taxes on consumption. The monarch's rents, rights and emphyteusis were also negotiated, albeit on far fewer occasions as they were far less attractive in terms of profitability and, in some situations, in the values involved. If we take, for example, the case of Guarda[28] in 1436, it is noteworthy that while the rents of the king in that city were capable of yielding 189,525 pounds that same year, toll revenues and royal rights in Trancoso, a small municipality within Guarda's fiscal jurisdiction, generated revenues of about 300,000 pounds for the same period. Not coincidentally, the first was not leased, while the second had been leased to a couple of interested parties. In Setúbal,[29] the king's emphyteusis were valued in 1439 at 12,022.5 pounds, and the *sisas* collected from bread, in the same year, leased to a group of partners, was worth 3,540,760 pounds, being the amount paid by the leasers. What is clear here is that this aspect was not something that could somehow limit or control the collection's efficiency, and that what would dictate direct management or tax farming will not be separated by the type of taxation but rather the profit factor and the King's political and financial ability to collect it himself, with a proper structure assembled.

In Portugal's case, despite the presence of Italian representatives of banking and business houses, the structure was still open for Jewish participation. The Jewish communes themselves, which often advanced contributions and revenues (Gonçalves, 1987: 53–55), demonstrate this financial capacity of the Jewish community. Their prominence in the tax farming business was notorious, which probably provided them the necessary condition to lend money, acting in parallel as small/informal bankers, moneylenders and moneychangers. In this sense, Portugal was developing, in a rudimentary way, its credit instruments, which, in some way, permeated the fiscal structure.[30] Effectively, tax leasing served as a medium-term liquidity mechanism for leaseholders, that is, it provided a constant and continuous cash flow to the leaser. This would fit them in a better position to lend large sums to the monarch (and others) from these collection rights. If running okay, they would have easy access to money, quickly recovering the primary investment, with profit, lending it at interest, making the capital circulate and grow. According to other scholars, the *sisas*' farming was the most common way to collect sales taxes (Barros, 1945: IX, 461). The disturbances that usually happened during its collection, such as default and corruption of collecting agents, for example, may have given rise to another approach in the sixteenth century: the *sisas* framed as a poll tax (Barros, 1945: IX, 489–490), i.e., *per capita*, known as the *cabeção* ("big head").

6.4 The *Cortes*: supervisory body or business desk?

The Parliament's authority mainly derives from its institutional solidity. Is this a logical way of thinking about parliamentary assemblies in the Middle Ages? Portuguese scholars dedicated to this topic observed that

> the difficulty in combining the profile of Portuguese medieval parliament with the image of the parliament transmitted by sociologists has its roots in the fact that the former was never completely structured and always depended on the king – as the convocation, local, agenda, enclosing and ratification of decisions. But the fact that it had important socio-political functions and that these functions were generally assimilated by the nation's collective conscience granted it a distinct status among related substructures.
>
> (Sousa, 1990: I, 271)

However, while relying on the king and never attaining a full political status, the Portuguese medieval parliament had a more political rather than a legal nature and based its prestige at the time of its legislative functions on its ability to write and propose general chapters for the king. For this reason, the *Cortes* really never depended politically or morally on the king; its strength and legitimacy "came from a strong political authority, and not from a legal status" (Duarte, 2003: 9). In any case, the institutional position of the *Cortes* is not really a central question, but rather the presence of municipal representatives in their sessions, the objectives to be reached and the issues discussed, and among these, the questions in which interests and real "people's power" actually reside: those of a financial nature (Sousa, 1990: I, 182–183). Early and prior to the formation of the French kingdom, the Languedoc region, like Portugal, also made use of the *Cortes* as a fundamental point of adjustment of its finances – that is, a representative assembly that discusses taxes and their applications (Larguier, 2008: 355).

In any case, Parliamentary discourses must be treated with caution. What is called "popular" can and should be carefully assessed in order to try to identify the origin of the voices heard in the assembly. Often, when we hear the people, especially in matters pertaining to oceanic expansion and the economy, what we are actually hearing is the voice of the merchants, those who are interested in securing their share of the riches that were abroad. In addition, it was as if Afonso V, according to some scholars, "had eyes only for Morocco and did not understand the economic, financial and civilizational magnitude of the ongoing overseas expansion, delivering to private initiative and for the benefit of a selected group, something that should belong to all" (Sousa, 1989a: I, 231). This would have been the representatives' main argument in the assembly of 1472–1473, gathered at Coimbra and Évora. The people complained, i.e., "the bourgeoisie of the commercial cities, through their representatives". They grumbled about the overseas' trade monopoly, granted to Fernão Gomes, on the exclusive rights of Martim Anes Boa Viagem regarding the ivory trade, on the slave sale to foreigners, as well as the "sugar and molasses trade that the Genoese and others had recently established with the inhabitants of Madeira Islands" (Sousa, 1989b: 232–233).

That being said, what, after all, would the *Cortes* be, from a fiscal point of view? A real body with real control over State finances, a place of deliberation aimed at perfecting and improving the Portuguese taxation system? Or a meeting, addressing some innocuous debates, purely pro-forma – a counter of complaints against the mistakes and abuses arising from the implementation of a proper fiscal mechanism in Portugal, which were essentially committed against economically important groups in specific regions and municipalities? In fact, what it appears to be, in financial terms, is objectively a little of both but more of the latter than of the former. That is to say, a control body which, from the taxation perspective, only acted when pushed by reports and complaints, when the boundaries between public and private deals were exceeded, disregarding the particular interests of a specific group or collective. The denunciations were then taken to the monarch, who took action as the grievances reached him, or only dragged his feet and avoided harsher measures against the offenders, especially if they were part of the social sector that assured his political sustainability, avoiding everything that could harm them in any way, although many of these protests were against the king himself.

In theory, municipal representatives were expected to produce chapters with grievances and requests, knowing that eventually they would be heard and that some of their appeals would be served and others not. However, what these representatives found during Afonso V's reign was a king who always tried to find a way to avoid addressing people's complaints as can be seen through the number of rejections and evasive responses to requests. This helped to create the image of a spendthrift king, belligerent and with advanced and expensive military technology at his disposal. This would certainly take a toll on how he was remembered, as well as on the Royal Treasury. With João II, this scenario would begin to change.

What results from all this is the fact that, effectively, the *Cortes* did little or almost nothing for the concrete improvement of the fiscal apparatus. In terms of taxation, collection, supervision and administrative organization, it did not express much more than the general yearning for paying less taxes, in the face of a monarch eager for an increase in revenues at all costs. On top of that, to approving (or not) extraordinary requests for more resources, since inadequate efforts had been made to improve the collection mechanism. Almost all important measures, such as the request that *sisas* judges should not be royal officials, which sought to improve a taxation system in desperate need of objective improvements, were rejected. That gives the exact measure of a Crown that, at the same time, thought that could be able to judge in own cause when making such resolutions and profit from it but that ended up backfiring and resulting in the opposite effect. The *Cortes* had very well-defined technical functions, focused on producing measures and information to help the king reinforce law and administer justice, as well as provide him with the financial means to fulfill his obligations and maintain his royal status. It is true, however, that their competence tended to be limited in matters of credit and resolving monetary matters. These were the most important elements for the king and the most uncomfortable for the cities (Sousa, 1990: I, 255). On the other hand, paradoxically, the technical function of the *Cortes* was the one that contributed most to the institution because that was how, in the majority of cases, pressure could be exerted for the assemblies to be called. Convocation of the *Cortes* depended on the monarch and was designed to deal with his interests. According to other scholars, when the kings from Manuel I onwards found themselves in a favorable financial position, which allowed them to request money less frequently, the *Cortes* stop being held as often (Sousa, 1990: I, 255–256). The first effects of this can actually be seen a little earlier, in the midst of João II's rule, with the development of S. Jorge da Mina's monopoly and the influx of gold and other revenues from that region. With those cornerstones established, parliamentary meetings would lose their importance and be strictly limited.

Although always intertwined with debates over the *sisas*' abolition, other important themes could emerge. For example, the maintenance of a military presence in Africa, dating back to the conquest of Ceuta in 1415. In the *Cortes* of 1459–1460, held at Lisbon and Évora, Afonso V requested the people's help to stabilize his finances. It is important to note that the monarch himself, in his speech to the representatives, acknowledged the troubles that afflicted the kingdom and its powerlessness to deal with its debt. In his rationale, he began by considering that after the death of his father, and because of some works and things that followed, the kingdom had gone through many ordeals, and that adding to that the expenses were so voluminous that such debts were made necessary, as well as the rewards that had to be given to those who served the Crown. For those reasons, the Royal Treasury was so diminished, and so was its state, that the sovereign was unable to meet the expenses which the kingdom's government and the maintenance of African dominions demanded (Barros, 1945: IX, 513–515). Justifying a defensive war before the *Cortes* was always easier than seeking to legitimize an offensive action. How to legitimize a tax for this purpose?

In any case, the people offered him a subsidy of 150,000 golden doubloons, at a rate of 230 reais each, but with certain conditions, namely that the king would moderate grants of rewards and cease asking for more money, unless duly justified (Barros, 1945: IX, 516–519). However, what had been previously promised was broken in the same year, according to one of the royal chroniclers. The expedition to Africa, which had been fumbled and quickly organized, had discomfited the monarch, putting the Crown in trouble. Some scholars suggested that "the kingdom was not amended there; and if it had little before, thereafter it had even less" (Sousa, 1990: I, 386–387), meaning that many (if not all) of the conditions which the people imposed on him in return for granting the subsidy were not respected in the end. The Crown did nothing more than protect the nobility's rights and privileges, as it was undoubtedly in a better position to lend money. On the other hand, it increased the people's burden, who had limited resources. This would eventually create a chain reaction in which people, heavily taxed, would not have resources and therefore would not be able to consume. Of course this contraction of demand would lead to a reduction in tax revenues, but this is something that still needs to be proven by other studies.

In the end, the *doubloons* granted clearly were not enough. Taking the perspective offered by the parliamentary debates, the problem was quickly diagnosed: to them (the people), what overtaxed and consumed the Treasury "was the many *tenças* that we gave to many, by the dowries and marriages we promised them, as well as for the service they rendered or other thing which they moved us" (Faro, 1965: 190), and that

> if the treasury were relieved of these rewards, its condition would be such that the lack of revenue would never torment or hinder us to incur in such expenses which the common good demanded, without ever having to over-burden our people as often as has been customary.
>
> (Faro, 1965: 190–191)

However, the state of mind of a crusader king in the second half of the fifteenth century was evident in his reply:

> that it is our duty to pay the dowries and other gifts which the said *tenças* which by us they should have about, and to please others for service or for another cause, that we had moved, we gave, according to the reason required.
>
> (Faro, 1965: 191)

Certainly, the king and his advisers had no clear idea of the effect this policy would have on the kingdom's finances. Expenditure on African possessions increased at a rate which the king might not have expected, if we bear in mind the essence of his speech in the *Cortes*. Some scholars quantified some of these extraordinary expenses and, if we consider the conquest of Alcácer Ceguer (*Ksar es-Seghir*) and the reconstruction of the city's walls the following year, the total amount would be 126,000 doubloons (Faro, 1965: 70), which is almost as much as the total amount of money requested by the king to revitalize the royal coffers a few years earlier. After that, the conquests of Asilah, Tangier and Larache followed, as costly as the previous one, or perhaps more so. And on top of all this, there was more to pay than just the military expansion.

6.5 Organizational difficulties

The definitive evidence that there were management problems is the amount of reforms, albeit superficial and unsuccessful, that the monarchs proposed in the course of the 1400s (Marques & Dias, 1998: 249). Those problems did not only concern the state finances' organic structure but also the linkages between its officials, and it was urgent to overcome them, especially from the point of view of increasing revenue. During this period, some measures were taken in order to seek a general improvement of the administrative fiscal apparatus. With João I, some modifications in the royal household were made, changes that would last until the 1480s (Barros, 1945: III, 204–208). The financial reform implemented by Duarte I (1433–1438) modified some positions within the fiscal system, to achieve greater oversight of procedures and a more effective presence of royal power (Silva, 2008: 550), in order to avoid corruption regarding the agents involved and the waste of resources, a tendency that Afonso V would try to follow, as he realized that the government was getting out of hand. Thus, organization and overhaul would become slogans for the *Contos'* staff.

However, there were also remarkable signs of an excessive number of people employed within the bureaucracy in this same period. Not by chance, the *Cortes* of 1465, gathered at Guarda, would try to limit the number of accountants and clerks, as well as their income (Rau, 2009: 57–58). But with this same monarch, as other scholars remarked, "the warfare clarion was calling" (Rau, 2009: 246), that is, a good part of the official class was requested to take up arms and offer their military services in Africa. On the other hand, in the meantime, bodies still needed to work. The pivotal point, according to the peoples' claims in *Cortes* and as previously observed, were the excesses, both in terms of donations and favors granted as a reward for the services rendered in Africa, for example in appointments. There were often reports of more positions promised than there were, leading to queues, forcing officers recently named to wait for a place within the administration, normally the nobility's favorites and, at the same time, "the inheritance of these positions would be customary" (Rau, 2009: 246–247). The king's words and his actions were sending contradictory signals, that is, he wanted to control expenditure, but they did not produce measures with this effect, fearing that such actions could threaten his relations with powerful political groups. Moreover, the wages paid would have their values unreasonably increased from this period until mid-sixteenth century. In 1452, the Lisbon *Contos'* accountant received 4,116 reais of maintenance. Fifty years later, with Manuel I in governance, the same accountants would receive 30,000 reais. The providers received even more: 50,000 reais, excluding other payments such as *tenças* and dwellings. This, in fact, serves to illustrate how in such a short time the unbridled wealth of Manuel I contributed to the Royal coffers' distressing poverty during João III's reign (1521–1557). In thirty years, Portugal's finances went from extreme abundance to a harsh shortage of funds (Rau, 2009: 369–370), particularly related to the needs of the effective occupation of Meridional America (Brazil).

In the *Cortes* of 1472–1473, held in Coimbra-Évora, the symptoms of these organizational problems were described. The assembly had been summoned for "reformation and correction of many things . . . for the necessity and good and profit of these kingdoms," something that had not happened for at least 40 years, since Duarte I's reign (Sousa, 1990: I, 395–396), and the difficulties that, according to some scholars, "implied an attempt to reduce expenditure, beginning precisely by limiting the number of individuals who, by virtue of their palatine functions, received money from the Treasury" (Faro, 1965: 221–222). The king would then limit the number of people who were part of his household, as well as the princes', a sign of financial dire straits. On top of that was a cut in the number of officers and residents of the royal household who, as of the respective law of May 1473, should no longer have pensions for marriages (Faro, 1965: 223–224). Moreover, the ordinance that fixed the sums of money that would be paid as the salary of certain officials of the same house, who were formerly remunerated with rations, wine, meat and fish (Faro, 1965: 230–233) and then served as a sort of "salary table" for royal officialdom.

During João II's reign, the reformist tendency went on, with much that had to be done within the scope of justice, defense and, especially, finances (Sousa, 1989a: 140). Reformation of the *forais* ("charters" that locally regulated administration, tax collection and other privileges), which started in the previous reign, kept going in order to send a strong message of municipal recovery, by listening to their demands and, also, minimizing chances for revenue evasion. The monarch set in motion his plans to restrain the nobility, revising a series of privileges, forcing a return of fortresses and castles, implementing the presence of a *corregedor* into the nobility's lands, as well as requiring the presentation of all donations, graces and privileges for the king's confirmation. With all this, João II incited a rebellion against himself, which he overcame in a forceful and effective way (Dias, Braga & Braga, 1998: 701–703). This prompt reply, in general lines, demonstrated to the people that the king would not submit to the nobility. Furthermore, in itself, with that action he would be able to accumulate immediately, political and economic dividends which his father was not able to collect from the people. From his extraordinary aid request for 100,000 *golden crusaders* (approx. 50,000,000 reais), in 1483 to pay a remaining debt and honor his progenitor's testament (Sousa, 1990: I, 428), he gathered about 38,000,000 reais, while Afonso V's request for 60,000,000 reais to wage war against Castile barely reached 27,000,000 reais (Faro, 1965: 243; Sousa, 1989b: 142).

To the people's eyes, at that point, there was a strong and assertive monarch (Sousa, 1989b: 143). On the other hand, the group that provided the political support that thwarted the insurrection got its fair share of rewards as well, including newly created nobility titles (Dias, Braga & Braga, 1998: 704), increasing the royal entourage and thus spending as it grew. A monetary reform was also implemented, as it was started, to normalize commercial transactions (Marques & Dias (1998: 258–259) due to the difficulty of acquiring silver and also because of the imbalance arising from the gold excess supply provided by the *Mina* region in Africa, which unbalanced prices in general (Tavares, 1981–1983: 30–31). But this reign appears a bit more untroubled, precisely as a result of the profits and revenues from overseas, a strong government and a stabilized situation from the point of view of public expenditure: the *Perfect Prince*, even while contributing to the enlargement of officialdom, though not in the same haughty way as his father, also balanced wages thanks to the currency intervention (Rau, 2009: 370). As noted by other scholars, "it would be the hard and heavy hands of this monarch, committed to reform and reformulate the kingdom's administration" (Magalhães, 2007b: 112), which would care for the overseas' expansion paths and the dividends that rose from such discoveries, mostly underpinned by the Crown's monopolies on gold, slaves, ivory and pepper. It would be this magnificence that produced the fundamental condition for the affirmation of administrative and fiscal policy, simultaneously *bureaucratic* and *mercantilist*, of the Portuguese state (Magalhães, 2007a: 98–99).

From that moment onwards, the reformist movement, which had been previously repressed, would be resumed with Manuel I, mainly due to the newly acquired economic capacity. That capacity would then allow not only the gratification of the nobility, more generously than of his predecessor but also the promotion, with a great abundance of resources, of interventions in assistance, art, urban renewal, wars in Africa, navies to India and, finally, an administrative reformation (Costa, 2005: 101). However, the fiscal apparatus was not covered by this restructuring at all. On the contrary, it remained static, with a structure almost unmodified since Afonso V but with more burdens to support and benefits to pay. As for the resources to match this, there would be no problem at all. The monarch would not even bother to request extraordinary aids from the people's representatives, a common practice among his predecessors. He had been bathed by luck, with India's fortune and riches. The collection structure, with the tax farming, remained almost the same, with the single difference of possessing then a complete collection of procedures, the *Regiment and Ordinances of the Treasury*, issued in 1516, that ran from the *Vedores* and the other higher spheres of finances, down to the simpler procedures of young messengers (Carneiro, 1818: 89–208). The conduct of those officers, to a large extent, did not change substantially, especially in relation to the former fiscal *praxis* of earlier reigns.

Although the kingdom's bureaucratic coordination had severe issues, the communication between the royal officers' different spheres of performance seemed to work with a reasonable degree of effectiveness. It is noticeable that network operated fluidly, albeit with the intermixing of the king's household and the kingdom's finances. That phenomenon can be attested through the acquittance letter granted to Diogo Álvares,[31] king's personal buyer of all resources received between 1441 and 1451. In this source, the royal household's esquire accounts for a series of sums that he raised with the messengers, receivers, tenants and other people, in several different combinations. But this document, by itself, does not prove the system operated smoothly. We have been able, with the help of some other sources, to track the origin or destination of these revenues by checking against each other and by cross referencing information.

In another acquittance given to Vasco Afonso,[32] receiver of the *almoxarifado* at Torre de Moncorvo, regarding the *pedidos* collected between 1441 and 1448, the same account reported having paid 3,600 reais "to Diogo Alvarez, our squire, concerning his provisions for the months of September, October, November, December of the year 1440, and of January and February of the following year of 1441". Here, it is noteworthy that those sums, which were at first intended for the extraordinary expenses related to the aid to the King of Castile, ended up directed in part to the payment for supplies due in arrears to the buyer of the monarch. In addition, Diogo Álvares himself says that he received, in 1441, 513,516 reais from "fernam gill from Monte Royo, knight of our house and our treasurer". This is the same Fernão Gil, who had received, in three consecutive years – 1440, 1441 and 1442 – resources from two of Beja's *almoxarifes*: João Rodrigues Costa,[33] and from Gonçalo Anes de Magalhães,[34] reporting sums of 150,840 reais, 363,050 and 114,091 reais, respectively, "to his duty's expenses". Yet, the same buyer cited earlier, Alvares, also reported having received, in 1445, "twenty thousand from Joham Roiz almoxarife of Beja" and, in 1448, another "thirty-three thousand from Joham Roiz Costa almoxarife of Beja". Apparently, it was the same officer who had paid the treasurer Fernão Gil a few years before, for his duty's expenses, and that comes referenced in the first source on these two occasions.

The same treasurer cited previously, Fernão Gil de Monterroio, was also mentioned as having delivered several amounts between 1441 and 1448, while exercising his treasury functions within the royal household. In the last years, between 1449 and 1451, his relative Álvaro Fernandes de Monterroio[35] replaced him in this role, and the new receiver indicates that he collected payments of 1,149,917 reais, 581,060 reais and 300,000 reais, in the respective years. However, the funds needed to carry out the new treasurer's duties were mentioned in another acquittance granted to João Cerveira,[36] *almoxarife* of Setúbal. There, the payments' accounting was done regarding the years 1449 and 1450, of 290,368 and 68,101 reais, respectively, "that we entrust it to the expenses of his office".

Other officers were also identified by means of the first mentioned source: in 1442, the king's personal buyer reported that he had received "ten thousand from Afonso Gonçalves Baldaya, *almoxarife* in the city of Oporto". This same Afonso Baldaya appeared in another acquittance granted to Gonçalo Pacheco,[37] treasurer of Ceuta's deeds in Lisbon, having paid 3,000 reais between July 1441 and January 1442 for the maintenance of that African outpost. Further, in the same document, in 1445, was reported a payment of "thirty thousand from Martim Zapata, our main treasurer in the city of Lisbon". Moreover, in 1447, appeared another "seventy thousand from Martim Zapata our main treasurer", the same Martim who received three payments, referenced in another acquittance granted to João Lourenço da Seara,[38] receiver at the *almoxarifado* of Lamego.

Still following the trail of the first source, i.e., the acquittance granted to Diogo Álvares, in the following years of 1443, 1445 and 1450, another official mentioned was Vasco Jusarte, *almoxarife* of Évora, who delivered to the king's personal buyer, for those years, 100,000, 20,000 and 2,184 reais respectively. Vasco himself appears in another acquittance granted to Pedro Eanes,[39] the king's factor in Flanders, regarding the financial resources and things he received and spent between April 1441 and January 1443. He did report receiving

> a thousand spears and with their extra iron tips of which there were twelve, which he says it was lost in the journey, plus fifty cannons, with hundred and four chambers for them, and three mobile cannons, loaded, with its butts

which seems to be bought to prepare for a potential conflict against Castile, previously debated in the *Cortes* also held in Évora in 1442. It is evident, thanks to these references, the many points of contact between the different layers of royal administration and the fiscal mechanism which, as we have seen, intersected and, on many occasions, even confused themselves about their competences.

On the other hand, things were not always going well. Another acquittance of 1457, granted to Álvaro Vaz,[40] *almoxarife* of Abrantes and the king's main chamberlain, for all that had been received and spent in the name of Princess Catarina, confirms this disorganization. He had not taken account of the money collected due to the disappearance of books. However, the acquittance document was given anyway. It should also be clarified that the *almoxarifes*, receivers of the *almoxarifados* and of the extraordinary aids and other officials, regardless of the accounts provided, were considered debtors. And what does this mean in practical terms? The total received, which appears at the beginning of each acquittance, refers, in fact, to an estimate made by the evaluators, from the tax farming contracts agreed between the tax farmers and the monarch. As a result, in many cases, the officers were unable to receive from the tenants the sums stipulated in the agreements, which required a "discount" in the final accounts, for example in the acquittance granted to João Rodrigues Costa,[41] Beja's *almoxarife*, when "it is discounted eighteen thousand and thirty-nine reais of the fifty thousand reais regarding the rents of Mourão and Monsaraz" because the rents of that locality had not yielded "more than twenty-two thousand five hundred and eighty six reais". Among the partners, only Estevão Afonso Junçeiro, Samuel Amarilho and Mossel Navarro, "leasers who made up three quarters of the income", had paid 9,375 reais each, "and another who had Salomon of that village, who now is a Christian, never did and he was arrested. And the others also for the more that they lose than they have tied", being later released, although no assets had been found to be pawned. When goods were found, they would be sold to cover the losses. And if the total spent did not match the total received, the *almoxarife* would be considered as a debtor, and he should repay that amount in some way, by giving up some of his income, as in the acquittance granted to Gonçalo Anes,[42] Guarda's *almoxarife*, or transferring the sum as part of the next year's revenue, out of the *almoxarife*'s pocket, as in the case of Vasco Afonso, receiver of the *pedidos* collected at Torre de Moncorvo's *almoxarifado*, previously mentioned. Or he could be considered even, as a mercy granted by the monarch, as in the case of Afonso Cerveira,[43] receiver of Lamego's *almoxarifado*. Essentially, the Crown would give up important sums at certain times, as part of a broader and pragmatic strategy.

The flaws and lack of coordination within the system are also evidenced in the mismatch of formatting and standards used by officials in royal accounting. As observed by other experts, it is not accurate to assume that, due to the simple fact that Portugal has constituted budgetary outlines based on estimates of revenues and expenses, some of them evidenced during the reign of Afonso V, that a new era would come, without issues and disturbances in fiscal organization. Especially when simple incongruities were still present among the clerks, those who produced, handled and, along with accountants and *almoxarifes*, organized state accounting. Furthermore, the delay in replacing ancient Roman peninsular numeric notation, which progressively advanced throughout the 1500s, would only come by express deliberation, representing a culture of resistance, a rooted reluctance to innovations, characterizing the "slow osmoses" mentioned by other scholars (Godinho, 2009: 150). Portugal's public finances would begin to use Indian-Arab notation only in late seventeenth century and, in the meanwhile, Lisbon's fiscal superintendents seized all ledger books from the Indies. And why? Because those were written adopting this new notation, while the central body, the one from which the good example and initiative was supposed to emanate, rejected it, and demanded "the original books, with the records made according to the traditional norm in the *Contos*: in full and in Roman-peninsular numbering" (Godinho, 2009: 150–151), to be rewritten and resent to Lisbon.

On top of that there were so many accounting problems owing to their disjointed way of computing the inputs and outputs, that an officer's accounting process so that he could receive his respective acquittance, "could take from three to four years after the end of his term of office, rarely would take only one and, not so unusually, could take eight". This phenomenon was happening still in the seventeenth century, as in the case

> of the Warehouse of Supplies' *almoxarife* in 1610 who, having been in office for eight years, had been seconded to another office and had not yet noticed, probably because he was not informed; of the treasurer-general of Goa, who had been given the post in 1624, and five years later, his account had not yet been taken; and finally that of the *Conselho da Fazenda* (Finance Council), which had found that it was not possible to know what the State had actually spent in each year separately.
>
> (Godinho, 2009: 151)

Such was the confusion and mixture of expenditure records.

An important hypothesis to explain the existing obstacles and the attempt to overcome them, and even a subject for further investigation of fundamental importance, concerns the appropriation of military orders' economic assets by the Royal Treasury, to help in reducing financial difficulties. Bearing in mind the association of their masters to members of the royal household, some evidences in this sense may be suggestive. João II's response to Princess Beatriz, his aunt, when she made a request to the monarch regarding the Order of Avis' masters for her son, Manuel, then Duke of Beja, and future king Manuel I, provides us with important information about the execution of Afonso V's testament. He affirmed that "for the payment of this year's settlement, that came of expenditure that the king, my lord, that God now has, was obliged to make in the settlement of the great, and *tenças* of nobles of this kingdom, lacks forty-two millions", that is, the increased spending on the nobility is manifest. Nevertheless, revenues must increase. In addition, there were the

> debts which His Highness orders to pay in his will, thirty million, and what I had in being Prince could not support my state, without being a debtor from one year to another, as she may well know, and for these reasons I am forced for some time to have in me these two masters.
>
> (Chaves, 1983: 306)

Furthermore, in the same line, the potential economic support provided by the military orders can be seen in the acquittance granted to Vasco Fernandes Leborato,[44] esquire of the royal household and *almoxarife* of Avis, a village 150 kilometers east of Lisbon and headquarters of the military order with the same name. The source reports everything that had received in the period that began on St. John's day, 24 June 1480, and closed on the same day of 1487. There seems to be no doubt here that there was an *almoxarifado* in that village that reported to the royal finances' central office. On the other hand, we are not able to determine the precise date of creation for that local branch fiscal, which does not appear in the sources seen prior to the fifteenth century, but only afterwards. Following the established subdivisions it would be under the jurisdiction of Évora's accounting office, deducible from the provenance of the revenues described: revenues received from the *almoxarifados* of Veiros, Estremoz and Portalegre, in addition to extraordinary revenues collected in that region, corresponding to less than 50% of that collection. The remaining

> 1,642,041, which is lacking to the fulfillment of the 3,010,936 *reais*, received the forementioned Vasco Fernandez, from the income of the rents that the Order has in that town and places that belongs to it, which yielded from the day of St. John of the year of 80, until another such day of the year of 87, which is seven years"

that is, more than half of this *almoxarifado*'s collection came from the Order of Avis. This should be no surprise at all, especially since the former prince and now King João II was the master and main administrator of the order (Fonseca, 2005: 204–209).

Notes

1 Previously, in some situations, they were paid in kind.
2 According to Henriques, Afonso IV's chancery records indicate someone named Pedro Esteves as a *Vedor*, already in 1341, practicing supervision activities, above the *Contos'* officers. Henriques (2008: 139).
3 ANTT, *Chanc. D. Afonso V*, liv. 23, fl. 30.
4 ANTT, *Chanc. D. Afonso V*, liv. 27, fl. 116v.
5 ANTT, *Chanc. D. Afonso V*, liv. 25, fl. 71–71v.
6 ANTT, *Chanc. D. João II*, liv. 19, fl. 91.
7 ANTT, *Chanc. D. João II*, liv. 20, fl. 174v-175.
8 ANTT, Leitura Nova, *Livro dos Extras*, fl. 13–13v.
9 ANTT, *Chanc. D. Manuel I*, liv. 30, fl. 106; copied at Leitura Nova, *Beira*, liv. 1, fl. 13v. Published in Freire (1904: II, 237).
10 ANTT, *Chanc. D. Manuel I*, liv. 31, fl. 46v; copied at Leitura Nova, *Estremadura*, liv. 1, fl. 129v. Published in Freire (1907: V, 478).
11 ANTT, *Chanc. D. Manuel I*, liv. 28, fl. 55; copied at Leitura Nova, *Guadiana*, liv. 5, fl. 196v. Published in Freire (1903: I, 279–280).
12 In the *Cortes* of 1472–1473 (Coimbra-Évora), the people petitioned for a broad reform of kingdom's government. The representatives wrote about 27 propositions

about judicial affairs, and another 162 chapters called Místicos (miscellaneous), with different proposals on diverse themes: justice, economy, fiscal affairs etc. They asked the king, for example, to punish officers already condemned for abuse, to forbid the *corregedores* ("supervisors") of forcing inhabitants to provide men, animals or wagons for different prices of those legally established and to empower judges to determine the restitution of that property forcibly obtained. Sousa (1990: I, 397–398; II, 384–434).

13 See Fonseca (1995).

14 By dry ports, we mean the land customs, checkpoints to control international trade and collect taxes from products coming from Castile. We used some references provided by Silva (2002: 210–211). See also Cosme (2002) and Rodrigues and Carqueja (2009).

15 See Costa and Castro (1998); Machado (1998).

16 We think it is very plausible, by an inquisitorial lawsuit to a Duarte da Costa, who was a barber and guard of dry ports' customs in Penamacor. See Mendes (2010: 49).

17 See Cardoso (1944, 1953, 1996).

18 See Pereira (1983) and Polónia (2002a, 2002b, 2007).

19 See Moreira (1984, 1992).

20 See Gomes (2009).

21 Pereira (2003: 175–177). See also Magalhães (1970, 1993, 2012).

22 ANTT, Leitura Nova, *Beira*, liv. 3, fl. 96–96v.

23 ANTT, *Chanc. D. Manuel I*, liv. 11, fl. 112; copied at Leitura Nova, *Estremadura*, liv. 12, fl. 18. Published in Freire (1905: III, 386).

24 ANTT, *Chanc. D. Manuel I*, liv. 15, fl. 72; copied at Leitura Nova, *Místicos*, liv. 5, fl. 140. Published in Freire (1905: III, 471).

25 ANTT, Leitura Nova, *Guadiana*, liv. 7, fl. 187.

26 In the *Cortes* of 1451 (Santarém), a petition overruled by the monarch claimed the punishment of *almoxarifes*, treasurers and royal receivers when they demanded extraordinary taxes (*peitas*) to those who were supposed to receive pecuniary mercies granted by the king; and the penalty had to be so powerful that it should dissuade them from their greed. Sousa (1990: II, 344).

27 Adjustment (*adiantamento*) by which indirect taxes' payers acquit before the fiscal authorities, by paying a previous fixed amount, proportional to the probable sales in that period, regardless of sales values or earned profits. Definition found in 2013/08/20, in the *Dicionário Houaiss da Língua Portuguesa*, online version – http://houaiss.uol. com.br/.

28 ANTT, *Chanc. D. Afonso V*, liv. 18, fl. 63–65.

29 ANTT, *Chanc. D. Afonso V*, liv. 23, fl. 2–3; copied at Leitura Nova, *Guadiana*, liv. 6, fl. 122v.

30 The acquittance letters granted to João Afonso, receiver of Lisbon's sales taxes (*sisas*) on colored cloth, accounts for Jewish merchants, alone or in partnerships with other Jewish businessmen, to lease the respective sales taxes.

31 ANTT, Leitura Nova, *Livro dos Extras*, fl. 118–119.

32 ANTT, *Chanc. D. Afonso V*, liv. 3, fl. 13v-15. Published in Gonçalves (1964: 246–257).

33 ANTT, *Chanc. D. Afonso V*, liv. 27, fl. 65–65v.

34 ANTT, *Chanc. D. Afonso V*, liv. 25, fl. 71–71v.

35 We don't know which the degree of kinship was. However, it is known his family bonds with Fernão Gil de Monterrorio. Gomes (1995: 133–134).

36 ANTT, *Chanc. D. Afonso V*, liv. 11, fl. 143v-144.

37 ANTT, *Chanc. D. Afonso V*, liv. 25, fl. 17v. Published in Azevedo (1915: I, 556–560).

38 ANTT, *Chanc. D. Afonso V*, liv. 36, fl. 123–123v. Published in Gonçalves (1964: 258–261).

39 ANTT, *Chanc. D. Afonso V*, liv. 27, fl. 122. Published in Marques (1988: I, 427).

40 ANTT, Leitura Nova, *Livro dos Extras*, fl. 91–91v.

41 ANTT, *Chanc. D. Afonso V*, liv. 27, fl. 65–65v.
42 ANTT, *Chanc. D. Afonso V*, liv. 18, fl. 63–65.
43 ANTT, *Chanc. D. Afonso V*, liv. 27, fl. 116v.
44 ANTT, *Chanc. D. Manuel I*, liv. 30, fl. 32v; copied at Leitura Nova, *Guadiana*, liv. 1, fl. 227 Published in Freire (1908: VI, 77–78).

Bibliography

Primary sources

ANTT, Chanc. D. Afonso V, liv. 3.
ANTT, Chanc. D. Afonso V, liv. 11.
ANTT, Chanc. D. Afonso V, liv. 18.
ANTT, Chanc. D. Afonso V, liv. 23.
ANTT, Chanc. D. Afonso V, liv. 25.
ANTT, Chanc. D. Afonso V, liv. 27.
ANTT, Chanc. D. Afonso V, liv. 36.
ANTT, Chanc. D. João II, liv. 19.
ANTT, Chanc. D. João II, liv. 20.
ANTT, Chanc. D. Manuel I, liv. 11.
ANTT, Chanc. D. Manuel I, liv. 15.
ANTT, Chanc. D. Manuel I, liv. 28.
ANTT, Chanc. D. Manuel I, liv. 30.
ANTT, Chanc. D. Manuel I, liv. 31.
ANTT, Leitura Nova, Beira, liv. 1.
ANTT, Leitura Nova, Beira, liv. 3.
ANTT, Leitura Nova, Estremadura, liv. 1.
ANTT, Leitura Nova, Estremadura, liv. 12.
ANTT, Leitura Nova, Guadiana, liv. 1.
ANTT, Leitura Nova, Guadiana, liv. 5.
ANTT, Leitura Nova, Guadiana, liv. 6.
ANTT, Leitura Nova, Guadiana, liv. 7.
ANTT, Leitura Nova, Livro dos Extras.
ANTT, Leitura Nova, Místicos, liv. 5.

Secondary sources, chronicles and dictionaries

Azevedo, P. de. (1915–1934). *Documentos das chancelarias reais anteriores a 1531 relativos a Marrocos*, 2 vols. Lisbon: Academia das Sciências de Lisboa.
Carneiro, M. B. (1818). *Resumo chronologico das leis mais uteis no foro e uso da vida civil publicadas até o presente anno*, vol. I. Lisbon: Impressão Régia.
Chaves, A. L. de. (1983). *Livro de Apontamentos (1438–1489)*. Códice 443 da Colecção Pombalina da BNL, introdução e transcrição de Anastásia Mestrinho Salgado e Abílio José Salgado. Lisbon: Imprensa Nacional – Casa da Moeda.
Dicionário Houaiss da Língua Portuguesa, Online version [http://houaiss.uol.com.br/].
Faro, J. (1965). *Receitas e despesas da Fazenda Real de 1384 a 1481: subsídios documentais*. Lisbon: Instituto Nacional de Estatística.

Freire, A. B. (1903–1916). "Cartas de Quitação del rei D. Manuel", in *Archivo Historico Portuguez*, 11 vols. Lisbon: Of. Typographica-Calçada do Cabra.

Marques, J. M. da S. (1988). *Descobrimentos Portugueses: documentos para a sua História*, 5 vols, 2nd ed. Lisbon: INIC.

Studies

Barata, F. T., & Henriques, A. C. (2012). Economic and Fiscal History, in J. Mattoso (dir.), M. de L. Rosa, B. V. e Sousa, & M. J. Branco (eds.), *The Historiography of Medieval Portugal (c.1950–2010)*. Lisbon: Instituto de Estudos Medievais, 261–281.

Barros, H. da G. (1945). *História da Administração Pública em Portugal nos Séculos XII a XV: 2ª edição dirigida por Torquato de Sousa Soares*, 11 vols. Lisbon: Livraria Sá da Costa Editora.

Bonney, R. (1995). Revenues, in R. Bonney (ed.), *Economic Systems and State Finance*. Oxford: Oxford University Press, 423–505.

Cardoso, J. (1953). *Castelo Branco e o seu Alfoz – Achegas para uma monografia regional*. Castelo Branco: Câmara Municipal de Castelo Branco.

Cardoso, J. (1996). *Foral da cidade de Castelo Branco*. Castelo Branco: Câmara Municipal de Castelo Branco [fac-simile of 1510's edition].

Cardoso, J. R. (1944). *Subsídios para a História Regional da Beira Baixa*. Castelo Branco: Junta Provincial da *Beira* Baixa.

Chevalier, B. (2002). Le financement de la première guerre d'Italie, in P. Contamine, J. Kerhervé, & A. Rigaudière (dir.), *L'impôt au Moyen Âge: l'impôt public et le prélèvement seigneurial, fin XIIe – début XVie siècle*. Actes du colloque tenu à Bercy les 14, 15 et 16 juin 2000. Paris: Comité pour L'Histoire Économique et Financière de la France, I, 41–66.

Coelho, M. H. da C. (1988). O poder e a sociedade ao tempo de D. Afonso IV, Revista de História, 8, 35–52.

Cosme, J. (2002). As Relações Económicas Entre Portugal e Espanha (1756–1759): O Movimento dos Portos Secos de Castelo de Vide e Campo Maior, População e Sociedade, 8, 179–201.

Costa, J. P. O. e. (2005). *D. Manuel I: um príncipe do Renascimento*. Mem Martins: Círculo de Leitores.

Costa, P. P., & Castro, J. I. C. C. A. de. (1988). A Alfândega de Freixo de Espada-à-Cinta em 1517, *Douro – Estudos & Documentos*, III (5), (1°), 95–108.

Cruz, M. L. G. da. (2001). *A Governação de D. João III: a Fazenda Real e os seus Vedores*. Lisbon: Centro de História da Universidade de Lisboa.

Dias, J. J. A., Braga, I. M. R. M. D., & Braga, P. D. (1998). A Conjuntura, in A. H. de O. Marques (dir.), de J. J. A. Dias (coord.), *Nova História de Portugal, vol. V – Portugal do renascimento à crise dinástica*. Lisbon: Ed. Presença, 689–760.

Duarte, L. M. (2003). The Portuguese Medieval Parliament: Are We Asking the Right Questions? e-journal of Portuguese History, 1, 2, winter, 1–12.

Duarte, L. M. (2006). A memória contra a História: as sisas medievais portuguesas, in D. Menjot & M. Sánchez Martínez (dir.), *Fiscalidad de Estado y fiscalidad municipal en los reinos hispánicos medievales: estudios dirigidos por Denis Menjot y Manuel Sánchez Martínez*. Madrid: Casa de Velázquez, 433–445.

Fonseca, C. S. (1995). *A centralização monárquica portuguesa: 1439–1495*. Ph.D. Thesis. Porto, Faculty of Arts.

Fonseca, L. A. da. (2005). *D. João II.* Mem Martins: Círculo de Leitores.

Godinho, V. M. (2009). A Formação do Estado e as Finanças Públicas, in V. M. Godinho, *Ensaios e Estudos: uma maneira de pensar*, vol. I, 2nd ed. Lisbon: Sá da Costa Editora, 123–173.

Gomes, R. C. (1995). *A Corte dos reis de Portugal no final da Idade Média.* Linda-a-Velha: Difel.

Gomes, S. A. (2006). *D. Afonso V: o Africano.* Mem Martins: Círculo de Leitores.

Gomes, S. A. (2009). Aveiro nos alvores de Quinhentos – breves considerações, in D. Bismarck (coord.), *História de Aveiro – Sínteses e Perspectivas.* Aveiro: Câmara Municipal de Aveiro, 143–147.

Gonçalves, I. (1964). *Pedidos e empréstimos públicos em Portugal durante a Idade Média.* Lisbon: Cadernos de Ciência e Técnica Fiscal: Centro de estudos fiscais da direcção-geral das contribuições e impostos – Ministério das Finanças.

Gonçalves, I. (1987). As finanças municipais do Porto na segunda metade do século XV. Porto: Câmara Municipal do Porto, 1987.

Henriques, A. M. B. de M. de C. (2008). *State Finance, War and Redistribution in Portugal (1249–1527).* Ph.D. Thesis. Department of History, University of York.

Homem, A. L. de C. (1978). Subsídios para o estudo da Administração Central no reinado de D. Pedro I, Revista de História, 1, 39–87.

Homem, A. L. de C. (1990). *O Desembargo Régio (1320–1433).* Porto: Junta Nacional de Investigação Científica.

Ladero Quesada, M. A. (1997). Las reformas fiscales y monetarias de Alfonso X como base del 'Estado Moderno', in M. Rodríguez Llopis (ed.), *Alfonso X: aportaciones de un rey castellano a la construcción de Europa.* Murcia: Consejeria de Cultura y Educación, 31–54.

Larguier, G. (2008). Fiscalité municipale, fiscalité royale, fiscalité provinciale en Languedoc (France), XIVᵉ-XVIIIᵉ siècles. Nature, poids, évolution, in *Actas La fiscalità nell'economia europea (sec. XIII-XVIII),* 39th Settimana di Studi dell'istituto "Francesco Datini" di Prato a cura di Simonetta Cavaciocchi. Firenze: Firenze University Press, 351–370.

Machado, M. de F. P. (1998). Freixo de Espada à Cinta: problemas e privilégios em finais da Idade Média, Revista da Faculdade de Letras: História, II, 15, 1, 275–286.

Magalhães, J. R. (1970). *Para o Estudo do Algarve Económico no Século XVI.* Lisbon: Ed. Cosmos.

Magalhães, J. R. (1993). *O Algarve Económico (1600–1773).* Lisbon: Ed. Estampa.

Magalhães, J. R. (2007a). A Fazenda, in J. Mattoso (dir.), *História de Portugal, vol. V – No Alvorecer da Modernidade.* Mem Martins: Círculo de Leitores, 98–112.

Magalhães, J. R. (2007b). A Guerra: os homens e as armas, in J. Mattoso (dir.), *História de Portugal, vol. V – No Alvorecer da Modernidade.* Mem Martins: Círculo de Leitores, 112–121.

Magalhães, J. R. (2012). Panorama social e económico do Algarve na época de D. Jerónimo Osório, in *O Algarve na época moderna: miúnças 2.* Coimbra: Coimbra University Press, 55–68.

Marques, A. H. de O., & Dias, J. J. A. (1998). As Finanças e a Moeda, in A. H. de O. Marques (dir.), de J. J. A. Dias (coord.), *Nova História de Portugal, vol. V – Portugal do renascimento à crise dinástica.* Lisbon: Ed. Presença, 249–276.

Mattoso, J. (2001). O triunfo da monarquia portuguesa: 1258–1264. Ensaio de História Política, Análise Social, 35, 157, 899–935.

Mattoso, J. (2006). A consolidação da monarquia e a unidade política, in J. Mattoso (dir.), *História de Portugal, vol. III: A Monarquia Feudal*. Mem Martins: Circulo de Leitores, 284–313.

Mendes, L G. (2010). *Os Judeus de Penamacor e a inquisição*. Penamacor: Câmara Municipal de Penamacor-Arquivo Municipal.

Menjot, D. (2008). Les enjeux de la fiscalité directe dans les systèmes financiers et fiscaux des villes castillanes aux XIVᵉ et XVᵉ siècles", in *Actas La fiscalità nell'economia europea (sec. XIII-XVIII)*, 39th Settimana di Studi dell'istituto "Francesco Datini" di Prato a cura di Simonetta Cavaciocchi. Firenze: Firenze University Press, 699–729.

Merêa, P. (2006). Organização Social e Administração Pública, in P. Merêa, *Estudos de História de Portugal*. Lisbon: INCM, 129–231.

Moreira, M. A. F. (1984). *O porto de Viana do Castelo na época dos descobrimentos*. Viana do Castelo: Câmara Municipal de Viana do Castelo.

Moreira, M. A. F. (1992). *A Alfândega de Viana e o comércio de importação de panos do século XVI*. Viana do Castelo: Câmara Municipal de Viana do Castelo.

Moreno, H. B. (1993). Dois concelhos medievais da Beira interior: Sabugal e Sortelha, Revista de Guimarães, 103, 345–358.

Ormrod, W. M., & Barta, J. (1995). The Feudal Structure and the Beginnings of State Finance, in R. Bonney (ed.), *Economic Systems and State Finance*. Oxford: Oxford University Press, 53–79.

Pedreira, J. M. (2010). Custos e Tendências Financeiras no império Português, 1415–1822, in F. Bethencourt & D. R. Curto (dir.), A Expansão Marítima Portuguesa, 1400–1800. Lisbon: Edições 70, 53–91.

Pereira, J. C. (1983). *Para a história das alfândegas em Portugal no início do século XVI: Vila do Conde – organização e movimento*. Lisbon: Nova University of Lisbon – FCSH.

Pereira, J. C. (2003). *Portugal na Era de Quinhentos: estudos varios*. Cascais: Patrimonia.

Polónia, A. (2002a). O Porto de Vila do Conde no séc. XVI: Depoimentos históricos e perspectivas cartográficas, in A. Polónia, I. Amorim, & H. Osswald (orgs.), *O Litoral em Perspectiva Histórica (Séc. XVI a XVIII)*. Porto: Instituto de História Moderna, 145–164.

Polónia, A. (2002b). *Vila do Conde no período manuelino: a reconstrução da memória*. Vila do Conde: Câmara Municipal de Vila do Conde.

Polónia, A. (2007). *Expansão e Descobrimentos numa perspectiva local. O porto de Vila do Conde no século XVI*. Lisbon: Imprensa Nacional-Casa da Moeda.

Rau, V. (2009). *A Casa dos Contos: os três mais antigos regimentos dos contos*. Lisbon: Imprensa Nacional-Casa da Moeda [re-edition of 1951 and 1959 original prints].

Rodrigues, A. V., & Carqueja, M. A. (2009). Relações Culturais Internacionais de Torre de Moncorvo (Séculos XV-XVII), in F. Sousa (coord.), *Moncorvo: da Tradição à Modernidade*. Porto: CEPESE-Ed. Afrontamento, 63–72.

Schulze, W. (1995). The Emergence and Consolidation of the 'Tax State'. I – The Sixteenth Century, in R. Bonney (ed.), *Economic Systems and State Finance*. Oxford: Oxford University Press, 261–279.

Silva, F. R. da. (2002). "Alfândegas lusas em finais de Setecentos: fiscalidade e funcionalismo", in A. Polónia, I. Amorim, & H. Osswald (orgs.), *O Litoral em Perspectiva Histórica (Séc. XVI a XVIII)*. Porto: Instituto de História Moderna, 205–216.

Silva, F. R. da. (2008). Transferring European Fiscal System Overseas: A Comparison between the Portuguese Home and Colonial Fiscal Systems, in *Actas La fiscalità nell'economia europea (sec. XIII-XVIII)*, 39th Settimana di Studi dell'istituto "Francesco Datini" di Prato a cura di Simonetta Cavaciocchi. Firenze: Firenze University Press, 545–567.

Sousa, A. de. (1989a). A Estratégia política dos municípios no reinado de D. João II, Revista da Faculdade de Letras: História, II, 06, 137–174.

Sousa, A. de. (1989b). O Parlamento na época de D. João II, in *Actas do Congresso internacional Bartolomeu Dias e a sua época*. Porto: University of Porto, I, 231–261.

Sousa, A. de. (1990). *As cortes medievais portuguesas: 1385–1490*, 2 vols. Porto: INIC.

Tavares, M. J. P. F. (1981–1983). Subsídios para o estudo da história monetária do séc. XV: 1448–1495, Nummus: Boletim da Sociedade Portuguesa de Numismática, 2ª série, 4–6, 9–59.

Viana, M. (2011). A metrologia nas posturas municipais dos Açores (séculos XVI-XVIII), *Actas do 5° Colóquio "O Faial e a periferia açoriana nos séculos XV a XX"*, Faial e São Jorge, 17 a 20 de Maio de 2010. Ponta Delgada: Universidade dos Açores, 279–312.

7 Conclusion

A contribution for further Portuguese early modern fiscal studies

Some scholars engaged in the history of economic thought, as well as social history, theory of history and history of historiography have, in recent works, meditated about the history of concepts as a fundamental tool to perform a more accurate analysis, a temporal beacon regarding history's scientific autonomy between past and present.[1] Beyond that, some of them approached the idea of history as the master of life, from its origins in the Roman Empire, with Cicero – *historia magistra vitae* – to the present day, in which the same story has been going through a crisis of meaning. When reflecting on the social function attributed to the writing of history by the Greeks, it was affirmed that history could be seen as a *monument*, that is, something that allows us to revisit past situations, a guarantor of triumph over forgetfulness, a function that would already be present in Herodotus, who wrote his *Histories* so that the deeds of men "would not fade with time, and great companies would not remain unrecognized", whether they were carried out by the Helenes or by the *barbarians* (Catroga, 2006: 13–14). Reflecting on this relationship between the judgment and writing of that Greek thinker and historian, it was ascertained that he left her under the tutelage of *Mnemosyne* – the goddess of memory – because only she was able to unite what individuals were with what they will be, in which the writing of history "proposed to defeat the amnesia produced by the corruption of time". That said, only *fame*, corroborated by memory, would give us the possibility to confront forgetfulness, obtaining effects similar to those of oral testimony, providing a collection of pedagogical examples (Catroga, 2006: 14–15; Marques, 2013: 66–67). Following this thread, would history still be the master of life? With regard to what we observed in the course of this fiscal analysis, would they then have these experiences and this course taught something in terms of a liable fiscal attitude? Let's examine, in parts.

First, from the point of view of an expenditure that exceeds revenue, this trend does not change, except for a gap of about forty years, between the consolidation in S. Jorge da Mina in the 1480s, and the decline of the Indian commercial monopoly in the 1520s. This was the turning point, especially regarding the analysis of tax system formation process, in its various moments, between the monarchical reigns covered by this chronology and, fundamentally, the transition from Manuel I to João III. That is to say, even the monarchs who, at a certain point had new forms of collection (Henriques, 2008: 147–149), found that the fiscal regime implemented were not capable of meeting the fiscal requirements of the state, whose expenses were based on the proceeds' redistributive component. Not even with new taxes, such as *sisas*, or tools that provided them extraordinary income, such as *pedidos* and *empréstimos*, or the resources from overseas' mercantilist outposts in Africa, Asia and Brazil could the fiscal need be met. On one hand, the phenomenon of redistribution analyzed by some scholars is indeed confirmed, particularly when we observe the high values found in the expenditure component related to annuities, weddings, dwellings and settlements. All those components far outstripped the real wages, which were intended for the payment of civil servants. It should be noted that we did not mention what was intended for public works and repairs in cities and towns, as well as military equipment located on border lines and throughout the kingdom. For that purpose, there were the extra requests, formalized in numerous *Cortes* meetings in the period analyzed which, on the other hand, disproves the idea that only the *sisas* would be sufficient for everything. They were not even close to enough. It would be inaccurate to insist on such a thesis.

Second, there was an increase in revenue, albeit on nominal terms. However, only through a more detailed analysis, converting those values into grams or tons of silver, would it be possible to determine whether there was an increase in the wealth accumulated by the state, even with currency debasement and inflation during that period. The fact is that, notwithstanding this analysis, the revenues' growth rate does not seem to be indexed only by the Portuguese economy's "ordinary" variables, nor by inflation, given the almost constant increase in revenue values, year after year, in each one of the *almoxarifados* observed. Noticeable was the variation of the amounts raised due to the demand (or lack thereof) of those interested in investing in tax farming. In the years when there were no leaseholders, for whatever reason, there was a tendency for reduced collections, usually performed by a local inhabitant or person linked to the king's service. On the other hand, when it is perceived that the collection can be profitable, and the investors' demand is numerous, the leasing values naturally accompany this trend.

However, this policy of *outsourcing* regarding tax collection does not seem to have generally benefited the state. Objectively, there was a revenue *freezing*, that is, from year to year, the resources' inflow into the Crown's coffers did not suffer great variations, except for leasing rates due to the supply and demand law applied to the deals in public auctions, which facilitated the organization of a budget by this predictability factor. On the other hand, the most appealing tax farming markets were the realm's big cities, main seaports and specific frontier's small towns. Moreover, there was no increase regarding most of the earnings throughout the kingdom, where most of the tax collection was not attractive to investors to the point of forcing the revenue increase by means of competition concerning tax farming initiatives. In other words, the treasury suffered from income stagnation, while expenditures increased sharply due to the simple preparation for military conflicts, or even worse when the wars actually occurred. See, for example, the enormous quantity of military equipment stored in Lisbon between 1438 and 1448, whose acquittance was granted to Gonçalo Afonso,[2] the warehouse's *almoxarife*, ranging from silver harnesses to bombards, chambers, stones, arrows, cross-bows and all kinds of weapons and supplies. Or even the resources expended for the defense of the conquered African outposts, as reported by Fernão Gonçalves,[3] Queen Isabel's servant, when rendering accounts of what he had received of artillery and other things to the army gathered to succor Ceuta in 1456.

On top of that, more bombards, trons, stones, tents and other equipment that would serve to defend sites that, in practice, did not yield the state any money and, at the same time, drained funds from the kingdom, much of which was already destined for redistribution among nobility for their political sustainability. The difficulties faced by those who remained in Africa were witnessed by Gomes Eanes de Zurara, and reported in the chronicle of Duarte de Meneses, Earl of Viana and Captain-Chief of Alcácer Ceguer (*Ksar es-Seghir*). He reported the difficulties to keep that outpost after more than forty-two days of siege,[4] operating a vanguard and expensive military apparatus which, on several occasions, forced the monarch to borrow beyond what was reasonable. That senseless policy was evidenced by the voyage of Diogo Dias de Abreu,[5] a royal household knight, and his envoy to Barcelona, in search for more money in the Catalans' *taulas de canvi* ("exchange tables") in 1458, in order to purchase gunpowder and other warfare equipment, following the king's order.

In 1450, Afonso V promulgated two charters. The first was related to the conditions in which the rents, rights and currency's profits were to be registered by Lisbon's officers: the treasurers, the *almoxarifes*, the receivers, the tenants and the clerks should record in their books all that rents and rights yielded, writing not only what they received but also what they spent, as well as the goods that were to pay *sisas*. In addition, the king complained of injurious practices by merchants, who recorded generically the goods in the books as theirs and "their partners' purchases", not identifying them and allowing them the possibility of getting involved in other businesses, avoiding the tax to be duly charged and reducing the collection. The second demanded that all scribes of rents and royal rights in Lisbon to keep their records relative to the years when taxes had been leased, six months after the leases had ended. The purpose was to ensure that tenants collected their debts and handed over all the ledger books of those leases and rights to the Lisbon *Contos*' doorkeeper, so that he may have them on his guard in order to confront any doubts that may have arisen in the service of the king or between the tenants and the people. If the clerks did not deliver it, the *Contador-Mor* ("Main/ Master Accountant") should oblige them to do so (Rau, 2009: 55–56). According to some scholars, these measures taken by the monarch explain how it became possible to account for the kingdom's revenues and expenditure and, at the same time, reflected a process of collection widening (Rau, 2009: 56–57), drawing conclusions that, from our perspective, characterize a half truth. The argument that revenue increased is true but, on the other hand, Afonso V's concerns regarding the accounting procedures were much more symptomatic of a king who wanted to control his expenditure, which notoriously soared under his reign, rather than the organization of royal accountability proceedings. In many ways, Portugal, as far as taxation is concerned, never took its destiny into its own hands. The

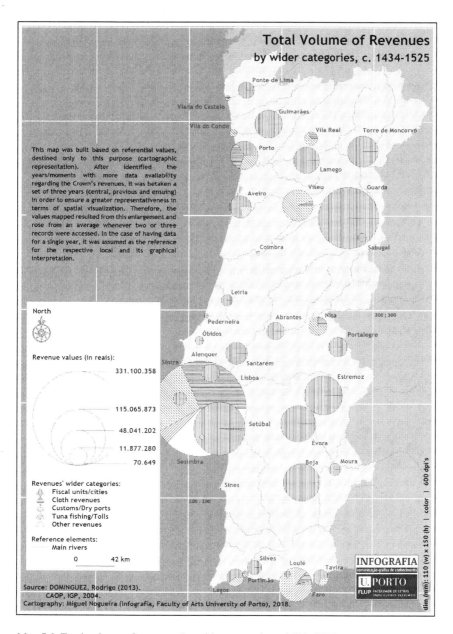

Total Volume of Revenues
by wider categories, c. 1434-1525

This map was built based on referential values, destined only to this purpose (cartographic representation). After identified the years/moments with more data availability regarding the Crown's revenues, it was betaken a set of three years (central, previous and ensuing) in order to ensure a greater representativeness in terms of spatial visualization. Therefore, the values mapped resulted from this enlargement and rose from an average whenever two or three records were accessed. In the case of having data for a single year, it was assumed as the reference for the respective local and its graphical interpretation.

North

Revenue values (in reais):

331.100.358

115.065.873

48.041.202

11.877.280

70.649

Revenues' wider categories:
Fiscal units/cities
Cloth revenues
Customs/Dry ports
Tuna fishing/Tolls
Other revenues

Reference elements:
Main rivers

0   42 km

Source: DOMINGUEZ, Rodrigo (2013).
CAOP, IGP, 2004.
Cartography: Miguel Nogueira (Infografia, Faculty of Arts University of Porto), 2018.

INFOGRAFIA
comunicação gráfica de conhecimento
U.PORTO
FLUP FACULDADE DE LETRAS
UNIVERSIDADE DO PORTO

dim. (mm): 110 (w) x 150 (h) | color | 600 dpi's

Map 7.1 Total volume of revenues by wider categories c.1434–1525

country's rulers decided, on key occasions, to be only a supervisor rather than to build something from scratch, an efficient and effective state reinforcement fiscal machine. Tax collection rights were sold and/or leased to whomever wanted them (and had the financial ability), even if the state had to compensate losses in many situations. Portugal sought, in this respect, the most comfortable way.

7.1 Mutatis mutandis

Earlier in this study we created a small dossier for the Portuguese state's revenue and expenditure analysis, following in the footsteps of scholars who noticed the tendency of tax systems to survive their periods of productivity and to properly serve not the interests of the state but rather its subjects in charge of administration, i.e., the elites (Ormrod, 1995: 157). In fact, what we observed is that this tendency also existed in Portugal, when we see that tax system set up in Portugal mainly served the most powerful subjects, the nobility, through the phenomenon of redistribution which, according to some scholars, "must be proportional to the monarch's ability to concentrate wealth in his hands" (Henriques, 2008: 13). However, the structured device was able to establish internal communications among its most varied layers and reasonably articulated in its many points of contact. On the other hand, the configuration was too dense, far more complex than other studies previously suggested, and clearly had an excessive staff. At some point, there were some attempts to avoid bureaucratic failures, an obvious case of *Contadores das Comarcas* ("County's Accountants"), and to compensate for certain blunders in the system's initial design, but it did not work; they were unable to cope with fissures and imperfections generated at the origin of the process. Essentially, those flaws were the roots of the abuses committed regarding functions' accumulation that may cause some strangeness, according to the modern notion of management, due to the evident conflict of interests. The corruption in the possible privileged information, evidenced in many complaints filed in *Cortes*, gave us a series of examples of how the State finances were drained by officers and leaseholders taking advantage of law breaches. But above all this was based on an origin's central problem: the fusion (or confusion, intentional or not, necessary or not) between public and private, an issue approached and analyzed by other scholars in a similar case study of Tuscany's public finances.[6]

More evidence of the process of ongoing building of the Portuguese tax mechanism is the development of taxation as situations and difficulties arose. Even with an administrative apparatus and a reasonable degree of evolution, Portugal seemed to have relied upon *ad hoc* finances, which are supported by some examples. First, there was the miscellany between short-term credit and mechanisms of tax farming. Second, there was the delay in the adoption of the public debt issuance mechanism, which only arose in the sixteenth century. Third, the debate about the origins of the *Vedor da Fazenda*, that is, regardless of who is right or wrong, whether or not the origins of his establishment in the royal officialdom were or not in 1370, or thirty years before or after, the fact is that they would only have a regiment to control and regulate their activity nearly 150 years later, in 1516. Until then the grievances were brought to the *Cortes'* meetings, to discuss the merits of each situation, and from there, the monarch, as supreme judge, would determine what would be done and how it would be corrected. Add to this the difficulties of accounting techniques in the composition of the Indian *almoxarifados'* ledger books previously mentioned, which give a bit of tone to the adjustments that the machine needed to undertake.

7.2 An embargoed state?

Some scholars already pointed out that the demand for income is based on two assumptions: the lack of the state's concern for constitutional and economic constraints in relation to its needs and the objectives set to satisfy them (Henriques, 2008: 11). Moreover, the tax system's exclusion from nonstate interests, based on the premise that expenditure is a state interest, i.e., the Crown's interest and its king's, ultimately.

Regardless of these premises, the way the tax system's constitution was conducted would determine the elements of an embargoed state. According to other scholars, the average court spending among Western European kingdoms and principalities in the fourteenth and fifteenth centuries varied from 10% to 40% of total expenditure, a percentage that fluctuated according to costs on internal and external security (Körner, 1995: 402). In Portugal, by sampling the expenditure collected, and considering only the cases where the acquittances allowed us to analyze expenditure in detail, particularly in the 1450s, even if a reference estimate were established or if an average was taken, the numbers would reach almost 80% in several situations. In a quick rationale account, it is possible to perceive the size of this problem.

In 1441, Prince João (one of the *Infantes*), son of João I, received from the *almoxarife* of Beja 279,883 reais of the 14,000,000 that constituted his settlement and graces that year.[7] If we take into account the Infante and his three brothers, in a more privileged position than him, receiving more money and aids, even admitting, by supposition, that they received the same, we would then have this value multiplied by four, resulting in 56,000,000 reais. Putting away the monarch, as well as the rest of his court, and bearing in mind that the kingdom's revenues summary of 1473, already studied and published, counted a total of just under 48,000,000, and if we considered this same value as the total revenue of thirty years before, which evidently was not, there would be no budget able to withstand such pressures for additional resources.

7.3 Portugal and the quest for a model

If we look to the first model proposed by Kersten Krüger in the 1980s, as discussed earlier, we would have no doubt in pointing to Portugal, according to its parameters, as a *tax state*. However, the analysis' instrument proposed and used followed new standards, rethought and refined (Bonney & Ormrod, 1999: 4–8). When comparing both, we found many points similar to the procedures adopted by the Portuguese Crown in its fiscal system, which would also frame it in the same way, in particular the issues related to its method of financing, with some payments in kind in areas where money circulation was reduced, despite a general trend toward to wider use of money. This was especially true for public finances, with an increasing importance of taxation, especially on consumption, with some remnants of dependence on rights and privileges granted. Expenditure, directly related to the scale of military efforts, whose costs for military and naval equipment would lead to uncontrolled spiral escalation and urgent cuts to other expenses in times of war. Furthermore, the tax mechanism's role in the economy, i.e., the use of taxation as a form of income redistribution, as well as the application of new forms of assessment and sophisticated credit structures, the state-owned enterprises, with guaranteed and fixed-price monopolies through royal or state-sponsored commercial enterprises, which also sought to secure supplies of grain and other commodities in times of scarcity. And last but not least, to political participation, which authorized and legitimized the collection of new taxes, later limited or removed by absolute rulers. On the other hand, criteria stipulated by this same model could still situate Portugal as a *domain state*, such as the occupation of public offices, in the hands of the noble families and the state's responsibilities with the maintenance of law and order, especially from the point of view of defending the *status quo*.

However, there are certain criteria which do not frame Portugal as a *domain state*: the form of government was personal and limited in its decision making, but it also had some legal procedures that were moving toward an advanced "fiscal constitution". The central administration was reasonably (and often excessively) equipped in terms of personnel but did not comprise a large, highly specialized apparatus but often disobeyed authority as a local administration with a certain autonomy, which suffered from frequent royal interventions. The income was made through an inefficient collection and political constraints, which played an important role, with a systematic degradation of coinage in times of war. Moreover, it uses direct and indirect taxes no longer limited to specific ends, with some attempts to unify the tax structure. On the other hand, there was an ongoing transition, as in the case of credit structures, in the economic policies adopted, in the use and application of accounting techniques and, finally, in the causes of instability and elements precipitating changes in the system.

All of this led us to say that Portugal closely resembles the model/concept proposed by other Portuguese scholars (Macedo, Silva & Sousa, 2006: 207–209; Pedreira, 2010: 78–79) of an *entrepreneurial domain state*. Based on the sources gathered, and especially on the type of data found, it is explicitly observed that the evolution of a state that would seek income through a colonial commercial empire would be the "alternative to evolution for a true state tax system", and at the same time, would hamper the development or correction of the already existing taxation mechanism in order to increase revenue and better manage its expenses, at least for some time. With wealth flowing significantly after 1480, the Crown would not need to worry about developing a suitable model until the 1550s, i.e., until the decline in the commercial value of Indian *commodities* pushed Portugal toward the colonization of Brazil. This forced the state to a small reformulation and later transposition of its tax system to the new colony and major source of income, an effect that, according to some scholars, was similarly generated by the way that the *sisas*' collection was implemented in the 1400s (Godinho, 2009: 148–149).

All of this structure, underpinned by short-term debts, was driving the Portuguese kingdom into a state of difficulty toward bankruptcy, but the overseas' revenues would mitigate this process and, at some times, even reverse it, allowing the state the privilege of not building an adequate tax system. Even so, and since the empire had grown extensively, the demand for fast money was greater and more urgent; that is, the state could no longer expect its long-delayed collection system to work. Consolidating their debt and negotiating government bonds, the *padrões de juro*, would then become the final solutions to a hungry, almost global, administrative system. In this sense, Portugal stands out from the rest of Europe as a kind of middle ground, a country that hosted an incomplete transition between the *domain state* and the *tax state* and, at the same time, was also somewhat of a *fiscal state*, that the transition to the early modern period suggests to us (Ormrod, 1995: 158–159).

Considering the current financial institutional framework of Portugal as compared to the guideline proposed at the beginning of this chapter, we come to one final conclusion: history does not seem to be the teacher of life because very little actually teaches us about the simple art of saving more than spending, according to the possibilities, individual and collective, within what is possible and that does not compromise, in the medium and long term, the collectiveness.

Notes

1 See Catroga (2006), Koselleck (2006), Pavez (2011) and Marques (2013).
2 ANTT, *Chanc. D. Afonso V*, liv. 15, fl. 26v-29.
3 ANTT, Leitura Nova, *Estremadura*, liv. 5, fl. 99–101v.
4 Duarte de Meneses ordered on that occasion, among other measures, the horses' slaughter so that, at the same time, wheat and barley were not consumed in their food, and their meat served as supply to the men serving there. Zurara (1978: 164–165).
5 ANTT, *Chanc. D. Afonso V*, liv. 36, fl. 223.
6 "Finances comprise the transformation of public resources into private ones and private resources into public ones. They are divided into a series of processes of acquisition and disposal that, implemented by the public and private subjects themselves, exert a reciprocal influence among themselves" Waquet (1990: 175).
7 ANTT, *Chanc. D. Afonso V*, liv. 27, fl. 65–65 v. This source mentioned the amount of "xiiij contos que recebeo o dito ano", without knowing exactly the currency. We do believe it was the reais brancos, considering the fact that the same source reported all other values in reais.

Bibliography

Primary sources

ANTT, Chanc. D. Afonso V, liv. 15.
ANTT, Chanc. D. Afonso V, liv. 27.
ANTT, Chanc. D. Afonso V, liv. 36.
ANTT, Leitura Nova, Estremadura, liv. 5.

Secondary sources, chronicles and dictionaries

Zurara, G. E. de. (1978). *Crónica de D. Duarte de Menezes: edição diplomática de Larry King*. Lisbon: Universidade Nova de Lisboa – Faculdade de Ciências Sociais e Humanas.

Studies

Bonney, R., & Ormrod, W. M. (1999). Introduction: Crises, Revolutions and Self-Sustained Growth: Towards a Conceptual Model of Change in Fiscal History, in W. M. Ormrod, M. Bonney, & R. Bonney (eds.), *Crises, Revolutions and Self-Sustained Growth: Essays in European Fiscal History, c.1130–1830*. Stanford: Shaun Tyas, 1–21.

Catroga, F. (2006). Ainda será a história mestra da vida?, Estudos ibero-Americanos. Revista do Departamento de História, Pontifícia Universidade Católica do Rio Grande do Sul, Edição Especial, 2, 7–33.

Godinho, V. M. (2009). A Formação do Estado e as Finanças Públicas, in V. M. Godinho, *Ensaios e Estudos: uma maneira de pensar*, vol. I, 2nd ed. Lisbon: Sá da Costa Editora, 123–173.

Henriques, A. M. B. de M. de C. (2008). *State Finance, War and Redistribution in Portugal (1249–1527)*. Ph.D. Thesis. Department of History, University of York.

Körner, M. (1995). Expenditure, in R. Bonney (ed.), *Economic Systems and State Finance*. Oxford: Oxford University Press, 393–422.

Koselleck, R. (2006). Futuro Passado: Contribuição à semântica dos tempos históricos. Rio de Janeiro: Contraponto-Ed. PUC-Rio.

Macedo, J. B. de, Silva, A. F. da, & Sousa, R. M. de. (2006). War, Taxes, and Gold: The Inheritance of the Real, in M. D. Bordo & R. Cortés-Conde (ed.), *Transferring Wealth and Power from the Old to the New World: Monetary and Fiscal Institutions in the 17th Through the 19th Centuries*. Cambridge: Cambridge University Press, 187–228.

Marques, J. B. (2013). A historia magistra vitae e o pós-modernismo, História Historiografia, 12, Agosto, 63–78, doi: 10.15848/hh.v0i12.618.

Ormrod, W. M. (1995). The West European Monarchies in the Later Middle Ages, in R. Bonney (ed.), *Economic Systems and State Finance*. Oxford: Oxford University Press, 123–160.

Pavez, L. A. (2011). *Historia Magistra Vitae: História e Oratória em Cícero*. M. A. Thesis. São Paulo: FFLCH-USP.

Pedreira, J. M. (2010). Custos e Tendências Financeiras no império Português, 1415–1822, in F. Bethencourt & D. R. Curto (dir.), A Expansão Marítima Portuguesa, 1400–1800. Lisbon: Edições 70, 53–91.

Rau, V. (2009). *A Casa dos Contos: os três mais antigos regimentos dos contos*. Lisbon: Imprensa Nacional-Casa da Moeda [re-edition of 1951 and 1959 original prints].

Waquet, J. C. (1990). *Le Grand-Duché de Toscane sous les derniers Médicis: essai sur le système des finances et la stabilité des institutions dans les anciens états italiens*. Rome: École Française de Rome.

Index

Abrantes (town) 71, 86, 98, 107, 142, 161
acquittance (letter of) 4–8, 66–67, 72,
    76, 80, 83–86, 88, 92, 96–100, 110,
    112–114, 117, 122–123, 127, 131,
    141–142, 152, 159–163, 171, 175
Afonso (1st Duke of Braganza) 82, 99
Afonso III (king of Portugal) 23, 55, 70, 139
Afonso IV (king of Portugal) 24, 141, 163
Afonso V (king of Portugal) 1, 3–5, 21,
    24, 56–57, 66, 69, 82–85, 87–88,
    92–95, 111, 129, 131, 138, 141, 143,
    145–148, 151, 153–155, 157–159,
    161–162, 172
Africa 57–58, 82, 87, 93, 97–99, 118,
    155–160, 171–172
African (the, Afonso V's epithet) 58, 82,
    87–88, 90
aide (tax) 47–48
alcabala 44
Alcácer-Ceguer (same as Ksar es-Seghir,
    city) 129, 156, 172
Alcácer do Sal (city) 72, 119, 129
Alenquer (city) 71, 107
Alentejo 71–72, 80, 84, 97, 108, 121
Alfândega 166, 168
Alfarrobeira, Battle of 57, 90, 92, 105
Alfonso X (king of Castile) x, 43–44
Alfonso XI (king of Castile) xi, 43
Algarve (region) 11, 57, 71, 81, 112–113,
    117, 121, 131, 145
Aljustrel (city) 108, 121
alliramento (tax) 19
Almada (city) 72, 119
almadravas 71, 113
Almeida (city) 32, 55, 72, 90, 135
almoxarifado 24, 55, 58, 67–68, 71–73,
    76, 82, 85–93, 95, 97–100, 106–108,
    110–115, 117, 121–122, 131, 141–144,
    146, 159–161, 163, 171, 175

almoxarife 6–7, 72, 80, 83, 86–87, 89,
    92–93, 95, 108, 111, 114, 119, 129,
    131, 139–142, 144–146, 148, 159–163,
    171–172, 175
Alvalade (city) 108, 121
aquantiadores 81, 82
Aragon, Infants of 57, 84
Aragon (kingdom of) 15, 26–27, 42,
    45–48, 52, 82, 98–99
Asilah (city) 68, 156
Assentamentos, Caderno de 66
Audiencia da Portaria 24
avaliador 81–82
Aveiro (city) 71, 107, 145
aver-do-peso 72–74, 114–115, 123–124
Avis, military order of 80, 94, 162–163
Avis (dynasty of) 15, 88, 100, 138, 163

Beira (region) 11, 71, 145
Beja, Duke of 162
Beja (city) 58, 71–73, 76, 79, 89, 93–95,
    107–108, 114, 118, 121–122, 141,
    145–146, 160–161, 175
Belmonte (city) 72
Benavente (city) 72
Bolognese (Afonso III's epithet) 70
Bonney-Ormrod (model) 5, 14, 16–21, 23
bovatge 46
Braganza (Duke of) 82, 99, 118
Braganza (dynasty of) 82
Brazil 3, 115, 157, 171, 176
Buoyancy (fiscal) 15
Burgundy (dynasty of) 53
burden (fiscal) 9, 14–15, 20–21, 51,
    53–54, 57–58, 155–156, 159

Campo Maior (city) 93, 145
capitation (tax) 19
Casa da Suplicação 25

Casa do Cível 25, 149
Casével (city) 108
Castelo Branco (city) 72, 97, 145
Castelo Mendo (city) 72
Castelo Rodrigo (city) 72
Castile (kingdom of) 1, 14–16, 42–44, 57, 67, 71–73, 80, 83, 88, 98–99, 106, 117, 122, 129, 141, 144, 147–148, 150, 160
Castilian kings 44
Castilla (diezmos de la mar de, tax) 44
Castro Verde (city) 72
Catholic kings 44–45, 115
censales 46
centralization/growth 24, 58, 138–139, 145
Ceuta 57, 68, 89–90, 92, 97–98, 114, 117–118, 123, 155, 172
Christ, Military Order of 80
Church, Catholic (institution) 28, 42, 76
city-state 28, 50–52, 150
cloth 21, 73, 83–84, 87, 92, 95, 108, 111, 114, 118–119, 122, 125–126, 129, 148
Coimbra (city) 71, 80, 82, 107, 112, 114, 129, 153
Colos (city) 108
Comptes, Chambre des 53
constitution (fiscal) 9, 16, 20, 23, 42, 150, 175–176
Contador 24
Contadorias das Comarcas 24, 58, 71, 92, 143
Contador-Mor 36, 143, 172
contado (tax) 19
contiadores (same as Aquantiadores) 82
Contos, *Casa dos* 1, 3, 24, 71, 83, 96, 140–141, 143, 147, 157, 162, 172
corregedor 158
Cortes (same as Portuguese medieval assembly) 21, 45, 70, 81–83, 87, 94, 97–100, 117, 141, 146–150, 153–157, 160, 171, 174–175
court 25, 55, 66, 72, 81, 88, 92, 96, 115, 139, 142, 145, 147, 175
Covilhã (city) 72
credit 1, 6, 8, 13, 17–18, 27–29, 44–45, 48, 51–52, 59, 81, 123, 127, 129, 150, 152, 154, 174, 176
Crown 3, 14, 26–27, 45, 47–50, 56, 68, 67, 70–71, 81, 85, 88–89, 96, 110, 112, 115, 122, 127, 129, 146, 149–150, 152, 154–155, 161, 176
Cruzaders, Golden (currency) 158
culture (tax) 16, 23

customs 2, 8, 15, 19, 24, 44, 47, 49, 51, 70–72, 76, 110, 112, 115, 143, 145–146, 151

dazi (tax) 51
decimas (tax) 42, 52
d'État (fiscalité) 16, 19
Dinis I (king) 9, 24, 131, 139, 143
direct (tax) 14, 19, 21, 28, 46–53, 69, 73, 118, 150, 152, 176
domain state 16–20, 47, 58, 121, 176–177
donativo (extraordinary tax) 81
doubloons, golden (currency) 21, 155–156
Douro (river) 71–72, 110–113, 117
draftsmen (same as Sacadores) 81–82
dry ports (same as Portos Secos) 71, 131, 145, 164
Duarte I (king of Portugal) 1, 88, 156
Duarte de Meneses (3rd Count of Viana) 90, 172

early modern x, 2–3, 13, 16–17, 21, 23, 26–30, 49, 54, 56, 71, 84, 150, 177
empire, the 56, 58, 88, 138, 170, 176–177
empréstimo 81–82, 127
encabezamiento 44
Enrique IV (king of Castile) 44
Entre-Douro-eMinho (region) 71–72, 113, 117
Entre-Tejo-e-Guadiana (region) 71–72, 84, 87, 121, 145
escrivães 81
estimo (tax) 51
Estremadura (region) 71–72, 145
Estremoz (city) 71, 80, 107, 114, 151, 163
exchequer 49–50, 71
expansion, maritime x, 7, 153, 158
expansion, Portuguese Oceanic 1–2, 4, 48, 56–57, 59, 145–146
extraordinary (revenues) 1, 3, 7, 14–15, 20–22, 25, 42, 44–49, 51, 53–54, 56, 67–69, 71, 73, 76, 81–86, 89, 92, 96–99, 110, 114, 117–118, 122, 127, 129, 141–142, 146, 154, 156, 158–163
Évora 71, 80, 87, 92, 98–99, 107–108, 114, 149, 153, 160

Faro (city) 66–68, 71, 80, 98, 106–107, 112–114, 146, 156–158
Ferreira do Alentejo (city) 72
feodale (fiscalité) 16, 19
finances, Recette générale de toutes les 53
First World War 17, 57

fiscal-military state 18
fiscal state (concept) 18
fodro (tax) 51
fogatge (tax) 47–48, 54
Fogos (demographic unit) 59
fonsadera (tax) 44, 59
Foral (charts) 69, 70, 72, 100
Fortunate (the, Manuel I's epithet) 58, 88
fouage (tax) 48, 54
Frederick III (Emperor of Germany) 69
fuego 59
Fuero Viejo 23

gabelle (tax) 47
Golden Penny (tax) 19
Gouveia (city) 72, 90
grace 85–86, 92, 94, 96–99, 139, 141
gravezze (tax) 51
Guadiana (river) 71–72, 84, 95, 97,
    121, 145
Guarda (city) 71–73, 76, 84, 89, 97, 107,
    110–111, 114, 118–119, 121, 123, 129,
    142, 149, 151–152, 157
Guimarães (city) 55, 71, 80, 84, 107,
    111–112, 114, 145
Guinea (Portuguese Outpost) 115

Henrique, Infante D. (same as Henry, the
    Navigator) 48, 89, 92–94, 99, 141
Henry the Navigator (Infante and Prince,
    Duke of Viseu) *see* Henrique, Infante D.
household 6, 15, 20, 24, 58, 66, 71–72, 81,
    86, 92–93, 96, 99–100, 125, 129, 143,
    145, 156–157, 159–160, 162–163, 172

imposicions/imposiciones (tax) 46
India x, 115, 117, 159
indirect (tax) 7, 15, 17, 20–21, 25, 42–44,
    46–54, 67, 69, 72, 89, 107, 150–152
Infanta 92, 131
Infante 86, 88, 175

Jean (king of France) 48
Jewish 5, 83, 95, 111, 113, 119, 122–127,
    129, 152, 164
Jews 5, 24, 45, 49, 67, 69, 97, 11, 118,
    123, 151
João I (king of Portugal) 15, 67, 82, 88, 93,
    97, 142, 147, 156, 175
João II (king of Portugal) 1, 3–5, 58, 73,
    80, 88, 96, 111, 115, 141–142, 145, 147,
    154–155, 158, 162–163
João III (king of Portugal) 67, 89, 157, 170

John (king of England) 50
Juan (king of Castile) 99
jugadas 72
Juíz dos Feitos do Rei 25
Juro, Padrões de (Portuguese debt) 129, 177
Juros al quitar (Spanish titles) 44–45

Ksar es-Seghir, kingdom of (Alcácer-
    Ceguer) 57, 68, 156, 172

Lagos (city) 71, 107, 112–114, 131, 146
Lamego (city) 68, 71, 73, 76, 84–86, 89–90,
    92, 96, 100, 107, 11, 114, 141, 160
Larache (city) 156
Leiria (city) 71, 107
Leonor of Aragon (Queen of Portugal) 69,
    82, 98
libranzas (Castilian bonds) 45
libras (same as Pounds, Portuguese
    currency) 73, 101, 121, 125, 127, 129
Lisbon (city) 2, 5, 8, 25, 29–30, 32,
    68–73, 76, 87, 93, 95, 97, 99–100, 107,
    113–115, 118, 123–126, 140–143,
    146, 148–151, 155, 157, 160, 162–163,
    171–172
Loulé (city) 71, 98, 106–107, 112–113, 146
low gain 125

Manuel I (king) 1, 3–5, 8, 58, 66, 70, 73,
    80, 88, 110, 114, 131, 138, 147, 155,
    157, 159, 162, 170
Marialva (city) 72, 90, 97
marriage (payment) 94, 99–100, 131
medieval x, 2–5, 8, 13, 17, 22–23, 26–30,
    56, 69–71, 75, 84, 126–127, 147, 153
mercy 86–87, 92, 122, 161
Mértola (city) 72, 97, 145
Messejana (city) 108
Middle Ages 2–3, 13, 16–17, 19, 21–22,
    27–30, 47, 49, 54, 56, 114, 116, 120,
    128, 130, 149, 153, 178
military orders 9, 58, 163
military revolution 20, 48
Mina, Casa da (overseas' fiscal branch) 117
Mina, S. Jorge da (Portuguese outpost) 170
Modern Age 28, 41
modern state 18, 26, 41
Mondego (river) 71
monedatge/monetaje (tax) 46
monetagium 25, 81
montazgo (tax) 44
Moors 24, 98, 122
Moorish 122

mordomo 139
Moura (city) 72, 93, 122, 145–146
Murcia (kingdom of) 72, 93, 122, 145–146

Navigator, Prince Henry the 48, 89,
    92–94, 99, 141
Noudar (city) 72, 97

Óbidos (city) 71, 80, 92, 107, 114
Odemira (city) 72, 108
ombudsman 140
Oporto (same as Porto, city) 69, 160
ordinary (revenues) 3–4, 15, 25, 43–45,
    45, 47, 52–54, 67–81, 83–87, 89–96,
    118–119, 129, 140, 146, 148, 171
Ouvidor 140
Ouvidor da Portaria 140
ovençais del-rei 139

Palmela (city) 72, 119
Panóias (city) 108
Pedido 68, 81–84, 96–100, 114, 131
Pedro (Portugal's *Infante*, Prince, Duke of
    Coimbra) 82, 86, 88, 97–100, 126
Pedro I (king of Portugal) 25, 82, 88,
    98–99, 141
Pedro III (king of Aragon) 52
Perfect Prince (the, epithet) 58, 117, 158
poll (tax) 14, 41, 45, 81, 152
Ponte de Lima (city) 71, 80, 107, 113
Portalegre (city) 71, 107, 163
porteiro 139
Porteiro-Mor 139
Portimão, Vila Nova de (city) 112
Porto (same as Oporto, city) 112, 146
portos secos (same as dry ports) 71
pounds (same as Libras, Portuguese
    currency) 73, 82–84, 87, 89, 92–94, 97,
    111, 152
prestanze (tax) 20
prestiti (tax) 51

questia (tax) 45

reais (currency) 73, 83–86, 89–90,
    94–110, 106, 110–113, 115, 117,
    121–122, 125, 127, 129, 131, 141,
    155–163, 175–177
Reais, White (currency) 73, 75, 83–85,
    101, 107, 114, 124–126, 177
reconquista 23, 115, 138, 143
redistribution 13, 23, 25, 43–44, 57, 59,
    87–90, 94, 96, 110, 117, 137, 171–172,
    174, 176

regedor 127
reguengos 72, 111
rendas rameiras (revenue) 108
royal 1, 4, 6–9, 14–15, 19–27, 41–43,
    45–59, 67–73, 76–78, 84–87, 92–96,
    106–111, 113–114, 121, 125–127, 131,
    137, 139–140, 142–149, 152, 154–163
royal household 6, 23–24, 45–50, 55–56,
    58, 71, 73, 81, 86–87, 92–93, 96–100,
    129, 139, 143, 145, 147, 157, 159–163
royal treasury 4–5, 23–24, 56, 68, 67–68,
    83, 87, 90, 96, 129, 154–155, 162

sacadores (same as draftsmen) 81–82, 84
Sabugal (city) 72, 145–146
Santarém (city) 71, 95, 110, 106–107, 114,
    141–142, 148–149
Santiago, Military Order of 80
Santiago do Cacém (city) 72, 108, 121
scribe 6, 88, 141
Seia (city) 72
Serpa (city) 72, 145
servicio (tax) 44
Sesimbra (city) 72, 119, 145
settlement (*assentamento*) 67, 87, 89, 92,
    94–95, 99, 102, 138, 162, 175
Setúbal (city) 71–73, 89, 107, 114,
    118–119, 121, 142, 152, 160
sheriffs 50
short-term (adj) 44–45, 52, 81–82,
    174, 177
side effects 146
Silves (port, city) 71, 98, 107, 112, 131, 146
Sintra (city) 71, 107
sisa 61, 114, 119, 121, 125–126
siseiro 149
situados (tax) 45
state, the 7, 14, 23, 26, 52, 58, 69, 73, 80,
    110, 114–115, 129, 137–139, 147, 150,
    156, 162, 171–172, 174, 176–177

Tagus (river) 27, 71
taille (tax) 19, 45, 48, 67, 81, 87
talha (tax) 67, 81
tallages (tax) 49
Tanger 68, 83, 88–89, 92–93, 96–97, 156
Tangier (same as Tanger) 68, 83, 88–89,
    92–93, 96–97, 156
taulas de canvi (Catalan currency
    exchange) 129, 172
Tavira (city) 71–72, 98, 112, 114, 146
Tavola delle Possesioni 20
taxation x, xi, 3–5, 7–8, 14–15, 17–22,
    24–30, 41–43, 45–57, 68–69, 73,

113–114, 118, 123, 127, 137, 140, 142, 144, 149–154, 172, 174
tax farming 7, 20, 44, 66, 70, 107–108, 118, 121, 124, 139, 150–152, 159, 161, 171, 174
tax state 16–20, 48, 50, 121, 175, 177
Tejo (same as Tagus, river) 71–72, 84, 97, 121, 145
Tenças, Livro das (primary source) 66
tença (tax) 85
tenentia 85
tithes 15, 42, 69, 71, 76, 89, 97, 99, 107–108, 114, 119, 148
Toro, Battle of 56
Torrão (city) 108
Torre de Moncorvo (city) 71–72, 80, 84–86, 100, 107, 113, 131, 159
Trancoso (city) 72, 129, 133, 152
Trás-os-Montes (region) 71, 88, 113, 131, 141, 145
Trastámara (dynasty of) 42
tribute 17–19, 59, 121, 147
tribute state 18

universitas (concept) 41, 45

Valencia (kingdom of) 15, 27, 46, 123
Vedor da Fazenda 55, 142, 148, 174
Venice 28, 51–52, 57
versus 84–85, 114, 126, 150
Viana do Castelo (same as Viana, city) 72
Vila Real (city) 71, 107, 113–114
violarios 46
Viseu (city) 71, 80, 92, 107, 141

war 8, 20, 43, 48–50, 84, 88, 96, 100, 115, 117, 127, 141, 144, 146–147, 155, 158, 176
war, civil 82, 88, 90
war, defensive 155
War, Hundred Years' 48–50
war, offensive 15
war, spoils of 81
warehouse (same as Armazém) 95, 132, 146, 162
warfare 42, 49, 54, 96, 99, 157, 172
Wars, Fernandine 8, 57

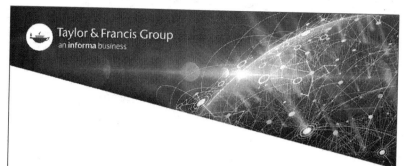